FRANCE
THE BEAUTIFUL
COOKBOOK

AUTHENTIC RECIPES FROM THE REGIONS OF FRANCE

SWISS CHARD PIE (top, recipe page 238), PASTRY PUFFS (right, recipe page 247) AND LEMON TART (bottom, recipe page 238)

AUTHENTIC RECIPES FROM THE REGIONS OF FRANCE

FRANCE
THE BEAUTIFUL
COOKBOOK

RECIPES
THE SCOTTO SISTERS

TEXT
GILLES PUDLOWSKI

PHOTOGRAPHY
PIERRE HUSSENOT
PETER JOHNSON
LEO MEIER

HarperCollins*Publishers*

First published in USA 1989
by Collins Publishers, Inc., San Francisco.
Reprinted 1991, 1993, 1998, 1999.
Produced by Weldon Owen Pty Limited
43 Victoria Street, McMahons Point,
NSW 2060, Australia
Fax (02) 929 8352
A member of the Weldon International
Group of Companies
Sydney • San Francisco • London

President: John Owen
General Manager: Stuart Laurence
Co-editions Director: Derek Barton
Publisher: Jane Fraser
Indexer: Jo Rudd
Production: Mick Bagnato
Design and Art Direction: John Bull,
The book Design Company
Map: Mike Gorman
Illustrations: Yolande Bull
Food Stylists: Janice Baker, Laurence Mouton

Library of Congress
Cataloging-in-Publication Data

Scotto, E. (Elisabeth)
  France the beautiful cookbook.

  "Authors, the Scotto sisters: Elisabeth
Scotto, Marianne Comolli, and Michèle
Carles" —

ISBN 0-00-215412-9

  1. Cookery, French. 2. France — Description
  and travel — 1975-   . I. Comolli,
  Marianne. II. Carles, Michèle. III. Pudlowski,
  Gilles, 1950-   . IV. Title.

[TX719.S388   1989]   641.5944   89-7189

ISBN 0-06-757593-5 (pbk.)

Printed by Toppan in China

A Weldon Owen Production

RIGHT: SAUERKRAUT WITH PORK AND SAUSAGES (left,
recipe page 180), BAKED MEAT AND POTATOES (center, recipe
page 180), PORK COOKED IN BEER (bottom right, recipe
page 178) AND OXTAIL STEW (top right, recipe page 168),
PHOTOGRAPHED IN ALSACE.
PIERRE HUSSENOT/AGENCE TOP

PAGES 2–3: THE PICTURESQUE COUNTRYSIDE OF THE
LOIRE VALLEY, ONE OF THE MOST FERTILE FARMING
REGIONS IN FRANCE.
LEO MEIER

PAGES 8–9: BAKED ZUCCHINI WITH TOMATOES AND
ONIONS (top left, recipe page 211), STUFFED ZUCCHINI
FLOWERS (top right, recipe page 199) AND VEGETABLE
FRITTERS (center front, recipe page 200),
PHOTOGRAPHED IN PROVENCE.
PIERRE HUSSENOT/AGENCE TOP

ENDPAPERS: DELIGHTFUL ST-EMILION IN BORDEAUX,
WHERE COBBLESTONE STREETS LEAD TO
ENTICING RESTAURANTS.
LEO MEIER

BOUILLABAISSE (top right, recipe page 110) AND BOURRIDE (recipe page 109), PHOTOGRAPHED IN PROVENCE

CONTENTS

INTRODUCTION 14
A particular approach to eating and drinking

NORMANDIE, BRETAGNE 22
Gateways to the sea

FIRST COURSES 28
To excite the appetite

VAL DE LOIRE 54
A gentle garden

SHELLFISH OF THE SEA AND RIVERS 60
The good fortune of the mollusks

THE NORTH, ALSACE, LORRAINE 82
Solid, rugged, joyful

FISH 88
The sea's great bounty

FRANCHE-COMTÉ TO DAUPHINÉ 114
From one mountain to another

POULTRY AND GAME 122
From the farmyard and elsewhere

PROVENCE, CORSE, LANGUEDOC-ROUSSILLON 144
Sun-drenched dishes

MEATS 152
Gang of four

FROM CHARENTES TO THE BASQUE COUNTRY 182
A joyous accent

VEGETABLES 190
A garden of Eden

AUVERGNE, BOURBONNAIS, ROUERGUE 216
Cheeses, mountains and plateaus

DESSERTS 222
How sweet they are!

GLOSSARY 252

INDEX 255

ACKNOWLEDGMENTS 256

THE REPUBLICAN *TRICOLORE*, SYMBOL OF FRANCE, REPLACED
THE *FLEUR-DE-LIS* AS THE FRENCH NATIONAL FLAG AFTER
THE REVOLUTION IN 1789.

INTRODUCTION

A particular approach to eating and drinking

France, this magnificent, many-hued country! A stroll along its narrow country lanes, a ramble through the woods by forest paths, yield the rewards of armfuls of perfumes, the scents of fresh grass, a thousand aromas. Nowhere else in the whole world, from arid deserts to luxuriant gardens, from golden beaches shaded by palm trees to vast untouched landscapes where the horizon appears infinite, can be found this sense of the exotic which takes the traveler directly from the countryside to the table.

In France, every road leads to a splendid food. From Flanders (Flandres) to the Basque country (Pays Basque), from Normandy (Normandie) to Nice, from the Ardennes to southernmost Bigorre, the worthy hexagon is unequaled in its flavors. But more than that, it is a store of fine ingredients which produce not only thousands of good recipes, but also the rich fragrances steaming from a simmering pot in a homely country inn, the aroma of sausages and hams hanging in a corner of an alpine chalet in winter, the characteristic iodine and seaweed scents in a bustling seaside port.

Without the piles of oysters, without *cassoulet*, without *hochepot*, without *bourride*, without the curly green Savoy cabbage, and without the wines and beers that go with them, France would not be France. It is no use denying its postcard image.

This book simply bears witness to an infinite richness, a richness that embraces ancient regional traditions (zealously retained in spite of new administrative boundaries), the landscape, the flavors of its foods and the methods of preparation particular to each small area.

FRANCE DIVIDED: OIL VS BUTTER

Do not protest if someone expresses it in a single word: "France." Just smile. And chant after me the lilting names of Rouergue and Auvergne, of Berry and Quercy, of Aunis and Saintonge. Small or large, each province is a piece in a huge jigsaw puzzle, to be divided like a cake.

And why not? Because throughout history, throughout administrative divisions and boundary changes, each region has maintained the originality of its culinary traditions. In truth, there is nothing unusual in this: culinary traditions very often correspond to a climate.

So beer and charcuterie predominate in eastern France, fresh vegetables and garden herbs in the south. It is easy to discern two faces in France: the domain of butter and the domain of oil, which correspond, more or less, to north and south. Butter cuisine is heavier; fresh oil is lighter, more digestible. *Andouillettes* and poultry sizzle in butter; oil — from the olive in the southeastern region, the walnut in the southwest — caresses the fish of the Mediterranean. And one can go further, to discover a France of potatoes, of the artichoke, of the beet, of the cabbage in all its forms — cauliflower, Savoy cabbage, green cabbage, red cabbage, Brussels sprouts, sauerkraut. A France that links together in a tightly packed crown the regions of the north, from Brittany (Bretagne) to Alsace, its tip directed towards northern Flanders, and in contrast, another France, with vegetables of bright, vibrant colors and robust flavors: garlic, sweet red and green peppers, pumpkin, tomato, zucchini and eggplant. And yet again one could divide France into rings and circles: a marine France, obligingly abundant in fish, and an earthy France, rich in poultry and charcuterie; or find common roots in Brittany and southern France, in the northern stretch of the Opal Coast and Le Touquet and its southern rival, the Basque coast. The same ingredients, microclimates born of the high and low tides: nothing better to bring together peoples who imagined themselves to be separated by thousands of kilometers.

From mountain to mountain, the roots meet, entwine and marry. Are not the cheeses of Auvergne, with their fresh, wholesome perfume of milk from alpine pastures, close cousins of the cheeses of Savoy (Savoie)? Are there not a few family ties between the Munster of Val d'Orbey and of Lapoutroie in the Vosges mountains of Alsace, and the Tamié cheese fabricated in the abbey of the same name by reclusive monks? Are

BOTH BUYERS AND SELLERS SEEM TO ENJOY THE ATMOSPHERE OF THE OPEN-AIR FOOD MARKETS — THE OLDEST AND SIMPLEST FORM OF RETAILING IN FRANCE, AND PERHAPS THE MOST PLEASANT.

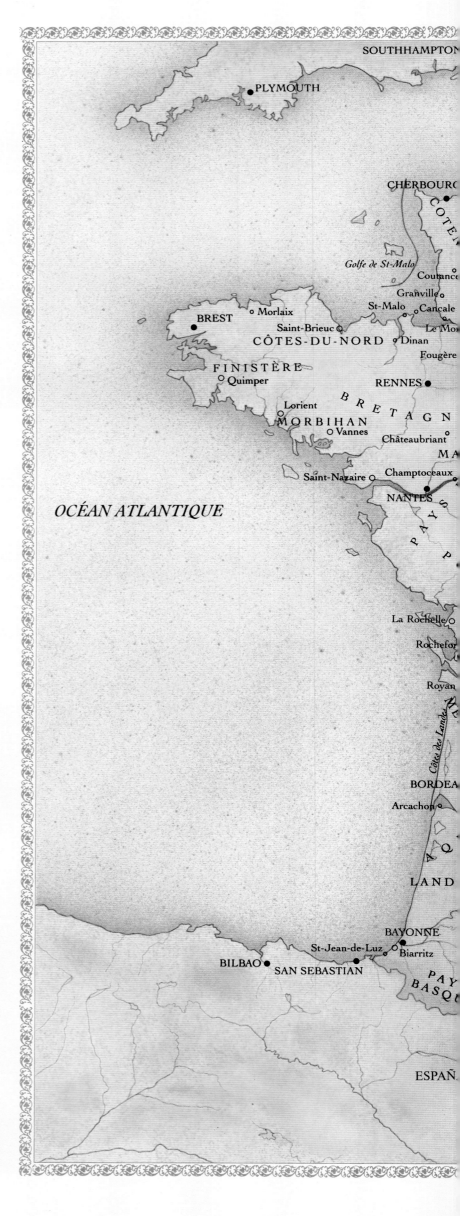

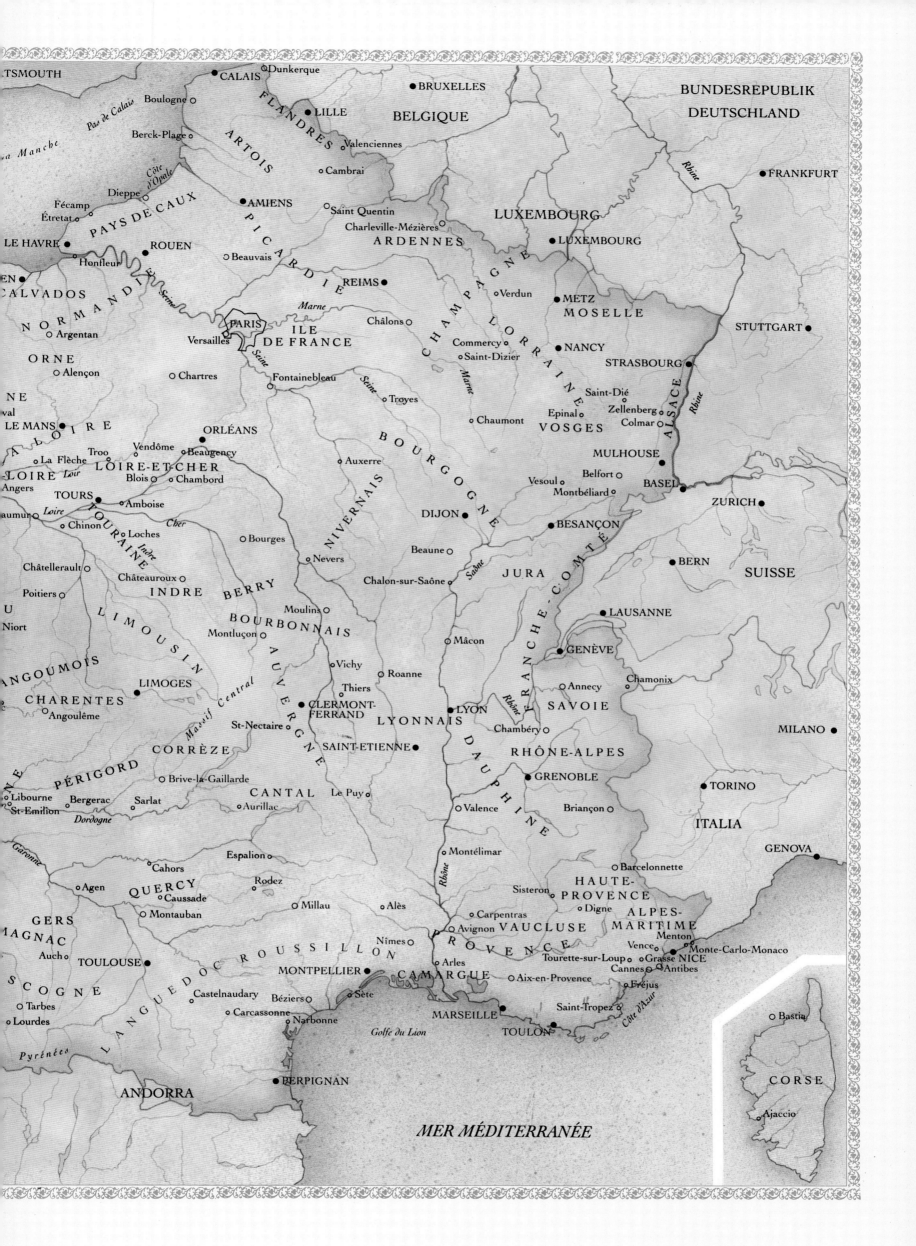

LEO MEIER

FRANCE IS FAMOUS FOR ITS *PÂTISSÉRIES*, AND IN EVERY VILLAGE OR TOWN
YOU CAN BE SURE TO FIND A SELECTION OF THE MOST POPULAR TARTS,
PASTRIES, CAKES AND COOKIES AS WELL AS THE REGIONAL SPECIALTIES.
HERE IN DINAN, BRETAGNE, *GALETTES BRETONNES* ARE ON DISPLAY.

ENJOYING A MOMENT TOGETHER
WHILE PICKING GRAPES IN CHAMPAGNE.

not the lambs of Haute-Provence related — however distantly — to the sheep of the Pyrenees?
Could not the free-range veal known as *broutard*
in Corrèze descend from the red cattle of the
Charolais mountains? In appearance, France may
be sectioned and subdivided, but between its
diverse blocks is woven a close fabric.

THE TRIUMPH OF THE NATURAL

The French predilection for fine cooking has never
faltered. Spices were highly esteemed in the Middle
Ages, but rejected at the start of the Renaissance,
when the flavors of exotic seasonings were
replaced by those of indigenous herbs: onions,
shallots, garlic, *rocambole*. Mushrooms were hon-
ored, truffles worshiped. The acidic, spicy
medieval sauces eventually gave way to more subtle
flavors, smoother textures, as butter entered into
the cuisine.

Thus the French discovered the resources of
their own country, but mostly kept them for themselves. The classic texts written around the end of
the seventeenth century — such as *Le Cuisinier
François* — advocate the selection of natural ingredients and the use of crunchy vegetables —
asparagus for example — with an *al dente* style of

LEO MEIER

WITH TWO MONASTERIES, THE TOWN OF ST-EMILION IN BORDEAUX OFFERS A WEALTH OF RELIGIOUS AND MEDIEVAL ARCHITECTURE, AND IT COULD EASILY BE FORGOTTEN THAT THESE BUILDINGS ARE ACTUAL HOMES.

cooking. Taste was becoming more refined. The prodigious quantities characteristic of medieval banquets were succeeded by a sense of elegance, which shines through such classics as the *Cuisinier Royal et Bourgeois*. The nineteenth century, the boomtime of the great Parisian restaurants (Café de Foy, Véry, Café Français), was also the century of rich and ornate cuisine: cleverly concocted dishes, all too often embellished, always highly sauced. No one hesitated to hide a food's natural taste by sophisticated preparations intended to benefit the eye more than the palate. Hence the vogue for dishes flamed in the dining room, and for *chartreuses* — elaborately fashioned preparations designed to hide the meats under a mass of vegetables — which served as counterparts to the pastrycook's *pièces montées*.

There was as little regional cuisine in the restaurants of Paris, or in the homes of the well-to-do, as there were tourists in the countryside. The twentieth century, from the decade of the '30s, is the era of the return to nature and, first of all, to regional virtues. The enemy — according to La Mazille who, in 1929, penned *La Bonne Cuisine du Périgord* — was Paris, which would accept nothing but a butter-based cuisine, which banished garlic and other strong flavors, and which rejected the traditional recipes of yesteryear.

It was Curnonsky, the elected Prince of Gastronomes, otherwise known as Maurice-Edmond Saillant, who decreed the proper and honorable principle according to which good cuisine means that "things have the taste of what they are." In 1946 he founded the magazine *Cuisine et Vins de France* which attempted to identify and promote regional specialties — recipes, quality ingredients, good restaurants. This insistence on the return to nature goes hand in hand with the rediscovery of the ancient treasure trove of French regional gastronomy.

Thirty years later, Henri Gault and Christian Millau, launching the slogan *nouvelle cuisine*, extolled the return to nature and issued a series of rules that have become a hallmark of modern cuisine: short cooking times, reduced sauces, elimination of unnecessary fats and flour, a ban on the roux that is fatal to digestion, *al dente* cooking of vegetables (as in the sixteenth century) and the marriage of sweet and savory flavors (as in medieval times). In addition, they initiated regional awards — *lauriers du terroir* — for the upholding of certain gourmand traditions.

AZAY-LE-RIDEAU IS CONSIDERED BY MANY TO BE THE MOST FEMININE OF THE LOIRE VALLEY CHATEAUX.
THE RIVER FORMS A WIDE MOAT AROUND THIS EPITOME OF RENAISSANCE GRACE AND PERFECTION.

In parallel fashion, top chefs were innovating, imaginatively creating new dishes based on the traditional recipes and products of their regions. Pike-perch with sauerkraut, from Emile Jung at Strasbourg; snails with nettles, from Bernard Loiseau in Burgundy (Bourgogne); peppers with cod, from Firmin Arrambide in the Basque country — all are illustrations of a regional cuisine reinterpreted. No longer satisfied simply to copy, or to combine goat cheese and cabbage, or duck and kiwifruit, these chefs are returning to the old framework and the time-honored products to give them a new savor.

"Rediscover yesterday's flavors with today's techniques": this could be the motto of the cuisine of the present era. While the regional renovation shakes the provinces, the capital and its leading chefs — most of whom have their roots in the country — amuse themselves by imitating a homely style of cuisine. The dish which was all the rage in Paris in the 1980s was a "common" pig's head simmered with sage and served with "simple" mashed potatoes. But it was prepared with impeccable style and subtle perfection. As if at all costs one had to return to the splendid taste of simple things.

So it seems that now, at the end of the twentieth century, all the traditions of France have been thoughtfully brought together: the diverse regional cuisines, the bourgeois cuisine restoring to honor the old, slow-simmered dishes (*blanquette, daube, navarin, pot-au-feu*), preserving with jealous care the great classics of the country. The *bouillabaisse* of Marseilles, the *aïoli* of Provence, the *bourride* of southern France, the *cassoulet* of the southwest — as well as the preserved goose and foie gras of Périgord, the *choucroute* of Alsace, the *potée* of Lorraine, the tripe of Normandy and the *aligot* of Auvergne — are but a few of the unique culinary masterpieces which the year 2000 should preserve and promote as supreme examples of French genius.

If French cuisine is today thought of as a major art — a daily art, constantly being renewed — it owes this status to the enormous riches of its countryside. Each generation has a duty of conservation and adaption. The last decades of the twentieth century will be seen as the era of a lighter cuisine, and at the same time as a period of authenticity. The genius of French cuisine will be seen as knowing how to adapt to new technologies (preserving, freezing, vacuum packaging) without in any way betraying its principles. Now will you believe me when I say that, from the gastronomic point of view, France has never been so rich, so thoroughly in control, as in the 1980s?

RIGHT: ONE OF THE MANY NARROW MEDIEVAL STREETS OF DINAN IN
BRETAGNE WHERE THE TINY SHOPS SEEM TO COMPETE FOR ATTENTION.

LEO MEIER

NORMANDIE, BRETAGNE

Gateways to the sea

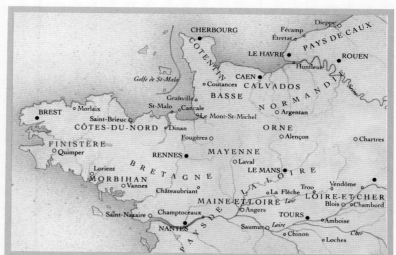

NORMANDIE, BRETAGNE

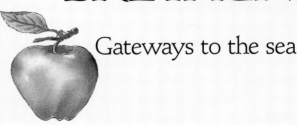

Gateways to the sea

Two regions facing the sea but still agricultural, still strongly tied to the soil; two sovereign provinces for seafood, yet both endowed with incomparable treasures from the land: how to explain it?

By the beauty of grassy meadows, of crooked white fences, and picturesque dwellings. Half-timbered Norman houses, Breton granite, handsome churches, tormented calvaries, wild hills running down to the sea, marshes: from Normandy through to Brittany, the beauty of the French countryside continues. It is noble, proud, even imperial, like Mont-Saint-Michel, adored by the Bretons but separated from them by the thin stream of the Coesnon and belonging to Normandy. As the Breton saying goes:

"The Coesnon in its folly
Placed the Mount in Normandy."

And there is Coutances, in the region of Cotentin situated between solemn Brittany and traditional Normandy and pointing towards Ireland and England. Norman it is, but the buildings of grey stone, the rough and jagged coast, the serenity of its wooded wilderness make it appear more Breton.

And again, Rouen, so happily Norman, devastated by the last war like so many other little villages in Normandy, has been able to retain its wonderful medieval quarter — with its street named after the ancient clock, the *Gros Horloge*; its Gothic houses with their wooden facades; its superb cathedral; the Saint-Maclou cemetery, where plague victims were buried; and the city has even reconstructed the site where Joan of Arc was burned. In the same way, Rouen has kept alive the

LEFT: ONE OF THE BEST PRESERVED TOWNS IN BRETAGNE, DINAN BOASTS MANY BEAUTIFUL HALF-TIMBERED HOUSES AND COBBLESTONE STREETS.

PREVIOUS PAGES: NESTLED IN THE BAIE DU MONT-ST-MICHEL, CANCALE, LIKE MANY OF THE COASTAL VILLAGES OF BRETAGNE, IS FAMOUS FOR ITS OYSTERS.
LEO MEIER

ENJOYING THE AMBIANCE OF THE LOCAL RURAL FAIR AT
LANDÉVANT, NEAR LORIENT.

nineteenth-century tradition of the *canard à la rouennaise,* reproduced in Paris under the name *canard au sang* by Frédéric Delair, the famous chef of the Tour d'Argent. The bird is roasted, then carved, after which the carcass is crushed in a special press to extract all its juices; they become the starting point for a smooth and fragrant sauce, thickened with cream and enriched with cognac. The authentic Rouen duck, its flesh fine-textured and reddish, should come from the village of Duclair.

Butter, cream and cheese: this is the holy trinity of the Normandy pasturelands. One need only detour into the hinterland of the Mother-of-Pearl coast, just behind the splendid resorts of Cabourg, Deauville, Trouville and Honfleur, to discover a picture-postcard Normandy, still virtually as it was during the last century: the old villages with their plaster-and-wood houses and ancient churches, the unforgettably green meadows with their grazing cows, the manors that watch over docile and agile horses.

Some fine cheeses reign there: camembert, invented by a young peasant girl, Marie Harel, whose memory remains very much alive around Vimoutiers; Livarot, choice and strong, found around the commune which bears its name, and also known as "colonel" because of the five bands of woven rushes that surround its red form; and Pont-l'Evêque, the most delicate, still made in the traditional craftsman style throughout the valley of the river Touques. The superb butter, golden yellow, churned on the farms of Isigny, Sainte-Mère-Eglise, Gournay, Neufchâtel-en-Bray or Valognes, and the pale cream, so thick you can cut it with a knife; these treasures can hardly be found elsewhere.

It is here, too, in the heart of the Pays d'Auge, this most Norman part of Normandy, nurtured by orchards of apple trees that blossom in the month of May, that the sparkling cider is produced, the best of which comes from Cambremer. Of farm-house origin, it is typically extra dry, and goes very well with savory dishes — like pork tripe cooked in the Caen style, stewed for hours in a special pot with carrots and onions; sole in the style of Dieppe (with mussels) or of Fécamp (with shrimp); turbot with sorrel; or chicken cooked with calvados and cream.

Distillation of the fermented apple juice, followed by its aging in wood, produces calvados, with its aroma of ripe apples, soft and mature; it is the best Norman digestive. The valleys of the Auge and the Orne are favored for its production, and the picturesque villages of Beuvron, Pierrefitte, Beaumont — all qualified by the suffix "en Auge" — indicate that this is the heart of the traditional farmland.

But good cider and fine apples are also found on the farms of the windy plateau of the Caux district, to the north of Rouen, near Etretat and Fécamp. This is also the realm of the chalky white cliffs and of the sea. Sole, turbot, John Dory, and shellfish — oysters, clams, shrimp — all go so well with thick farmhouse cream and orchard-fresh apples.

Exactly the same varieties are found in Brittany, though there the countryside is more reserved. Too often the milk is pasteurized, converted to industrial cheeses that are distributed over the whole of France. But this is where the great kingdom of the sea opens up. Its character is determined in the Cotentin, the Norman boundary next to the the lands of Brittany. There are white, sea-smelling oysters from Saint-Vaast-la-Hougue, scallops from Erquy, and shrimp from the waters off Granville.

Further inland, the landscape is somewhat harsher, its charm more on the wild side, like the wind that blows relentlessly around the point of Penmarch, situated at the country's far western tip. Here the Atlantic Ocean marks the end of Brittany, and this most maritime department of France bears the name Finistère which, in the Breton tongue, means "the end of the earth." Guilvinec offers squirming shrimp; the huge nurseries of Audierne provide lobsters and crayfish, and an abundance of fish is brought into Saint-Guénolé — mackerel, mullet, sardines, tuna, as well as sea bass, sole large and small, salmon and sea trout. It is easy to imagine Brittany as a huge bowl of salt water where only fishermen have rights of citizenship — and yet this is a region which, together with its Norman neighbor, produces the world's best cider, at Forêt-Fouesnant in the sunny south of the Finistère. It is also an agricultural region, famous for its artichokes, potatoes and cauliflower. To the north are Finistère-nord, Côtes du Nord, and the Léon — a vast market garden, where once again the tides bring in the bounty of the sea.

Like that of Normandy, Breton cuisine is constantly bringing together the land and the sea, the harvest of one with that of the other. Oysters from the bay of Quiberon and the gulf of Morbihan served with crisp-cooked lettuce, or with shallot juice and vinegar; lobster with artichokes; turbot with potatoes; these are the ingredients of some happy marriages. Cotriade — which is the local version of bouillabaisse — combines conger eel, halibut, anglerfish and whiting with carrots and onions, all cooked in stock and white wine — muscadet, the only wine of Brittany, which comes from the region around Nantes (already almost the Loire).

The art of charcuterie, country-style, is highly regarded in Brittany — pork pâtés described as "Breton," the highly flavored *andouilles* which, in both Brittany and Normandy, are prepared in distinctive and characteristic styles. The Norman *andouille,* known as "Vire," is made from finely chopped pork tripe, whereas for the Breton *andouille* — labeled "of Guéménée" — the lengths of tripe are wound around one another and finally wrapped in a piece of beef membrane. A real craftsman's job! Today the farmers of both Normandy and Brittany, proud of their skills and of their rich, fertile territory, have begun to produce their own foie gras, starting with geese and ducks imported from the Gers *département*, raised in their grassy meadows, fattened with the customary corn, then slaughtered in the traditional way. To differentiate between the products of the two regions is impossible.

On the other hand, there are some treasures that really belong to only one particular province. One such treasure is the salt-meadow lamb from pastures bathed by the sea breeze where the grass itself has a faint salty taste, by right belonging to the Bay of Mont-Saint-Michel. It was here, on Mont-Saint-Michel, that Mère Poularde, who ran a celebrated inn, invented the omelette that still bears her name: eggs beaten long and rhythmically, then cooked in plenty of butter in a long-handled iron pan over an open fire, and finally served, thick, warm and creamy, to revive the weary traveler who has arrived late, and on foot, to this miracle of a mountain in a watery land.

Butter shows the dividing line betwen the two provinces; it is invariably salted in Brittany, unsalted in Normandy. In the Breton region, it goes into the caramels of Morbihan as well as the brioches and regional cakes, like the butter cake or *quatre-quarts, kouigh amann*, and lacy pancakes or crêpes-dentelles, all of which are characterized by their fresh, buttery flavor. The two regions come together again around their common assets: crêpes, made with wheat flour if sweet, with buckwheat flour if savory. With either type, the proper drink is cider, with its distinctive aroma of ripened apples, its deep golden color and its head of light foam. A fair and friendly way to celebrate the union of two neighbors, rivals, each jealously guarding its own fame, and yet cousins.

BUILT FROM THE ELEVENTH TO THE SIXTEENTH CENTURIES BY BENEDICTINE MONKS, MONT-ST-MICHEL, ONE OF THE GREATEST RELIGIOUS BUILDINGS IN EUROPE, IS AN INSPIRING AND AUSTERE SIGHT.

LEO MEIER

FIRST COURSES

To excite the appetite

THE CHARCUTERIE TOURON, IN THE TOWN OF CAUSSADE, DISPLAYS TYPICAL GASCOGNE
SPECIALTY MEATS, SAUSAGES, PÂTÉS AND *PLATS CUISINE.*

FIRST COURSES

To excite the appetite

A typical meal in France today would consist of a first course, a main dish, cheese (which is eliminated by those in a hurry or considered as the final course by those on a diet) and dessert. For a special occasion, three dishes would be served before the cheese — generally a cold hors d'oeuvre, a hot first course and then the main dish. The great chefs very skilfully manage both the hot and the cold. Soup, for example, is reputed to have a beneficial effect on digestion, whether it be a hot consommé or chicken broth, or a creamy vegetable soup that is served cold.

Likewise, soup makes an excellent first course when it helps the diner to understand the region in which he is eating. Emile Jung, the famous chef of Le Crocodile at Strasbourg, likes to serve a goose soup with pearl barley, whose basic components — meat and cereal — are strongly representative of both the originality and the variety of the products of Alsace. The pale, garlic-flavored *tourain* (or *tourin*) in the Landes, the Provençal *soupe au pistou* from the inland regions and the *soupe de poissons* of the coast from Marseilles to Nice, fulfil the same introductory functions; you learn about where you are, while you experience the aromas and flavors of the region that welcomes you.

Hot first courses often take the form of *tourtes*, quiches, pâtés, *hures* and soufflés: all of which rely on forcemeats, pastries, jellies and other components designed to enrich an ingredient which the land offers au naturel. These are rich, contrived dishes that typically demand a complicated, or at least elaborate, preparation. It is a mark of respect to one's guests to offer them such a dish, to which much care and attention will have been devoted in the kitchen well before their arrival.

First courses are not necessarily based on meat and fish, but they often depend heavily on such ingredients. Eggs, too, are treated in a multitude of styles, according to region: with peppers in the Basque country, as *pipérade*; as truffle omelettes in Provence and Tricastin; poached in red wine as *oeufs en meurette* in Burgundy or *couilles d'âne* in the Berry. These dishes are perfect examples of the diversity of preparations which the richness of the French countryside allows for a single ingredient.

Often it is vegetables which make the difference, either as one component of a recipe, or as a complete dish. Tomatoes, zucchini, olives, peppers and eggplant from the Midi are opposed to the cabbage, beets and potatoes of the north and east. Mediterranean artichokes, which might be stewed in oil, *à la barigoule*, contrast with Breton artichokes, which are simply eaten with a vinaigrette sauce. Asparagus, whether from the Vaucluse, the Loire Valley or Alsace, here slender and green, there large and white, is always served with the same accompaniments — mousseline sauce, mayonnaise or vinaigrette. Yet in the east it will be accompanied by ham, and in the Midi it will be served as a vegetable, nobly accompanying a main dish. In general, the first courses offered north of the Loire — the line which divides France both climatically and gastronomically — are more substantial, more robust, richer than in the south. But it is all a matter of the weather, and therefore of the season. Naturally, summer dishes are often cold, and their wintertime counterparts are usually intended to be served hot — even if both furnish exactly the same amount of energy to the body.

A few first courses have become quite separate dishes, like the foie gras that is served cold as an hors d'oeuvre, but which might be pan-fried and served warm, accompanied by fruits which also have been tossed in butter. Similarly a meat-filled pasta like ravioli, which might become the center-piece of the meal when servings are substantial.

Contrarily, and with the help of fashion, certain dishes that might otherwise have been served as the main course have been accepted as light first courses: like marinated raw fish, either Scandina-vian- or Tahitian-style, or raw meats prepared in the manner of the Italian *carpaccio*. Such relative newcomers prove that in gastronomy nothing is ever fixed. According to individual appetites, tastes and habits, a first course will or will not be effectively considered as such.

It is all a question of era and custom. Some regions have a reputation for abundant first courses, as prelude to a rich and copious meal. This is equally true of the Périgord and of Alsace, both of which share a love of foie gras — and both claim

EVERY FRENCH VILLAGE AND TOWN HAS A RESIDENT *BOULANGER* WHO PRODUCES THE STRAIGHT AND NARROW *BAGUETTE* THAT APPEARS ON THE TABLE AT EVERY MEAL.

TO TEMPT THE PASSING SHOPPER, THIS STALL IN THE MARKETS OF NICE OFFERS A RANGE OF POPULAR FRENCH CHEESES. THEY INCLUDE CANTAL AND COMTÉ, AS WELL AS SOME ITALIAN SPECIALTIES FROM ACROSS THE BORDER.

LEO MEIER

THE FRENCH ARE CONVINCED THAT GARLIC, LIKE WINE, IS GOOD FOR YOU.
GARLIC STALLS ARE PROMINENT IN EVERY MARKETPLACE, AND FEATURE THE THREE
MAIN VARIETIES, WHITE, VIOLET AND ROSE.

MUSHROOM PÂTÉ IS EVIDENTLY POPULAR
IN THE VILLAGE OF DIGNE IN HAUTE PROVENCE.

LEO MEIER

to have created it. Could this be related to the fact that many Alsatians emigrated to the southwest in 1940, just before the German annexation of their region?

On the other hand, certain regions in France have retained a tradition of light, fresh-tasting first courses. Often these are the maritime regions, where salads — such as the *salade niçoise* at Nice — or seafood (oysters, shellfish, mussels, alone or in combination) constitute the most natural of preludes to a meal.

Actually, in any self-respecting French meal, the first course has one single role: to inspire in the diner the desire to pursue his pleasant task. And everyone knows that there are a thousand and one ways of doing it.

Provence

ANCHOÏADE
Anchovy Spread

12 anchovies preserved in salt
6 cloves fresh, young garlic, finely chopped
3 fresh, young French shallots, finely chopped
1 tablespoon red wine vinegar
¾ cup (6 fl oz/200 ml) extra virgin olive oil
6 sprigs parsley, stemmed and finely chopped
slices of baguette (French bread), toasted
raw vegetables: celery, cauliflower, radishes, fennel,
  artichokes, peppers (capsicums)…

❖Rinse the anchovies under cold running water and rub them to remove all traces of salt. Separate into fillets, removing the head and backbone. Cut each fillet into small pieces.

❖Combine the chopped anchovies, garlic and shallots in a food processor. Add the vinegar and blend until smooth. With machine running, pour in the oil in a thin stream, then add the parsley and blend for 10 seconds longer. Serve the *anchoïade* spread on toasted slices of bread or as a dip for raw vegetables.

SERVES 6   *Photograph pages 28 – 29*

ANCHOVY DIP

PETER JOHNSON

Provence

BAGNA CAUDA
Anchovy Dip

Bagna cauda *is very similar to* anchoïade*, but as its Provençal name indicates (*bagna cauda *means hot bath), it is served hot.*

12 anchovies preserved in salt
4 cloves fresh, young garlic
2½ oz (75 g) butter
3 tablespoons extra virgin olive oil
slices of baguette (French bread), toasted
raw vegetables: celery, cauliflower, radishes, fennel,
  artichokes, peppers (capsicums)…

❖Rinse the anchovies under cold running water and rub them to remove all traces of salt. Separate into fillets, removing the head and backbone. Cut each fillet into small pieces.
❖Force the garlic through a garlic press into a small saucepan. Add the anchovies, butter and oil and stir over very gentle heat until the mixture forms a smooth, homogeneous paste. Serve immediately, on slices of toast or as a dip for raw vegetables.

SERVES 6

Bourgogne

OEUFS EN MEURETTE
Poached Eggs with Red Wine Sauce

The term meurette *in Bourgogne applies to any preparation based on red wine, whether it is for use with fish, meat or eggs.*

2 cups (16 fl oz/500 ml) red Burgundy
3 French shallots, finely chopped
2 carrots, each about 3 oz (100 g), peeled and finely chopped
5 oz (150 g) butter, cut into small pieces
1 generous cup (300 ml) red wine vinegar
12 eggs
salt and freshly ground pepper

❖Pour the wine into a nonaluminum saucepan, add the shallots and carrots and bring to boil. Reduce by boiling over high heat for 5 minutes.
❖Reduce heat to very low and whisk in the pieces of butter one or two at a time. Strain the sauce into a small saucepan and keep warm over hot water.
❖Combine 2 qt (2 l) water and the vinegar in a skillet and bring to a gentle simmer. Break the eggs into a bowl, one after the other. As soon as the water begins to bubble, delicately slide in the eggs. Carefully turn the eggs over with a skimming spoon to bring the white over the yolk. Poach for 4 minutes.
❖When the eggs are cooked, remove them with the skimming spoon and transfer to a clean cloth. Trim the ragged edges of each egg to give a nice oval shape. Divide the sauce among six warm plates and arrange 2 eggs in the middle of each. Season with salt and pepper and serve immediately.

SERVES 6   *Photograph page 35*

Bourgogne

JAMBON PERSILLÉ

Parsleyed Ham

This is the traditional Easter Sunday dish in Bourgogne.

2 lb (1 kg) unsmoked raw ham
2 calf's feet
10 oz (300 g) veal knuckle
2 French shallots, halved
1 clove garlic, halved
1 sprig dried thyme
1 bay leaf
2 sprigs tarragon
3 sprigs chervil
10 sprigs flat-leaf parsley
salt and freshly ground pepper
3 cups (24 fl oz/750 ml) white Burgundy
2 tablespoons white wine vinegar

❖In a large bowl, cover the ham with cold water and soak for 12 hours to remove excess salt.

❖Blanch the calf's feet in boiling water to cover for 5 minutes, then drain. Drain the ham and rinse under running water. Combine the calf's feet, ham and veal knuckle in a large pot; add the shallots, garlic, thyme, bay leaf, tarragon, chervil and 3 sprigs of parsley. Season lightly with salt and pepper, and pour in the wine. Bring to boil over gentle heat and simmer slowly for 2 hours, stirring from time to time.

❖Snip the leaves from the remaining parsley. Drain the ham and the veal knuckle meat and roughly crush the meat with a fork. Strain the cooking liquid and stir in salt, pepper and the vinegar. Let cool until the stock is thick and viscous.

❖Pour a layer of the stock into a mold just large enough to accommodate the meat and liquid. Let cool, then refrigerate until firmly set. Cover with a layer of meat, then sprinkle with parsley. Pour more stock over and again refrigerate to set. Repeat the layers until all ingredients have been used, ending with a layer of stock. Cover the mold and refrigerate for 12 hours before unmolding. Serve in slices, accompanied by salad.

SERVES 8

Lyonnais/Ile de France

GRATINÉE À L'OIGNON

French Onion Soup

In days gone by, this thick, fragrant soup, invigorating and robust, was enjoyed late at night and into the small hours of the morning at the old markets of Les Halles, in Paris. The recipe is thought to have originated in Lyon.

3 oz (100 g) butter
1 lb (500 g) large onions, thinly sliced
1 tablespoon all purpose (plain) flour
1½ qt (1.5 l) beef or chicken stock
salt and freshly ground pepper
12 slices of baguette (French bread)
3 oz (100 g) grated Emmenthaler cheese

❖Melt the butter in a heavy 4-qt (4-l) saucepan. Add the onions and cook over low heat, stirring constantly, for 20 minutes or until they become soft and golden. Sprinkle in flour and stir for 2 minutes. Pour in the stock, season with salt and pepper and bring to boil. Cover and cook over very low heat for 45 minutes, stirring from time to time.

❖Toast the slices of bread on both sides under the broiler (griller). Divide them among four flameproof soup bowls and sprinkle with the cheese. Pour the soup into the bowls and slide the bowls under the broiler, close to the heat source; broil just long enough to melt and lightly brown the cheese. Serve immediately.

SERVES 4

BOUILLON DE VOLAILLE

Chicken Stock

For approximately 4¾ cups (1.2 l) stock:
4 lb (2 kg) chicken carcasses and bones
1 small onion (about 2 oz/50 g)
1 clove
8 cups (2 qt/2 l) cold water
1 carrot (about 3 oz/100 g), peeled
1 celery stalk
1 leaf of leek
1 sprig dried thyme
1 bay leaf
½ teaspoon sea salt
12 black peppercorns

❖Wash carcasses and bones under running water. Stud the onion with the clove. Place the carcasses and bones in a large pot. Add the cold water and bring to boil over low heat, skimming off the first brown scum. Add the vegetables, thyme, bay leaf, salt and pepper and simmer gently, half covered, for 2 hours or until reduced to about 4¾ cups (1.2 l). Strain.

❖This delicate, aromatic stock is used in the preparation of many dishes. It may be frozen in small containers for future use.

FRENCH ONION SOUP (top) AND OLIVE SPREAD (recipe page 36)

PETER JOHNSON

RIGHT: PARSLEYED HAM AND POACHED EGGS
WITH RED WINE SAUCE (recipe page 33)

PIERRE HUSSENOT/AGENCE TOP

Lyonnais

CERVELLE DE CANUT
Herbed Cheese Spread

This is a dish traditionally served in the mâchons — *the bistros of Lyon. The name* mâchon *originally referred to a small meal that was eaten mid-morning. It is also known as* claqueret, *from the expression "claquer le fromage," meaning to beat or whisk the cheese.* Canut *was the name of the silk workers who for a long period represented a true gourmet tradition.*

8 oz (250 g) fresh *fromage blanc* or ricotta cheese
¼ cup (2 fl oz/60 ml) olive oil
3 tablespoons white wine vinegar
3 tablespoons dry white wine
¾ cup (6 fl oz/200 ml) chilled cream
2 French shallots, finely chopped
6 sprigs flat-leaf parsley, leaves only, finely chopped
6 sprigs chervil, leaves only, finely chopped
10 chive stalks, finely chopped
salt and freshly ground pepper

❖Set the cheese to drain, in the container or a colander, 12 hours before commencing preparations. Turn the drained cheese into a bowl and mash with a fork. Mix in the oil, vinegar and wine.
❖Whip the cream until stiff and fold into the cheese mixture. Mix in the shallots, herbs, salt and pepper. Chill thoroughly. Serve the cheese with whole-grain country bread or rye bread.

SERVES 6

Provence

SOUPE DE POISSONS
Fish Soup

Saffron and fennel are the indispensable seasonings for this thick broth with its characteristic flavor. It is served all along the coast of the Mediterranean, and particularly in Marseille.

3 lb (1.5 kg) small white-fleshed fish of several types
1 green bell pepper (capsicum) (about 7 oz/200 g)
¼ cup (2 fl oz/60 ml) olive oil
1 onion (about 3 oz/100 g), finely chopped
4 cloves garlic, coarsely chopped
1 leek, white part only, washed and sliced
1 lb (500 g) ripe tomatoes, quartered
2 sprigs dried fennel
1 sprig dried thyme
2 pinches of saffron threads
3 sprigs parsley
1 bay leaf
2 qt (2 l) water
salt and freshly ground pepper
5 oz (150 g) vermicelli or 18 slices bread from a
    baguette (French bread)
grated Emmenthaler cheese
For the *rouille* sauce:
3 cloves garlic, coarsely chopped
2 to 3 fresh red chili peppers, halved and seeded

½ teaspoon coarse sea salt
1 slice of bread, crusts trimmed (from a sandwich
    loaf, about 3 oz/100 g)
¾ cup (6 fl oz/200 ml) extra virgin olive oil

❖Scale and gut the fish; wash and pat dry. Cut the green pepper into quarters. Remove the stem, seeds and white ribs, then slice the pepper thinly.
❖Heat the oil in a heavy 6-qt (6-l) saucepan. Add the onion, garlic, pepper and leek and cook, stirring, over low heat for 2 minutes. Add the tomatoes, fennel, thyme, saffron, parsley, bay leaf and fish and stir for 1 minute. Cover and cook over low heat for 10 minutes.
❖Bring 2 qt (2 l) water to boil in a saucepan and add to the fish mixture. Season the soup with salt and pepper. Cover and let simmer for 20 minutes over low heat.
❖Prepare the *rouille* sauce: combine the garlic, chilies and salt in a food processor or blender and grind to a smooth paste. Crumble in the bread and blend again. With machine running, pour in the oil in a thin stream; blend until the sauce is thick and smooth.
❖Strain the cooked soup through a sieve, pressing down well to extract all the flavor of the fish. Rinse the pan and return the soup to it, straining through a fine sieve. If you are using vermicelli, bring the soup to boil, add the pasta and cook until *al dente*. If you prefer to use bread, lightly toast the slices on both sides and offer them separately.
❖Pour the soup into a tureen and serve it immediately, with the *rouille* and cheese passed around separately.

SERVES 6

INGREDIENTS FOR FISH SOUP

PETER JOHNSON

Flandres

SOUPE DE POTIRON
Pumpkin Soup

2 tablespoons (50g) butter
4 leeks, white parts only, washed and thinly sliced
1½ lb (750g) peeled pumpkin, cut into 1-in (2-cm) cubes
3 cups (24 fl oz/750 ml) chicken stock
salt and freshly ground pepper
1 cup (8 fl oz/250 ml) milk

❖Melt half the butter in a heavy 4-qt (4-l) saucepan and cook the leeks until soft and golden, about 5 minutes, stirring constantly with a wooden spoon. Stir in the pumpkin cubes, stock, salt and pepper and simmer for about 30 minutes, or until the pumpkin is very soft.
❖Transfer the mixture to a food processor and blend to a smooth puree. Reheat gently, adding the remaining butter and the milk. Stir well and remove from heat. Pour the soup into a tureen and serve immediately.

SERVES 6

Picardie/Ile de France

POTAGE CRÉCY
Carrot Soup

The towns of Crécy-en-Brie in Picardie and Crécy-en-Ponthieu in Ile de France both claim credit for the creation of this soup, and indeed both are famous for the quality of their carrots. The rice is sometimes replaced by 9oz (300g) of potatoes, peeled, cut into small cubes and cooked in the same way.

2 oz (50g) butter
1 onion (about 3oz/100g), finely chopped
2 leeks, white parts only, washed and thinly sliced
2 qt (2l) water
2 lb (1 kg) small, young carrots, peeled and cut into ¼-in (5-mm) slices
salt and freshly ground pepper
⅓ cup (2oz/50g) long-grain rice
6 tablespoons (3 fl oz/100 ml) heavy (double) cream or crème fraîche

❖Melt half the butter in a heavy 4-qt (4-l) saucepan. Add the onion and leeks and cook, stirring, for about 3 minutes or until golden. Pour in the water and bring to boil. Add the carrots and season with salt and pepper. Cover and cook over low heat for 30 minutes or until the carrots are very soft.
❖Pour the contents of the pan into a food processor and blend at high speed for 1 minute or until the mixture is smooth and creamy. Return to the saucepan and bring to boil. Stir in the rice and simmer gently for 20 minutes or until the rice is cooked. Stir in the cream and the remaining butter. Pour the soup into shallow soup bowls and serve immediately.

SERVES 4

MILK SOUP (top, recipe page 40), CARROT SOUP (right)
AND BREAD AND GARLIC SOUP (bottom)

Languedoc

TOURAIN
Bread and Garlic Soup

Tourains, or tourins, are prepared all over the Languedoc and the recipes for these hearty soups — based on foie gras, garlic, onion or tomatoes — vary from one place to another. This recipe comes from Toulouse.

⅓ cup (2½ oz/75g) goose fat
8 cloves fresh young garlic, finely chopped
2 qt (2l) boiling water
bouquet garni: 1 sprig thyme, 1 bay leaf, 2 sprigs sage (tied together)
salt and freshly ground pepper
6 bread slices
3 oz (100g) grated Emmenthaler cheese
3 eggs

❖Melt the goose fat in a heavy 4-qt (4-l) saucepan. Add the chopped garlic and stir over low heat until golden, about 2 minutes. Add the boiling water, bouquet garni, salt and pepper. Return to boil, then cover and simmer gently for 30 minutes.
❖Meanwhile, toast the slices of bread and lay them in a soup tureen. Add the grated cheese.
❖Separate the eggs into two bowls. Discard the bouquet garni. Beat the egg whites with a fork until foamy, then whisk them into the boiling soup until they coagulate. Remove 2 tablespoons of soup and beat into the yolks with a fork. Quickly stir this mixture back into the soup and remove from heat; the yolks should not cook, but serve simply to thicken the soup. Pour the boiling soup into the tureen and serve immediately.

SERVES 6

PUMPKIN SOUP
PIERRE HUSSENOT/AGENCE TOP

Ardennes

SOUPE AU LAIT
Milk Soup

8 oz (250 g) baking potatoes
1 tablespoon (25 g) butter
1 onion (about 3 oz/100 g), finely chopped
3 leeks, white parts only, washed and thinly sliced
  diagonally
1 qt (1 l) milk
salt and freshly ground pepper
4 pinches of freshly grated nutmeg
8 slices baguette (French bread)

❖Peel and wash the potatoes; slice into thin rounds.
❖Melt the butter in a heavy 4-qt (4-l) saucepan and cook the onion and leeks over low heat, stirring with a wooden spoon, for about 5 minutes or until soft and golden. Pour in the milk and bring to boil. Add the potatoes, salt, pepper and nutmeg, cover the pan and cook over gentle heat for about 20 minutes or until the potatoes are tender.
❖Divide the slices of bread among four shallow soup plates. Pour in the boiling soup and serve immediately.

SERVES 4   *Photograph page 38*

Provence

SOUPE AU PISTOU
Vegetable Soup with Basil

In the Provençal dialect, pistou *means not basil, but* pilé — *the Italian* pesto *of Genoese origin — a paste that includes ground basil and garlic, bound with olive oil. This soup is made all along the Mediterranean coast in summer, when the fresh haricot beans arrive at the markets. Each family has its favored recipe, and different vegetables are often used. But they all have in common that light paste with its incomparable flavor which is added to the soup before serving.*

2 lb (1 kg) fresh haricot beans or 1 lb (500 g) dried
  haricot beans, soaked overnight and drained
8 oz (250 g) fresh broad beans or 4 oz (125 g) dried
  broad beans, soaked overnight and drained
4 oz (125 g) green beans
8 oz (250 g) small zucchini (courgettes), trimmed
2 cloves fresh, young garlic
8 oz (250 g) boiling potatoes
8 oz (250 g) ripe tomatoes
2 onions, about 3 oz (100 g) each, chopped
1 sprig basil
salt
3 oz (100 g) soup pasta or small macaroni
3 oz (100 g) Emmenthaler or Parmesan cheese,
  freshly and finely grated
For the *pistou*:
8 oz (250 g) ripe tomatoes
1 large bunch of basil, about 3 oz (100 g), stems
  removed
4 cloves fresh, young garlic, quartered
6 tablespoons fruity olive oil

❖Shell the haricot and broad beans, if fresh, and remove the soft green skin that covers them. String the green beans (if necessary); wash and pat dry. Quarter the zucchini lengthwise, then cut into ¼-in (5-mm) slices. Crush the garlic with a blow of the hand or with the side of a cleaver. Peel and wash potatoes; cut into ½-in (1-cm) cubes. Drop the tomatoes into boiling water for 10 seconds, then cool under running water. Peel, halve and squeeze out the seeds; coarsely chop the flesh.
❖Combine all the vegetables with the garlic, onions and basil in a 4-qt (4-l) saucepan and cover with cold water. Bring to boil over gentle heat. Season with salt, cover and let simmer very slowly for 1 hour.
❖When the soup is cooked, remove the garlic and basil. Add the pasta and cook until *al dente*.
❖Meanwhile, prepare the *pistou*: drop the tomatoes into boiling water for 10 seconds, then cool under running water. Peel, halve and squeeze out the seeds; coarsely chop the flesh and let drain in a colander.
❖Combine the basil, garlic, oil and tomatoes in a food processor or blender and blend to a smooth puree. When the pasta is cooked, pour the soup into a tureen. Add the *pistou*, stir well and serve immediately, passing the cheese separately.

SERVES 6   *Photograph pages 28 – 29*

MUSHROOM SOUP

PETER JOHNSON

Poitou/Charentes

POTAGE AUX CÈPES
Mushroom Soup

1 lb (500 g) fresh cèpes or *porcini* (boletus) mushrooms
1 tablespoon (25 g) butter
1 level tablespoon all purpose (plain) flour
1 qt (1 l) chicken stock
salt and freshly ground pepper
4 pinches of freshly grated nutmeg
6 tablespoons heavy (double) cream or crème
　　fraîche

❖Trim the ends of the mushroom stems. Rinse the mushrooms quickly under running water, pat dry and slice thinly. Melt the butter in a heavy 4-qt (4-l) saucepan and cook the mushroom slices until they are golden and have stopped giving out moisture. Add the flour and mix, stirring, for 1 minute.
❖Stir in the stock and return to the boil. Add salt, pepper and nutmeg, cover and cook for 30 minutes over gentle heat, stirring from time to time.
❖Pour the contents of the saucepan into a food processor and blend at high speed for 1 minute to produce a smooth puree. Return to the pan and bring to boil. Add the cream and boil the soup for 1 minute. Pour into a tureen and serve immediately.

SERVES 4

Alsace

TARTE FLAMBÉE
Alsatian Tart

This tart used to be baked in the ovens of bakeries, where it would be licked by the flames — hence its name. There is another version in which fromage blanc *(fresh cheese) and eggs are added to the cream filling.*

2 tablespoons peanut oil
1 onion (about 3 oz/100 g), finely chopped
1 cup (8 fl oz/250 ml) heavy (double) cream or crème
　　fraîche
salt and freshly ground pepper
4 pinches of freshly grated nutmeg
3 oz (100 g) streaky bacon
13 oz (400 g) bread dough (recipe this page)

❖Heat half the oil in a nonstick 10-in (26-cm) skillet. Add the onion and cook, stirring, over low heat for 5 minutes or until golden.
❖Combine the cream, salt, pepper and nutmeg. Stir in the onion. Remove the rind from the bacon and cut bacon into thin matchsticks. Heat the remaining oil in the skillet and fry the bacon until lightly browned, about 3 minutes, stirring constantly. Drain on paper towels and set aside.
❖Heat the oven to 450°F (230°C). Oil a 14 x 9-in (35 x 22-cm) baking sheet. Roll out the bread dough until slightly smaller than the baking sheet; place it on the sheet. Spread the onion mixture over the dough and dot with the bacon. Bake for 20 minutes or until the tart is lightly browned. Serve hot.

SERVES 6

PETER JOHNSON

EGGS WITH TOMATO AND PEPPERS (top, recipe page 42)
AND ALSATIAN TART

PÂTE À PAIN
Bread Dough

For approximately 1½ lb (750 g) dough:
1 teaspoon superfine (caster) sugar
6 tablespoons (3 fl oz/100 ml) lukewarm water
1 envelope (½ oz/15 g) dry yeast
1 lb (500 g) all purpose (plain) flour
1½ teaspoons salt
⅔ cup (5 fl oz/150 ml) lukewarm milk

❖Place the sugar in a teacup. Add the lukewarm water and stir until the sugar is dissolved. Sprinkle the yeast over, stir in, and let rise in a warm place for about 10 minutes, or until the mixture reaches the edge of the cup.
❖Sift the flour onto a work surface and sprinkle with salt. Mix the two together and make a well in the middle. Pour in the milk and the yeast mixture.
❖Mix all ingredients together, using the fingertips in a quick movement from the center to the edges, then roll the dough into a ball. Knead it by stretching out the dough in front of you, then folding it in two, giving it a quarter turn in a counterclockwise direction and repeating the operation. Continue to knead the dough in this way for about 10 minutes, or until it is smooth, elastic and no longer sticky.
❖Place the dough in a floured bowl and cover with a clean, damp towel. Let rise in a warm draft-free area until doubled in volume, about 1½ hours.
❖Turn the risen dough onto a floured work surface and flatten with the palm of the hand, then knead as before for about 3 minutes. The dough is then ready for use.

Pays Basque

PIPÉRADE
Eggs with Tomatoes and Peppers

The pipérade *is traditionally made with the very fine-skinned small, sweet green peppers, shaped like little horns, that are found in the markets in summer and fall.*

2 red bell peppers (capsicums), each about 5 oz (150 g)
2 green bell peppers (capsicums), each about 5 oz (150 g)
3 oz (100 g) onions
2 lb (1 kg) perfectly ripe tomatoes
4 tablespoons extra virgin olive oil
2 cloves garlic, finely chopped
1 fresh red or green hot (chili) pepper, seeded and
    coarsely chopped
salt and freshly ground pepper
pinch of sugar
6 eggs
6 medium-size slices of raw ham, such as Bayonne

❖Preheat broiler (griller). Place the peppers on the broiler rack and grill, not too close to the heat source, for about 20 minutes or until the skins are black, turning often.

❖Meanwhile, peel and thinly slice the onions. Drop the tomatoes into boiling water for 10 seconds, then cool them under cold running water. Peel, halve and squeeze out the seeds; coarsely chop the flesh.

❖When the peppers are charred, place them in a bowl, cover and cool to lukewarm. Peel away blackened skin; discard the stem, seeds and white parts. Rinse peppers briefly, then slice into fine strips.

❖Heat 3 tablespoons oil in a nonstick 10-in (26-cm) skillet. Add the onions and cook, stirring, for 5 minutes or until golden. Add the garlic, hot pepper and pepper strips and cook, stirring, for a further 2 minutes. Add the tomatoes and season with salt, pepper and sugar. Cover and cook over gentle heat for 30 minutes, stirring from time to time. Break the eggs into a bowl, season with salt and pepper and beat with a fork until blended. Pour into the skillet and cook, stirring, until the eggs have set. Keep warm.

❖Heat the remaining oil in another nonstick 10-in (26-cm) skillet and cook the ham slices over high heat for 30 seconds on each side.

❖Turn the *pipérade* into a shallow serving dish, arrange the slices of ham on top and serve immediately.

SERVES 6   *Photograph page 41*

Picardie

PÂTÉ DE CANARD D'AMIENS
Duck Pâté, Amiens-style

In Amiens, pâtés have a tradition going back to the Middle Ages, and duck pâté is certainly the most representative and the most authentic recipe of all. Reference to this pâté was made by Madame de Sévigné in her Letters, *written in the seventeenth century.*

1 duck, about 2½ lb (1.2 kg), with its liver
3 oz (100 g) fresh pork belly
8 oz (250 g) pork fillet

PIERRE HUSSENOT/AGENCE TOP

8 oz (250 g) boneless rabbit or chicken meat
8 oz (250 g) mushrooms
1 oz (25 g) butter
1 onion (about 3 oz/100 g), finely chopped
2 French shallots, finely chopped
2 tablespoons juniper eau-de-vie or gin
3 eggs
salt and freshly ground pepper
½ teaspoon *quatre-épices* (see glossary)
3 oz (100 g) shelled unsalted pistachio nuts
1 lb 6 oz (700 g) short (shortcrust) pastry (page 50)
1 tablespoon milk
1 calf's foot, split in two

❖Ask the butcher to bone the duck completely, without cutting through the skin; reserve the bones. After the tail and wing tips are removed, what should remain is a large pocket.

❖Cut the pork belly and fillet and the rabbit (or chicken) into ½-in (1-cm) cubes. Trim the duck liver and cut into large cubes. Trim the mushroom stalks, then wash and thinly slice the mushrooms.

❖Melt the butter in a nonstick 10-in (26-cm) skillet. Add the onion and shallots and cook, stirring, over moderate heat for 2 minutes or until golden. Add the mushrooms and cook over high heat until they have rendered all their liquid and it has evaporated. Add the three meats and the duck liver and cook, stirring, for 5 minutes or until lightly browned. Pour in the eau-de-vie and ignite, shaking the pan gently until the flames subside.

❖Turn the contents of the pan onto a chopping board and chop finely. Transfer to a bowl and mix in 2 whole eggs and 1 egg white (reserve remaining yolk), salt, pepper, *quatre-épices* and the pistachios. Fill the duck with ⅔ of this mixture.

❖Preheat oven to 400°F (200°C). Divide the short pastry in half. On a work surface, roll out half of the pastry into an oval shape somewhat larger than the duck. Spread half the reserved filling on the pastry to within ¾ in (2 cm) of the edges. Moisten the edges with a pastry brush dipped in cold water. Place the duck on top of the filling and spread the remaining filling over the duck. Roll the remaining pastry into an oval and lay it over the duck, reserving any pas-

try trimmings. Firmly press the pastry edges together to seal. Roll the edges towards the center and crimp with the tines of a fork. Whisk the reserved egg yolk with the milk and brush this mixture over the entire surface of the pâté. Cut three small holes in the top of the pâté and insert small "chimneys" of aluminum foil or waxed paper. Decorate the pâté with the pastry trimmings, cut into leaf shapes.

❖Bake the pâté for 2½ hours, reducing the oven temperature to 375°F (190°C) after 1 hour when the pâté is nicely colored.

❖Meanwhile, place the duck bones and the split calf's foot in a saucepan, cover with cold water and bring to boil. Season with salt. Simmer for 2 hours, then strain the resultant stock. When the pâté is cooked, remove it from the oven and pour the stock into the pâté through one of the chimneys; remove chimneys. Pour any leftover stock into a shallow dish to a depth of ½ in (1 cm) and refrigerate until set. Cut this jelly into small cubes and use to garnish the pâté. Let the pâté cool overnight before serving.

SERVES 8

43

Picardie

FLAMICHE AUX POIREAUX
Leek Tart

The word flamiche *(formerly* flamique*) is of Flemish origin and means a savory or sweet cake. In Picardie,* flamiches *are also made with pumpkin and onions, and the puff pastry may be replaced by the short pastry known as* pâte brisée.

2 oz (50 g) butter
1 lb (500 g) leeks, white parts only, washed and thinly sliced
    diagonally
salt and freshly ground pepper
2 tablespoons water
8 oz (250 g) puff pastry (recipe this page)
3 egg yolks
¾ cup (6 fl oz/200 g) heavy (double) cream or crème fraîche
6 pinches of freshly grated nutmeg
1 egg yolk
1 tablespoon water

❖Melt the butter in a nonstick 10-in (26-cm) skillet. Add the leeks, season with salt and pepper and cook, stirring, over low heat for 5 minutes or until the leeks begin to turn golden. Add 2 tablespoons water, cover and cook over very low heat for 30 minutes or until the leeks are very soft and transparent.

❖Meanwhile, divide the pastry into two portions, ⅔ and ⅓. Roll out the larger portion into an 11-in (28-cm) circle. Brush a straight-sided 8-in (20-cm) tart pan with water and line with the pastry, leaving ½ in (1 cm) overlapping the sides.

❖When the leeks are cooked, remove from heat and let cool. Beat 3 egg yolks in a medium bowl with a fork until blended. Add the cream, salt, pepper and nutmeg. Stir in the leeks.

❖Preheat oven to 400°F (200°C). Roll out the remaining third of the pastry into an 8-in (20-cm) circle. Pour the leek mixture into the pastry case and cover with the pastry circle, pressing the edges together to seal. Roll the edges of the pastry back over the pastry lid and crimp the edges of the roll with the tines of a fork.

❖Beat 1 egg yolk and 1 tablespoon water with a fork in a small bowl. Brush over the whole surface of the pastry. Cut out a small circle from the center of the pastry lid and insert a "chimney" of aluminum foil or waxed paper to keep it open. Bake the tart for 40 minutes or until golden brown. Serve hot or lukewarm.

SERVES 6   *Photograph page 43*

PÂTE FEUILLETÉE
Puff Pastry

For approximately 2 lb 6 oz (1.2 kg) pastry:
1 lb (500 g) soft butter
4 cups (1 lb/500 g) all purpose (plain) flour
1 teaspoon salt
about 1 cup (8 fl oz/250 ml) water

❖Remove the butter from the refrigerator 1 hour before using. In a large bowl, cream the butter until smooth and soft.

Sift the flour onto a work surface. Make a well in the center and add the salt and ¾ of the water. Blend the flour and water together with the fingertips of one hand, while the other hand gradually pushes the flour from the edges towards the center. Working with the fingertips, gradually blend in just enough of the remaining water to make a dough of the same consistency as the creamed butter; this dough is called *détrempe*. Roll it into a ball and let rest for 15 minutes.

❖Roll out the *détrempe* on a floured work surface to form a circle ¾ in (2 cm) thick and 6 in (15 cm) in diameter. With moistened fingers, spread the butter, in a layer again about ¾ in (2 cm) thick, in the center of the circle. Fold the edges of the dough over the butter, allowing an overlap of ¾ in (2 cm). You will now have a kind of envelope enclosing the butter; this is called the *pâton*. Dust both the *pâton* and the rolling pin with flour and roll out the *pâton* to a rectangle approximately 12 x 4 in (30 x 10 cm); apply only light pressure to the *pâton* so that it rolls out smoothly and the butter is not squeezed out.

❖ Now the operation known as *tourage* begins. Lift the lower edge of the pastry and fold it over to 4 in (10 cm) from the opposite edge. Press down this fold lightly with the rolling pin. Fold the remaining third of the pastry over the two layers and again lightly press down with the rolling pin: the pastry has just been given its first *tour*, or turn. The *tours* are done two at a time, but the *pâton* must always be turned a quarter of a circle, in a clockwise direction, so that the folds are no longer at the top and bottom, but on the left and right. Once more, roll out the *pâton* and fold it in thirds; it has now been given another turn. With the thumb and index finger, make two small indentations on the surface of the rectangle to indicate that the pastry has had two turns. Cover with a tea towel and refrigerate for 20 minutes.

❖Give the pastry two more turns as before, making four indentations with the fingers to show that the pastry has had four turns. Classic puff pastry is given six turns, but it is preferable to give the last two just before the pastry is to be used. After four turns, the pastry should rest for at least another 20 minutes; it may be kept in the refrigerator for 48 hours before use.

❖After the sixth turn, roll out the pastry and cut as required. When cutting the pastry, the knife should be kept vertical to avoid breaking the fine layers and allow maximum rise during baking. Puff pastry is always baked on a moistened, not buttered, baking sheet.

Savoie

SOUFFLÉ AU COMTÉ
Comté Cheese Soufflé

3 egg yolks
4 egg whites
salt
1 cup (8 fl oz/250 ml) milk
1½ oz (40 g) butter
¼ cup (1½ oz/40 g) all purpose (plain) flour
1 tablespoon heavy (double) cream or crème fraîche
freshly ground pepper
2 pinches of freshly grated nutmeg
3 oz (100 g) finely grated Comté cheese (or Emmenthaler)

COMTÉ CHEESE SOUFFLÉ

❖Preheat oven to 425°F (215°C). Generously butter a 6-in (16-cm) ovenproof porcelain soufflé dish. Place the egg yolks in one bowl, the whites in another. Sprinkle 2 pinches of salt over the whites. Bring the milk to boil in a small saucepan.

❖Melt the butter in a medium saucepan, add the flour and stir for 1 minute over low heat. Pour in the boiling milk in a thin stream, stirring constantly. Cook the mixture over low heat, stirring constantly, for 5 minutes or until it is the consistency of heavy cream. Remove from heat and whisk in the yolks one at a time. Blend in the cream, salt, pepper and nutmeg.

❖Beat the egg whites until firm but not too stiff. Whisk ¼ of the whites into the mixture in the saucepan, then pour this mixture back into the remaining egg whites. Gently fold together with a spatula, at the same time incorporating the cheese a spoonful at a time. Pour the mixture into the prepared soufflé dish, which should be about ¾ full. Bake for 30 minutes or until the soufflé has risen and is golden brown on top. Bring to the table immediately, in the dish, and serve with a large spoon.

SERVES 3-4

Corse/Côte d'Azur

RAVIOLIS

Ravioli

Traditionally, the filling for this ravioli is prepared from leftover daube (beef stewed in tomato sauce). It can also be made with veal that has been browned briefly in oil and ground.

For the pasta:
2½ cups (10 oz/300 g) all purpose (plain) flour
4 pinches of salt
2 eggs
2 tablespoons olive oil

For the filling:
1½ lb (750 g) cooked beef, finely chopped
1 egg
2 oz (50 g) Parmesan cheese, freshly and finely grated
1 lb (500 g) beet greens, Swiss chard or spinach
salt and freshly ground pepper
For serving:
tomato sauce
freshly and finely grated Parmesan cheese

❖Prepare the pasta: sift the flour and salt onto a work surface. Make a well in the center and add the eggs and oil. Combine all ingredients, using the fingertips in a quick movement from the middle towards the edges. When the dough is homogeneous, knead by pushing it out and then bringing it back into a ball, working it until it is elastic and comes away from the fingers. Roll out the dough into a ball, wrap in plastic and let rest for at least 30 minutes in a cool place.

❖Meanwhile, prepare the filling: combine the meat, egg and cheese in a bowl and mix well. Drop the greens into boiling water for 30 seconds, then drain and squeeze dry. Let cool slightly, then chop finely with a sharp knife. Stir into the meat mixture with salt and pepper.

❖Divide the pasta dough in half; roll out into equal-size rectangles. Place level teaspoons of the filling in small mounds on one rectangle, spaced 1 in (2 cm) apart. Moisten the dough between the mounds, using a pastry brush dipped in water, then cover with the second rectangle of dough. Seal the two sheets of dough together along the edges and around each mound of filling, pressing firmly. Cut out the ravioli using a sharp knife or a smooth-edged or crimped pastry wheel. Arrange the ravioli on a clean tea towel, taking care that they do not overlap.

❖Bring a large pot of water to boil. Add salt, then drop in the ravioli and cook for 5 minutes. Drain and turn the ravioli into a shallow dish. Cover with tomato sauce and toss lightly, then sprinkle with a little grated Parmesan. Serve immediately, with more Parmesan offered separately.

SERVES 6

RAVIOLI

45

POTATO OMELETTE, AUVERGNE-STYLE (top)
AND CHEESE AND WALNUT OMELETTE

Quercy

OMELETTE QUERCYNOISE
Cheese and Walnut Omelette

10 eggs
salt and freshly ground pepper
2 teaspoons armagnac
12 walnuts, coarsely grated
4 oz (120 g) Roquefort cheese, crumbled
1 tablespoon goose fat

❖Break the eggs into a bowl and beat with a fork until blended, adding salt, pepper and armagnac. Mix in the walnuts and crumbled Roquefort.

❖Melt the goose fat in a nonstick 10-in (26-cm) skillet. Pour in the egg mixture and cook the omelette over low heat, delicately stirring the surface, until it is firm on the bottom. Turn it over and cover the skillet until the other side is cooked. Slide the omelette onto a plate and serve immediately.

SERVES 5-6

Côte d'Azur

PISSALADIÈRE
Pissaladière

The name comes from the Niçoise dialect word pissalat *meaning a puree of anchovies flavored with thyme, cloves, fennel and a dash of olive oil. But this remains strictly a local combination and is usually replaced by anchovy fillets.*

5 tablespoons extra virgin olive oil
4 lb (2 kg) large onions, thinly sliced
4 cloves fresh, young garlic, finely chopped
2 tablespoons water
salt
13 oz (400 g) bread dough (see page 41)
16 anchovy fillets in olive oil
4 oz (125 g) black Niçoise olives

❖Heat 4 tablespoons olive oil in a nonstick 10-in (26-cm) skillet. Add the onions and garlic and cook, stirring, over low heat for 10 minutes or until the onions are golden. Add the water and season with salt. Cover and cook gently for 30 minutes or until the onions are transparent and very soft, adding a little more water if necessary during cooking.

❖Preheat oven to 425°F (215°C). Lightly oil a 14 x 9-in (35 x 22-cm) baking sheet or a 12-in (30-cm) round tart pan. Gently roll out the bread dough to fit and lay it in the pan. Spread the cooked onion mixture on the surface. Arrange the anchovy fillets in a lattice pattern on top, placing an olive in the center of each square. Sprinkle with the remaining oil. Bake for 30 minutes or until the crust is golden.

❖Serve the pissaladière hot or warm, cut into large squares or wedges.

SERVES 6

Auvergne

OMELETTE BRAYAUDE
Potato Omelette, Auvergne-style

This recipe comes from the town of Riom in the Auvergne. It is also popular in the Bourbonnais, where it is sometimes served without cream and sometimes without cheese. Bacon may be used in place of ham.

13 oz (400 g) baking potatoes
1 tablespoon lard
1 thick slice raw ham (7 oz/200 g), cut into small cubes
10 eggs
salt and freshly ground pepper
2 oz (50 g) Cantal cheese or aged cheddar
3 tablespoons cream

❖Peel and wash the potatoes; pat dry. Cut into ½-in (1-cm) cubes. Melt the lard in a nonstick 10-in (26-cm) skillet. Add the potatoes and cook, stirring, for 2 minutes or until lightly browned. Cover the pan and cook over very low heat until the potatoes are tender, about 15 minutes, stirring from time to time. Stir in the ham and cook for 2 minutes.

❖Break the eggs into a bowl, season with salt and pepper and beat with a fork until blended. Pour the beaten eggs into the skillet and stir for 1 minute. Cover and cook the omelette over low heat for 5 minutes or until the bottom is just set. Turn and cook the other side.

❖Meanwhile, grate the cheese using a coarse grater. When the omelette is cooked, pour the cream over and sprinkle with cheese. Slide onto a plate and serve immediately.

SERVES 6

PISSALADIÈRE (top), ALLYMES TART (bottom left, recipe page 48)
AND HERB PIE (bottom right, recipe page 48)

PETER JOHNSON

Lyonnais

TÂTRE DES ALLYMES

Allymes Tart

The tâtre *(a regional word for tart) is a specialty of the village of Allymes. It may also be made with* pâte brisée.

2 tablespoons peanut oil
1 lb (500 g) large onions, thinly sliced
½ cup (4 oz/125 g) well-drained *fromage blanc* or
 ricotta cheese
salt and freshly ground pepper
4 pinches of freshly grated nutmeg
½ cup (4 fl oz/125 ml) heavy (double) cream or crème
 fraîche
2 eggs
13 oz (400 g) bread dough (page 41)

❖Heat the oil in a nonstick 10-in (26-cm) skillet. Add the onions and cook, stirring, over low heat for 10 minutes or until golden. Set aside.
❖Beat the cheese in a bowl with a fork, adding salt, pepper, nutmeg and cream. Break the eggs into a separate bowl and beat with a fork until blended, then add to the cheese mixture and beat until smooth. Stir in the onions.
❖Preheat oven to 425°F (215°C). Lightly oil a 16 x 9-in (35 x 22-cm) baking sheet. Roll out the bread dough to the same size and lift the dough onto the sheet. Spread the onion mixture over the dough. Bake for 30 minutes or until the tart is lightly browned. Serve hot.

SERVES 6   *Photograph page 47*

Val de Loire

TOURTE AUX HERBES

Herb Pie

This is a specialty of Tours.

1 lb (500 g) fresh spinach
8 oz (250 g) sorrel
8 oz (250 g) beet greens or spinach
1 lettuce heart
2 oz (60 g) butter
salt and freshly ground pepper
1 lb (500 g) boiling potatoes
4 sprigs parsley
4 sprigs tarragon
2 cloves garlic, finely chopped
1 lb (500 g) puff pastry (page 44)
1 egg yolk
1 tablespoon water
1 cup (8 fl oz/250 ml) heavy (double) cream or crème
 fraîche

❖Wash the spinach and sorrel and trim the stalks; drain. Wash and drain the beet greens and lettuce. Coarsely chop all four greens. Melt half the butter in a nonstick 10-in (26-cm) skillet and gradually add the vegetables. Season with salt and pepper and cook over high heat, stirring constantly, for 5 minutes or until all liquid has evaporated. Turn vegetables out onto a plate and set aside.

❖Peel and wash the potatoes, pat dry and slice into ¼-in (5-mm) rounds. Rinse and dry the skillet. Melt the remaining butter in the skillet, add the potato and cook, turning often, for 15 minutes or until golden.
❖Finely chop the parsley and tarragon leaves. Add the chopped herbs and garlic to the potatoes, season with salt and pepper and cook, stirring, for 2 minutes. Remove from heat.
❖Preheat the oven to 425°F (215°C). Divide the pastry into two portions, ⅔ and ⅓. Roll out the larger portion into a 12 x 6-in (30 x 15-cm) rectangle and transfer it to a greased baking sheet. Spread half the potato mixture on the pastry to within 1 in (2 cm) of the edges. Cover with half the green vegetable mixture, then the remaining potatoes and finally the remaining green vegetable mixture. Roll out the remaining pastry into a 12½ x 6¾-in (32 x 17-cm) rectangle and place it over the filling. Press the two edges of the pastry together to seal.
❖To gild the pastry, beat the egg yolk and water with a fork in a small bowl. Brush this mixture over the entire surface of the pastry, using a pastry brush. Cut two small holes in the center of the pastry lid and insert small "chimneys" of aluminum foil or waxed paper to keep them open. Bake the pie for 45 minutes or until the pastry is golden brown.
❖Meanwhile, season the cream with salt and pepper. When the pie is baked, pour in the cream through the two chimneys. Let rest for 10 minutes before serving.

SERVES 6   *Photograph page 47*

Bourgogne

CORNIOTTES

Cheese Pastry "Hats"

8 oz (250 g) *fromage blanc* or ricotta cheese, drained
salt and freshly ground pepper
½ cup (4 fl oz/125 g) heavy (double) cream or crème fraîche
7 oz (200 g) Emmenthaler cheese, coarsely grated
2 eggs
1 lb (500 g) short (shortcrust) pastry (page 50)
1 egg yolk
1 tablespoon water

❖Turn the cheese into a bowl and mash it with a fork, adding salt, pepper and cream. Mix well. Add the Emmenthaler and eggs and mix well.
❖Preheat oven to 425°F (215°C). Roll out the pastry to a thickness of ⅛ in (3 mm). Cut out 26 circles, each 4 in (10 cm) in diameter.
❖Dip your finger in cold water and moisten the edges of the first pastry circle. Place a walnut-size mound of filling in the center of the pastry and turn up the edges of the circle on three sides to make a three-cornered "hat". Press the edges of the pastry firmly together at the corners so that the filling is enclosed. Repeat with the other pastry circles, arranging the *corniottes* on two nonstick baking sheets.
❖Beat the egg yolk and water and brush this mixture over the surface of the *corniottes*. Bake for 25 minutes or until the pastries are nicely browned. Arrange on a platter and serve hot or lukewarm.

SERVES 6

CHEESE PASTRY "HATS" (left) AND HERBED CHEESE
SPREAD (right, recipe page 37)
PIERRE HUSSENOT/AGENCE TOP

Pâte Brisée
Short (Shortcrust) Pastry

For approximately 8 oz (250 g) pastry: *
1¼ cups (5 oz/150 g) all purpose (plain) flour
3 oz (100 g) soft butter
1½ tablespoons water
½ teaspoon salt

❖If possible, prepare the pastry the day before, so that it loses all elasticity and is easy to roll out.
❖Place the flour, butter, water and salt in the bowl of a food processor. Mix for 30 seconds, or until the pastry comes together into a ball. Wrap the ball of dough in plastic wrap, without further kneading, and chill thoroughly. Remove the pastry from the refrigerator 1 hour before it is to be used, and let rest at room temperature.
❖Roll out pastry on a lightly floured surface according to instructions in recipe; transfer to pan. If possible, return pan to the refrigerator for an hour before baking; although this is not absolutely necessary, the pastry will cook better if prechilled.
Makes enough to line one 9- to 10-in (24- to 26-cm) pan.

Provence

Salade Niçoise
Niçoise Salad

This typically southern dish is made with raw vegetables, tuna, garlic, basil and olive oil. Neither cooked vegetables nor potatoes should be included.

6 eggs
1 lb (500 g) fresh broad beans
1 red bell pepper (capsicum), (about 5 oz/150 g)
2 small artichokes
½ lemon
1 clove garlic
1 lb (500 g) firm-ripe tomatoes, cut into eighths
1 small cucumber, thinly sliced
3 green (spring) onions, thinly sliced
2 tender celery stalks, strings removed, cut into fine strips
12 anchovy fillets in olive oil, halved lengthwise
1 can (6½ oz/195 g) tuna in olive oil, drained and coarsely flaked
2 oz (50 g) black Niçoise olives
12 large basil leaves
salt
6 tablespoons extra virgin olive oil

❖Place the eggs in a saucepan of cold water, bring to boil over low heat and simmer for 10 minutes. Drain the eggs and cool under running water. Shell them and cut into quarters.
❖Shell the broad beans and remove the green outer skins. Halve the red pepper and remove the stem, seeds and white ribs, then slice the pepper into fine slivers. Remove the outer leaves of the artichokes and trim the points of the remaining leaves. Cut each artichoke into quarters and rub the surfaces with lemon.
❖Rub a shallow bowl with the peeled clove of garlic. Arrange in it the tomatoes, pepper, cucumber, artichokes, onions, celery and broad beans. Garnish with anchovies, tuna, olives and hard-cooked eggs. Using scissors, snip the

basil leaves over the salad. Sprinkle lightly with salt. Drizzle with olive oil and serve immediately.

SERVES 6   *Photograph pages 28 – 29*

Provence

Petits Farcis Provençaux
Stuffed Vegetables of Provence

3 eggplants (aubergines), 7 oz (200 g) each
3 zucchini (courgettes), 3 oz (100 g) each
6 firm-ripe tomatoes, 5 oz (150 g) each
6 onions, 3 oz (100 g) each
salt and freshly ground pepper
3 tablespoons extra virgin olive oil
2 cloves garlic, finely chopped
1 lb (500 g) boneless veal from the neck or shoulder, trimmed of fat and finely chopped
3 oz (100 g) fresh pork belly, finely chopped
10 sprigs flat-leaf parsley, stemmed and chopped
3 tablespoons boiled rice
2 oz (50 g) Parmesan cheese, freshly and finely grated
2 eggs
2 sprigs thyme

❖Wash the eggplants and zucchini and pat dry. Cut in half lengthwise and remove most of the flesh, leaving ¼ in (5 mm) next to the skin. Cut off the top quarter of each tomato and hollow out the inside with a small spoon. Peel the onions, cut off the top quarter and scoop out a hollow in the center. Season the insides of all the vegetables with salt and pepper and brush lightly with oil. With a sharp knife, finely chop the flesh removed from the vegetables.
❖Heat 1 tablespoon oil in a nonstick 10-in (26-cm) skillet. Add the garlic, chopped vegetables and meat and cook, stirring, over moderate heat for 5 minutes or until lightly browned. Transfer to a bowl and let cool.
❖Preheat oven to 400°F (200°C). Using 1 teaspoon oil, brush the inside of a shallow baking dish large enough to hold all the vegetables side by side.
❖Add the parsley to the bowl with the rice, Parmesan, eggs, thyme, salt and pepper and mix well. Divide the filling among the vegetables and arrange them in the prepared dish. Sprinkle with the remaining oil and pour ¼ cup (2 fl oz/60 ml) water into the dish. Bake for 45 minutes or until the vegetables are tender, basting them from time to time with the pan juices and adding a little more water if the liquid evaporates too quickly.
❖When the vegetables are cooked, arrange them on a platter, spoon over the remaining cooking juices and serve immediately.

SERVES 6   *Photograph pages 28 – 29*

Languedoc

Petits Pâtés de Béziers
Little Pies from Béziers

It is said that in 1766 Lord Clive went to Pézenas to convalesce, and had these little pies made by his Indian cook. The original ownership of the recipe has been disputed ever since by Pézenas and Béziers; the version made in Pézenas does not contain currants.

For the pastry:
2½ tablespoons (50 g) lard
2 cups (8 oz/250 g) all purpose (plain) flour
2 pinches of fine sea salt
3 tablespoons water
For the filling:
grated rind of 1 lemon
1 egg
2 oz (50 g) dried currants
1 tablespoon brown sugar
salt and freshly ground pepper
3 oz (100 g) veal kidney fat or suet, coarsely chopped
10 oz (300 g) lamb shoulder or loin, finely chopped
1 egg yolk
1 tablespoon water

❖First prepare the pastry: melt the lard in a small saucepan and let cool to lukewarm. Sift the flour and salt onto a work surface. Make a well in the center and pour in the melted lard and 3 tablespoons water. Combine all together with the fingertips to make a smooth homogeneous dough. Roll into a ball and wrap in plastic. Refrigerate for 30 minutes.

❖Meanwhile, prepare the filling: wash and dry the lemon and grate its peel into a bowl. Add the egg, currants, sugar, salt and pepper and mix well.

❖Place the fat in a nonstick 10-in (26-cm) skillet and melt over low heat. Add the meat and cook, stirring, for 5 minutes or until well browned. Remove meat with a slotted spoon and add to the currant mixture, mixing well. Preheat the oven to 425°F (215°C).

❖Lightly butter six small custard cups or brioche tins 1½ in (4 cm) in diameter and 1¼ in (3 cm) high. Roll out the pastry thinly and cut out six 3-in (8-cm) circles and six 2-in (5-cm) circles. Line the cups or tins with the larger circles, then add the filling. Brush the edges of the pastry with water and cover with one of the smaller circles. Press the edges together to seal and make a few slits in the top of each pie with the blade of a knife to allow the steam to escape.

❖Beat the egg yolk and 1 tablespoon water with a fork in a small bowl. Brush this mixture over the surface of the pies. Bake for 20 minutes or until golden. Remove from tins and serve hot.

SERVES 6

PETER JOHNSON

LITTLE PIES FROM BÉZIERS (top) AND EGG AND BACON QUICHE

Lorraine

QUICHE LORRAINE
Egg and Bacon Quiche

The word quiche comes from the German küche, *meaning cake. The origins of* quiche lorraine *go back to the seventeenth century, but today the name quiche is used for savory tarts that are served warm.*

8 oz (250 g) short (shortcrust) pastry (page 50)
8 oz (250 g) thinly sliced streaky bacon
2 oz (50 g) butter
3 eggs
1 cup (8 fl oz/250 ml) heavy (double) cream or crème fraîche
salt and freshly ground pepper
6 pinches of freshly grated nutmeg

❖Heat the oven to 425°F (215°C). Lightly butter a deep 9- to 10-in (24-cm) tart pan. Roll out the pastry and line the tin, crimping the edge. Refrigerate until needed. Remove rind from the bacon and cut the bacon into small pieces. Drop these into a small saucepan of boiling water and blanch for 1 minute. Drain, rinse under cold running water and pat dry. Melt half the butter in a nonstick 8-in (20-cm) skillet and lightly fry the bacon, stirring constantly with a wooden spoon. Drain on paper towels.

❖Break the eggs into a bowl and beat with a fork until blended, adding the cream, salt, pepper and nutmeg.

❖Remove the tart pan from the refrigerator. Scatter bacon over the bottom of the pastry. Pour in the egg mixture and dot with the remaining butter. Bake for about 30 minutes or until the quiche is lightly browned. Serve hot.

SERVES 6

Lorraine

FOIE GRAS EN TERRINE
Cooked Whole Duck Liver Terrine

The much sought-after delicacy, foie gras, *whether of goose or duck, is traditionally made in two regions, the Landes and Alsace, according to recipes dictated by fashion or by the region. At one time, for example, it used to be served at the end of the meal instead of at the beginning, as we know today.*

1 uncooked duck *foie gras,* about 1¼ lb (600 g)
1 teaspoon fine sea salt
1 teaspoon crushed pepper
scant ½ cup (100 ml) cognac

❖Carefully separate the two lobes of the liver and, using a small, sharp-pointed knife, remove the fine outer membrane, the blood vessels and other filaments. Place the two lobes, side by side, in a shallow dish just large enough to hold them. Season with salt and pepper and sprinkle with cognac. Cover the dish and refrigerate for 12 hours, turning the liver once or twice.

❖Remove the liver from the refrigerator and let stand at room temperature for 1 hour. Preheat the oven to 350°F (180°C). Pat the liver dry and arrange the pieces in a covered baking dish just large enough to hold them. Top with the lid.

❖Place the dish in a pan of hot, but not boiling, water and bake for 40 minutes.

❖Place the two lobes of liver in a stainless steel colander resting over a bowl; let drain for about 15 minutes.

❖In a small container just large enough to hold them, rearrange the two lobes into the original form of the liver. Press down to firm, using the back of a spoon. Cover with a sheet of waxed paper, then with a board or a sheet of cardboard. Top with a 1-lb (500-g) weight and let stand for 1 hour.

❖Remove the weight, the board and the paper. Cover the liver by ¼ in (5 mm) with the fat collected in the bowl. Let the fat set, then cover the dish and refrigerate.

❖Chill the liver for 2 to 3 days before serving, in slices, accompanied by toasted country bread.

❖This terrine may be kept for a week in the refrigerator.

SERVES 6

COOKED WHOLE DUCK LIVER TERRINE
PIERRE HUSSENOT/AGENCE TOP

VAL DE LOIRE

A gentle garden

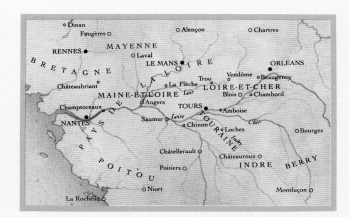

VAL DE LOIRE

A gentle garden

How soft and sweet it is, the garden of France! Following the length of the seemingly endless and capricious river, dotted with friendly colors: it is a cameo of grey, blue and green, tricking the eye with its contrasts, resisting clear definitions. It would be fascinating to follow its course.

Yet the Loire has become useless. No longer does it convey the flat-bottomed river barges, nor those sailing ships which once transported cargo to Nantes, the former "ebony" port, port of the Antilles. It gives an impression of indolence, but in reality it is frolicsome and reckless, forever swirling feverishly.

It is impossible to speak of the Loire Valley without first invoking the landscape. The bridge of Beaugency, the roofs of Blois, the levee banks that go as far as Tours, the tributaries — the Cher, the Indre, the lazy Cosson, the warm Sauldre — lapping at manors and châteaux. Back at Beaugency, behind the high-humped bridge, a dungeon watches over nothing more than the flights of birds. At Orléans, an island is lost in the middle of the river. Further on, towards Nantes and the sea, Champtoceaux, the promenade of Champalud, forms a panorama that spreads out and goes on and on. And then, the colors of the Loire, soft and muted, and of the fields . . . a garden of beauty! No matter whether you take leave of the river near Loché or near Ouchamps, whether you reach the low forests of Sologne or the high hedges of the park at Chambord, with its hundred bell turrets, or whether you wander towards the nearby Berry, awaiting, from across the flat green expanse of the countryside, the sight of the spire of the tower of Bourges cathedral; or whether you traverse the

LEFT: IN THE CALM OF TWILIGHT THE ENTRANCING FOURTEENTH-CENTURY CHÂTEAU DE SAUMUR IS REFLECTED IN THE WATERS OF THE LOIRE.

PREVIOUS PAGES: THE LOIR, A TRIBUTARY OF THE FAMOUS LOIRE RIVER, FLOWS THROUGH THE TINY VILLAGE OF LES ROCHES-L'ÉVÊQUE.

57

LIKE THE BUILDINGS IN TROO, THE ARCHITECTURE THROUGHOUT THE
LOIRE VALLEY EVOKES FAIRY-TALE IMAGES.

savored, they are forgotten. But it is only right to
begin with the fruits of the vine, which accompany to perfection the fruits of the earth.

The white asparagus and the green endive
grown between the Loire and the Sologne are the
most delicate in the world. The miniature
tomatoes, in the form of tiny cherries and mini-
pears, are common. There are innumerable garden
herbs, credited with medicinal virtues: balm,
camomile, tarragon, wild and cultivated thyme,
basil, chives, savory and simple parsley.
Everywhere, charcuterie reigns supreme, from the
rillons of Vouvray and the *rillettes* of Maine and
Anjou, to the *andouillette* of Jargeau and crumbed
pig's trotters, to chicken liver terrine and a variety
of sausages.

A few pâtés are based on game, since this is
hunting country: red deer and roe deer gallop
across fields, partridge and pheasant thread their
way through the heather of the moors, hares start
up and streak away along the roadsides, and wild
mallard ducks, or *cols verts*, fly over the ponds
between Bracieux and Romorantin. The vast,
gentle Sologne, with its expanses for hunting on
horseback; the flat Berry, where the châteaux
stand out on the horizon like spurs; the region of
Orléans with sandy soils and immense forests
wedded to the canals: these are the companions
of the river Loire.

WHILE CHINON IS WELL-KNOWN FOR ITS WHITE WINE (CELEBRATED IN
THE SIXTEENTH-CENTURY WORK *GARGANTUA AND PANTAGRUEL* BY FRANÇOIS
RABELAIS), FISHING REMAINS A POPULAR PASTIME.

deserted terrain of the Nivernais, which flirts with
the strict architecture of the château of Serrant . . .
behind the verdant serenity of a landscape shaped
by man beams an innocent appeal to the appetite.

If, once upon a time, the kings of France abandoned Paris for Chinon, where they established
their court, where they awaited the faltering steps
of the maid of Orléans on the smooth-worn
stones of the Grand-Carroi, it was because they
were certain of finding fine foods, fine wines and
festivity in the Loire Valley. Is it the richest region
of France? If so, it is also the most modest, for it
does not boast — except perhaps that the French
spoken here is the purest in the country and is free
of any provincial *patois*.

And here the miracle of wine occurs. After the
pleasant muscadets of Nantes come the full-
bodied Chaume of Anjou; the honorable Layons,
which improves with age, splendidly deep in
flavor in good years; the proud Savennières, with
a nose of almond and linden, of verbena and
acacia; the fresh red wine from Chinon, made
from the Cabernet Franc grape, smelling of green
peppers and pea pods; and its first cousins, from
Saumur-Champigny and Bourgueil, the mellow
Vouvray with enormous aging potential, the like-
able Montlouis, the light Gamay, the easy-drink-
ing Sauvignon, the fruity Sancerre and its flinty-
flavored cousins from Menetou-Salon and Reuilly.
All these wines are nurtured religiously in the region's white limestone caves, which become even
more white with age. They are drunk, they are

THE CHÂTEAU CHENONCEAUX IS PERHAPS THE MOST ELEGANT OF THE LOIRE VALLEY JEWELS. ITS BEAUTIFUL GARDENS AND SURROUNDING BUILDINGS MAINTAIN A STYLE FAITHFUL TO THE TIME OF HENRI II, WHEN THE CHÂTEAU WAS BUILT.

And here gambol the goats from which come such fine cheeses: the pyramids of Valençay and of Pouligny-Saint-Pierre, the cylindrical forms of Sainte-Maure-de-Touraine, the ash-covered loaves of Selles-sur-Cher. All make admirable marriages with the white wine pressed from the Sauvignon grape. Start with the *crottin* of Chavignol, firm to the touch, sandy-textured in the mouth, with a grassy, curdy taste, a product of the Sancerre region, where it finds its natural ally in the wine of the same name. All these cheeses make a fine prelude to the fruits harvested in this gentle climate: pears primarily, but also greengage plums, raspberries, strawberries and peaches. The sandy soils on either side of the river support a natural orchard, its offspring the quince or apple jelly known as *cotignac*, the caramelized upside-down apple tart invented by the Tatin sisters in their hotel (situated in the Sologne town of Lamotte-Beuvron), and the pancakes from Anjou, flavored with the locally produced, orange-scented liqueur, Cointreau.

Would these make us forget the other riches of the countryside? The Loire's tender fish include beautifully pink salmon, the pike with its estimable flesh but plentiful bones, the shad, the eel that is typically prepared with the red wine of Chinon *en matelote* or accompanied with a white butter sauce flavored with white wine, vinegar and shallots and said to be a specialty of Nantes. The eels were thought to have vanished long ago, eagerly seized by the few odd fishermen along the canals, but mostly chased away by pollution. But the opposite has occurred: they are proliferating in the river, now warmed by the discharge water of the nuclear power stations at Saint-Laurence-des-Eaux (near Beaugency) and Avoine (near Chinon).

Nor should we forget the diversity of mushrooms cultivated in underground caves. The grey *pleurotes* are of vaguely rubbery appearance, and the little cultivated mushrooms known as *champignons de Paris* are grown easily in the natural vaults found in the wine region of Saumur and along the banks of the Cher; pale in appearance, they take on flavor when fried with garlic. Poultry, too, has a high reputation here. Tender-fleshed guinea fowl, flavorful rabbit, and the succulent hen-chicken called *géline*, are still prepared in the same way as they were in the days of François I in the châteaux of Chambord and Ussé, when the art of combining sweet and salty flavors was highly esteemed. They are served with local heather honey or combined with the orchard-fresh fruits, lightly fried or roasted like choice vegetables.

Two typical dishes that epitomize this ancient sweet-sour style (which has nothing to do with the fad of *nouvelle cuisine*, but rather represents an underlying influence persisting since the Middle Ages) are noisette of pork with prunes and hindquarter of rabbit with honey. Here ingredients which would otherwise clash are gently and judiciously married. Is not the Loire Valley, after all, the land of soft colors, of subdued and apparently fragile landscapes, of bold wines and peaceful digestion?

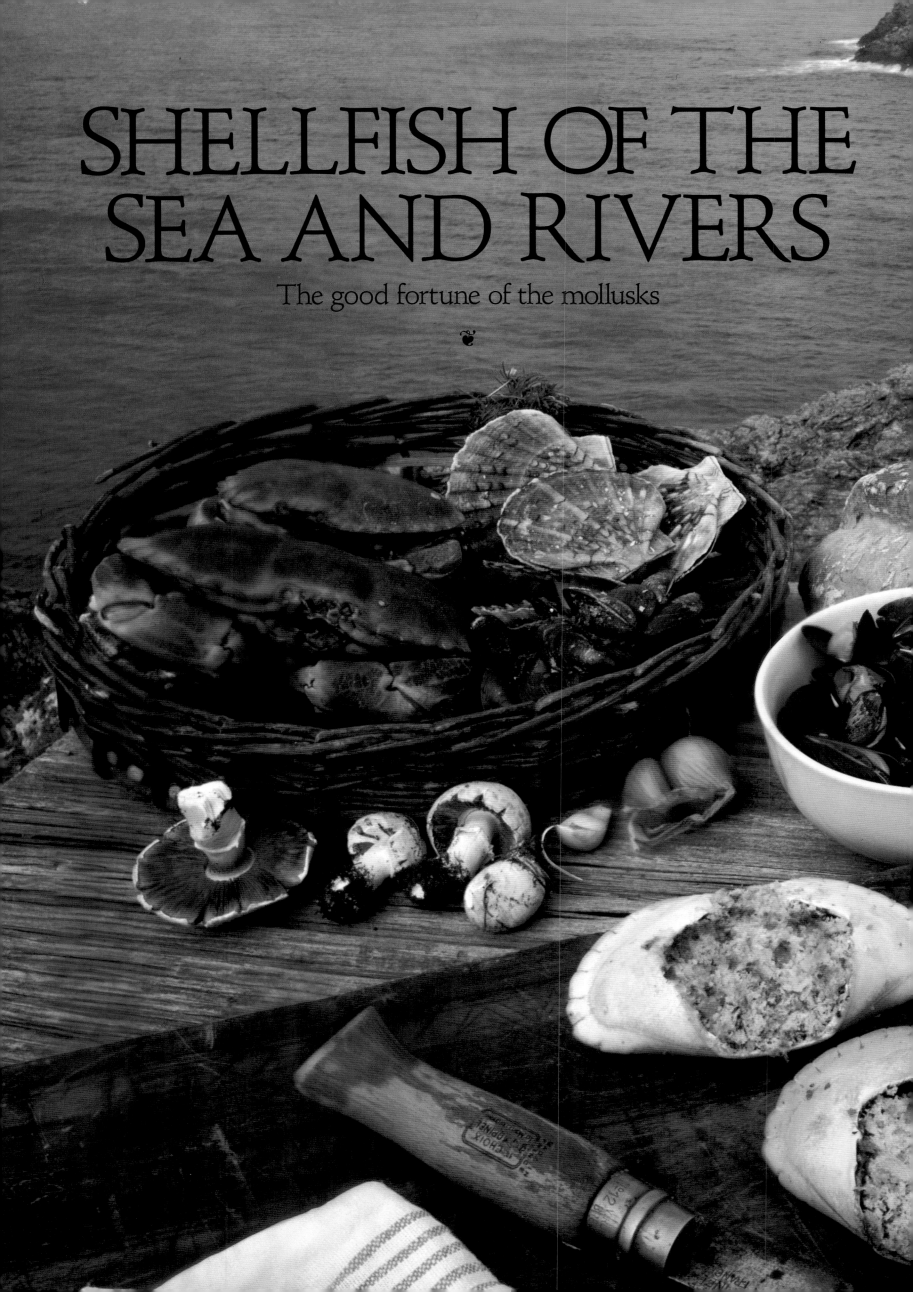

SHELLFISH OF THE SEA AND RIVERS

The good fortune of the mollusks

CULTIVATED IN THE BAIE DU MONT-ST-MICHEL, *MOULES DE BOUCHOT*,
SMALL HIGHLY-PRIZED MUSSELS, ARE GROWN ON STAKES DRIVEN
INTO THE SEDIMENT OF ITS SHALLOW COASTAL BEDS.

SHELLFISH OF THE SEA AND RIVERS

The good fortune of the mollusks

It is an utter mystery. Why on earth does the gourmet, and in particular the French gourmet, rave so much about white-fleshed mollusks? In the nineteenth century there were clubs and oyster-eating competitions at which honest, bourgeois citizens would be encouraged to overindulge in chorus, stuffing themselves with seafood.

Oysters from Cancale, from the bay of Morbihan, from Belon, from Saint-Vaast-la Hougue, from Marennes-Oléron: to say that they do not all have the same flavor is not enough. The flat oyster, which gave Cancale its fame, has almost disappeared as the result of an epidemic known as *bonamia*. The deep-shelled oyster, or *huître creusé*, although also decimated, was better able to survive than its more highly reputed neighbor. The Portuguese oyster, or *portugaise*, so named because a Portuguese ship once tipped its copious cargo of shellfish onto the Atlantic coast, has been replaced by a species of Japanese origin, the *gigas*. Apart from all this, the oyster has a solid reputation, and even dieters appreciate it.

The texture of the oyster can be deceptive. During the "R" months — in other words, from September to April — the mollusks are fresh and lively. In July and August, the period of egg-laying and reproduction, they are plump and milky — but should not be confused with those oysters that are naturally fatter because they are older (called *spéciales* by the vendors), in contrast to the *claires* which are younger and thinner in flavor.

Mussels are generally cultivated on fixed wooden stakes in the waters off Oléron and La Rochelle; these are the best. Others are grown in special "parks" at Croisic or, in the Mediterranean, on ropes, as are those from Bouzigues, on the Etang de Thau. Their tender, orange-red, flavorful flesh lends itself to many cooking variations: *marinière* style, or with cream, or in the preparation known as *éclade*, where a quick fire directly on top of the mussels causes them to open, or *mouclade*, which is nothing more or less than a mussel stew with white wine and cream.

It is no mystery why shellfish are well treated in cuisine: over-complicating the recipes entails a risk of losing their prime freshness. Scallops, firm-fleshed and delicate, and their baby sisters the *pétoncles*, white-fleshed mollusks with an almost-sweet flavor, can take only a very brief cooking, which preserves their iodine and their savor.

Lobster and crayfish, which are the kings — albeit rare — of the Breton coasts (the true Mediterranean crayfish are scarcely found any more) and which are trapped in pots, are served in a way that is both attractive and simple: grilled, with *beurre blanc* sauce. Spices and strongly flavored sauces should be used sparingly. The old ways which involved flaming, or outdated preparations such as "Thermidor" (covered with a white wine- and mustard-flavored sauce, then topped with grated cheese and grilled), or "Newburg" (cooked in a creamy, American-style sauce) have

PREVIOUS PAGES: STUFFED CRAB (left, recipe page 80), MUSSELS IN CREAM
(center, recipe page 66) AND SCALLOPS ÉTRETAT-STYLE (right, recipe page 68),
PHOTOGRAPHED IN NORMANDIE
PIERRE HUSSENOT/AGENCE TOP

BARGAINING FOR FRESHLY HARVESTED MUSSELS AND OYSTERS AT
VIVIER-SUR-MER ON THE BAIE DU MONT-ST-MICHEL.

A VARIETY OF SHELLFISH FOR SALE AT LES HALLES IN QUIMPER, BRETAGNE.
DELIGHTS INCLUDE *TOURTEAUX* (LARGE CRABS), *BOUQUET CUITS* (COOKED SHRIMP),
LANGOUSTINES CUITS (COOKED CRAYFISH), *HOMARDS* (LOBSTER), AND
ARAIGNÉES (SPIDER CRABS).

the effect of masking the shellfish's natural flavor.
Perhaps the reason that certain restaurateurs persist
with them is that such preparations hide the lack
of flavor of an inferior product.

Shrimp — the tiny ones, *grises*, and the larger
ones, *bouquets* — make excellent first courses,
whether as a salad, lightly fried, or cold with *sauce
verte* or mayonnaise. Langoustines, which resem-
ble baby lobsters in shape, are easily cooked —
but watch the time! A few seconds too long, and
a firm, crisp-textured flesh becomes soft and
stringy. Only the tail is used, pan-fried. The great
chef Joël Robuchon used to serve them as an
extremely elegant salad which was all the rage in
Paris in the early '80s; he would pan-fry them just
before serving, then dress them with a small
amount of goose fat.

There is a whole family of crabs, all hiding soft,
pinkish flesh under a hard red shell. The *tourteau*
(common crab) is the most hardy; the *étrille* (swimmer) is smaller and more delicate; the *araignée*
(spider crab) is the most fragile of all, but also the
rarest and tastiest. All are rich in vitamins, low in
calories and exquisite served cold with a lemony
mayonnaise.

To complete this diverse range of marine
shellfish, mention should be made of the sea
cockle, which must be cleaned of sand before
being eaten raw or cooked; the *palourdes*, or clams,
translucent and delicate, with their lightly striped
shell, excellent served raw with a dash of lemon;

the *praires*, or warty venus, which are usually stuffed and grilled with garlic butter or made into a soup.

Freshwater crustaceans are gradually disappearing from French rivers as a result of pollution. The crayfish, or *écrevisses*, that were once plentiful in small streams, lakes and reservoirs, now usually come from other countries (Turkey, in particular). The most highly reputed are the *pattes rouges*, the red-legged variety. It should be added, however, that in spite of the attraction of their delicate, firm-textured flesh, the taste depends more on their mode of presentation, which often involves extracting the flavor of the crushed shells to make a sauce or soup.

Contrary to popular opinion, squid (*calamars*, *calmars* or *chipirons*, to give them their Basque name, and the larger *encornets*) and small cuttlefish (*supions* in the Mediterranean) are not fish but mollusks. According to region, they may be stuffed, cooked with sweet peppers or tomatoes, or served with a sauce, their firm flesh retaining its distinctive taste and appearance regardless of recipe.

BUSINESS IS BRISK IN THE OPEN MARKETPLACE AT BLOIS WITH BOTH LOCAL FRESH AND OCEAN SEAFOOD FOR SALE.

THIS ENTICING DISPLAY OF LOCAL MEDITERRANEAN SEAFOOD IN NICE INCLUDES MUSSELS, CLAMS, SEA-URCHINS AND SPINY CRAYFISH.

MUSSELS IN WINE AND CREAM SAUCE

Charentes

MOUCLADE

Mussels in Wine and Cream Sauce

In Charentes, the mouclade *is made with the same basic ingredients as in Aunis and Saintonge: cultivated mussels, wine, French shallots, cream and egg yolk. The flavors vary, however: the curry powder may be replaced by saffron, and sometimes* Pineau des Charentes *is added. This is a delicious fortified wine made from grape must and cognac.*

5 lb (2.5 kg) mussels
1½ cups (12 fl oz/400 ml) dry white wine (in Charentes, Muscadet or Gros-plant would be used)
1 sprig thyme
1 bay leaf
6 sprigs parsley
1 oz (25 g) butter
3 French shallots, finely chopped
1 teaspoon curry powder
pinch of cayenne pepper
⅔ cup (5 fl oz/150 g) heavy (double) cream or crème fraîche
3 egg yolks

❖Scrape the mussels and remove the beards. Wash mussels in several changes of water, then drain.
❖Pour the wine into a large nonaluminum saucepan. Add the thyme, bay leaf and parsley, bruising them between the fingers. Bring just to boil over high heat and add the mussels, moving them around in the liquid with a slotted spoon. Remove them with the slotted spoon as soon as they open, and set aside in a bowl. Boil the mussel cooking liquid over high heat until reduced by half, then strain it into a bowl. Discard any unopened mussels.
❖Meanwhile, melt the butter in a small saucepan and

lightly cook the shallots, stirring constantly, for 2 minutes or until they are golden. Add the mussel liquid and bring to boil; boil for 1 minute.
❖Strain the contents of the small saucepan back into the pot used for cooking the mussels, add the curry, cayenne and ⅔ of the cream and boil for 1 minute. Beat the egg yolks in a small bowl with the remaining cream. Whisk 2 tablespoons of the hot liquid into the beaten yolks, then pour into the large saucepan. Add the mussels and reheat for 1 minute, stirring, over very low heat; do not allow the sauce to boil.
❖Ladle the mussels into shallow soup bowls, pour the sauce over and serve immediately.

SERVES 4

Provence

MOULES AUX ÉPINARDS

Mussels with Spinach

3 tablespoons milk
2 oz (50 g) fresh bread, crusts trimmed
2 lb (1 kg) spinach, washed and drained
1 lb (500 g) small mussels
2 lb (1 kg) large mussels
salt and freshly ground pepper
1 lb (500 g) ripe tomatoes
2 tablespoons olive oil
2 onions, each about 3 oz (100 g), finely chopped
pinch of sugar

❖Warm the milk in a small saucepan and crumble in the bread. Let cool.
❖Place the spinach in a large saucepan with the water clinging to its leaves. Cook over high heat for 4 minutes or until tender. Drain very well and squeeze dry, then chop finely.
❖Wash the mussels. Scrape the small ones and remove the beards, then transfer them to a large saucepan and place over high heat just until opened, turning them over constantly with a wooden spoon. Drain, reserving the cooking juices, and let the mussels cool. Discard any unopened mussels.
❖Open the large mussels by pulling on the beard, but do not separate the two halves of the shell. Reserve the juices, remove the small mussels from their shells and chop coarsely with a knife. Strain the cooking liquid, as well as the juices from the large mussels. Add the bread mixture and the spinach and mix well, mashing with a fork. Add the chopped mussels with a little salt and pepper and mix well. Fill the raw mussels with this mixture and tie the two halves of the shells together to retain the stuffing.
❖Drop the tomatoes into boiling water for 10 seconds, then cool under running water. Peel, halve and squeeze out the seeds; mash the flesh with a fork.
❖Heat the oil in a nonstick 11-in (28-cm) sauté pan. Add the onions, stirring, and cook for 2 minutes or until golden. Add the tomatoes, salt, pepper and sugar and cook, stirring, for 2 minutes. Add the stuffed mussels and cook for 5 minutes, turning over once. Remove the strings and arrange the mussels in a shallow soup dish. Pour the tomato sauce over and serve immediately.

SERVES 6 *Photograph page 67*

Normandie/Bretagne

MOULES MARINIÈRE
Mussels in White Wine

This is a traditional dish served all over France. It is usually made with a local white wine.

6 lb (3 kg) mussels
bouquet garni: 1 bay leaf, 1 sprig thyme, 6 sprigs parsley
2 oz (50 g) butter
6 French shallots, finely chopped
1 clove garlic, finely chopped
2 cups (16 fl oz/500 ml) dry white wine such as Muscadet
freshly ground pepper
2 tablespoons chopped flat-leaf parsley

❖ Scrape the mussels and remove the beards. Wash in several changes of water and drain. Tie together the herbs for the bouquet garni.
❖ Melt the butter in a saucepan large enough to hold all the mussels. Add the chopped shallots and garlic and cook over low heat, stirring, for 1 minute or until softened. Pour in the wine, add the bouquet garni and season with pepper; bring to boil. Boil for 2 minutes, then add the mussels and stir with a slotted spoon. As soon as they open, remove them with the slotted spoon and keep warm in a large bowl. Discard any unopened mussels.
❖ Boil the cooking liquid over high heat until reduced by half, then return the mussels to the pan and add the chopped parsley. Mix all together just long enough to reheat the mussels, about 30 seconds. Remove the bouquet garni.
❖ Divide the mussels and liquid among four large shallow soup plates and serve immediately.

SERVES 4

Normandie

MOULES À LA CRÈME
Mussels in Cream

Mussels are cultivated in different ways in different regions. The best known are those grown in Charentes on wooden stakes or bouchots, to which they attach themselves in clusters. In Bretagne mussels are cultivated like oysters — flat, in beds. In the south they are grown hanging, and in the Etang de Thau the famous Bouzigues mussels live permanently submerged, but without contact with the bottom of the lagoon.

8 lb (4 kg) mussels
2 cups (16 fl oz/500 ml) dry cider
4 French shallots, finely chopped
¾ cup (6 fl oz/185 g) heavy (double) cream or crème fraîche
salt and freshly ground pepper
3 egg yolks
1 tablespoon chopped parsley

❖ Scrape the mussels and remove the beards. Wash in several changes of water and drain.
❖ Pour the cider into a pot large enough to hold the mussels and place over high heat. Add the shallots and boil for 2 minutes. Add the mussels and stir with a slotted spoon. As

soon as they open, remove the mussels with the slotted spoon and keep warm in a large bowl.
❖ Pour half the cream into the pot and cook over high heat until the sauce is smooth and slightly thickened. Strain into a small saucepan and keep warm. Season with salt and pepper.
❖ Beat together the remaining cream and the egg yolks with a fork. Pour this mixture into the small saucepan and whisk over low heat until the sauce becomes thick and creamy; take care that the sauce does not boil and become grainy. Stir in the parsley. Divide the mussels among four warm plates and pour the sauce over. Serve immediately.

SERVES 4   *Photograph pages 60 – 61*

Charentes

HUÎTRES EN BROCHETTES
Grilled Oysters on Skewers

Whether they originated in Charentes or the kitchens of Queen Victoria, these delectable "angels on horseback" are equally popular in England and France, and bear the same name in both countries.

24 large oysters
6 slices of white sandwich bread
24 paper-thin slices of bacon
1 oz (40 g) butter
4 tablespoons dry breadcrumbs
2 pinches of cayenne pepper

❖ Open the oysters, pouring their juices into a large saucepan through a fine sieve lined with dampened cheesecloth. Remove the oysters from their shells.
❖ Place the saucepan over low heat. As soon as the liquid begins to bubble, add the oysters. Poach them for 7 seconds, then drain in a sieve.
❖ Preheat broiler (griller). Trim the crusts from the bread and lightly brown the slices on both sides under the broiler. Cut each slice into 4 squares. Place in a baking dish, in 4 rows of 6 squares.
❖ Remove the rind from the bacon and cut each slice in half crosswise. Wrap each oyster in a piece of bacon and thread 6 onto each of 4 wood or metal skewers, not too closely together. Arrange the skewers in the baking dish so that each oyster rests on a square of bread. Broil until the bacon is nicely crisp, about 2 minutes, turning after 1 minute.
❖ Meanwhile, melt the butter in a nonstick 8-in (20-cm) skillet, over low heat. Add the breadcrumbs and fry, stirring constantly with a wooden spoon, until golden. Turn into a fine sieve to drain.
❖ Carefully withdraw the oysters from the skewers. Sprinkle the oysters with cayenne and breadcrumbs and serve immediately.

SERVES 4

MUSSELS WITH SPINACH (top left, recipe page 65), GRILLED OYSTERS ON SKEWERS (top right) AND MUSSELS IN WHITE WINE (bottom)
PETER JOHNSON

Bretagne

COQUILLES SAINT-JACQUES AU BEURRE BLANC
Scallops with Beurre Blanc

Beurre blanc sauce is a reduction of French shallots and vinegar with butter incorporated into it. In Anjou, and in the Nantes area where it is a specialty, it is made with unsalted butter, which has a delicious nutty flavor, and accompanies pike or shad. In Bretagne it is made the same way, but with a semi-salted butter that has a subtle taste of iodine and is used to coat crustaceans and fish.

1 lb (500 g) scallops (without their coral)
salt and freshly ground pepper
4 French shallots, finely chopped
6 tablespoons dry white wine
3 tablespoons white wine vinegar
7 oz (200 g) butter

❖Rinse the scallops and pat dry. Cut each in half, into 2 thinner discs. Season with salt and pepper.
❖Combine the shallots, wine, vinegar and salt and pepper in a small saucepan. Simmer gently over low heat until only 2 teaspoons of liquid remain.
❖Meanwhile, cut the butter into ¾-in (1.5-cm) cubes; set aside ¾ oz (20 g). Over a very low heat, vigorously whisk the butter into the saucepan, piece by piece. When all the butter has been incorporated and the *beurre blanc* is light and foamy, set it aside and keep warm.
❖Melt the remaining butter in a nonstick 10-in (26-cm) skillet and cook the scallops over very low heat for 20 seconds on each side. Divide among four hot plates and pour the sauce over. Serve immediately.

SERVES 4

SCALLOPS, LANDES-STYLE (top) AND SCALLOPS WITH BEURRE BLANC

Aquitaine

COQUILLES SAINT-JACQUES À LA LANDAISE
Scallops, Landes-style

2 oz (50 g) pine nuts
1 lb (500 g) scallops, with their coral
salt and freshly ground pepper
2 tablespoons vegetable oil
1 tablespoon wine vinegar
1 tablespoon water
2 oz (50 g) butter
1 tablespoon chopped flat-leaf parsley

❖Lightly brown the pine nuts over low heat in a dry skillet. Set aside in a bowl.
❖Rinse the scallops and pat dry. Cut the white parts horizontally in half making two thin discs; season both the white parts and the coral with salt and pepper.
❖Heat the oil in a nonstick 10-in (26-cm) skillet. Lightly brown the scallops and coral over moderate heat for 1 minute on each side. Set aside and keep warm.
❖Discard the cooking oil. Add the vinegar and water to the pan and boil until reduced by half. Add the butter and whisk over low heat until it softens and becomes incorporated into the sauce. Add the parsley and pine nuts and stir again. Pour this sauce over the scallops and serve immediately.

SERVES 4

Normandie

COQUILLES SAINT-JACQUES D'ÉTRETAT
Scallops Étretat-style

With its shingle and tall cliffs making it one of Normandie's prettiest "postcards," Etretat is also a gastronomic mecca, famous for its shellfish and crustaceans.

1 lb (500 g) scallops, with their coral
salt and freshly ground pepper
8 oz (250 g) mushrooms
6 tablespoons heavy (double) cream or crème fraîche
2 egg yolks
2 oz (50 g) butter
2 French shallots, finely chopped
1 tablespoon calvados
1 cup (8 fl oz/250 ml) dry white wine

❖Rinse the scallops and pat dry. Season with salt and pepper. Trim the stems of the mushrooms; wash them, pat dry and chop finely. Beat the cream and egg yolks together with a fork in a small bowl.
❖Melt the butter in a nonstick 10-in (26-cm) skillet and cook the chopped shallots and mushrooms over very low heat, stirring, for 5 minutes. Add the scallops and cook for 30 seconds on each side. Sprinkle in the calvados and ignite, shaking the pan gently until flames subside. Remove the scallops and set aside in a warm place.

PETER JOHNSON

STUFFED SQUID (top) AND SQUID COOKED IN THEIR OWN INK (bottom, recipe page 70)

❖Pour the wine into the skillet and boil over high heat until the sauce is syrupy and reduced by ⅔. Add the egg yolk mixture and stir until the sauce thickens; do not allow it to boil.

❖Preheat the broiler (griller). Divide the scallops among four individual broilerproof dishes and cover with sauce. Slide under the broiler, close to the heat source, for about 30 seconds or until lightly browned. Serve immediately in the same dishes.

SERVES 4   *Photograph pages 60 – 61*

Provence

CALMARS FARCIS

Stuffed Squid

2 squid, about 11 oz (350 g) each
2 lb (1 kg) ripe tomatoes
2 onions, about 3 oz (100 g) each, finely chopped
1 tablespoon olive oil
salt and freshly ground pepper
1 teaspoon sugar
For the stuffing:
5 tablespoons milk
2 oz (50 g) stale bread, crusts trimmed
1 tablespoon dried currants
1 tablespoon chopped flat-leaf parsley
salt and freshly ground pepper
1 tablespoon olive oil
1 onion, about 3 oz (100 g), finely chopped
1 clove garlic, finely chopped
3 oz (100 g) prosciutto or other raw ham, finely chopped
2 eggs, beaten

❖Place one squid on a work surface. Hold the body with one hand and pull away the tentacles with the other. Discard the insides and the internal quill. Cut the tentacles off the head at the level of the eyes and reserve, discarding the rest of the head. Wash the tentacles and body; if the latter contains eggs or roe, leave them, as they have an excellent flavor. Prepare the second squid in the same way. Finely chop the tentacles.

❖Prepare the stuffing: heat the milk in a small saucepan over low heat. Crumble in the bread and stir. Remove from heat and let cool. Rinse the currants under warm water. Combine the soaked bread, currants, parsley, salt and pepper in a bowl.

❖Heat the oil in a nonstick 10-in (26-cm) skillet. Add the chopped onion and garlic and cook, stirring, for 2 minutes or until golden. Add the ham and chopped tentacles and continue to cook over low heat, stirring, for 5 minutes. Add the soaked bread mixture and eggs and cook, stirring, for 1 minute or until the eggs begin to set. Stir until smooth and remove from heat. Loosely fill the squid bodies with the stuffing; sew the opening closed with kitchen thread.

❖Drop the tomatoes into boiling water for 10 seconds. Cool under running water, then peel, halve and squeeze out the seeds. Finely chop the flesh.

❖Place the squid in an enameled saucepan over low heat and turn with a wooden spoon until they give out no more liquid. Add the onions and cook, stirring, until any liquid has evaporated. Pour in the oil and continue to cook, still turning the squid, for 3 minutes or until lightly browned. Stir in the tomatoes, salt, pepper and sugar and bring to boil. Cover and cook over low heat for 2 hours, turning the squid from time to time.

❖Remove the squid from the pan and slice into ¾-in (1.5-cm) rounds. Pour the sauce into a shallow serving plate and arrange the slices of squid on top. Serve immediately.

SERVES 4

Pays Basque

CHIPIRONS EN SU TINTA
Squid Cooked in Their own Ink

Chipirons is the regional Basque name for squid.

2½ lb (1.2 kg) small squid
8 oz (250 g) ripe tomatoes
3 tablespoons olive oil
1 onion, about 3 oz (100 g), finely chopped
1 clove garlic, finely chopped
1 cup (8 fl oz/250 ml) dry white wine
salt and freshly ground pepper
4 pinches of cayenne pepper
For the stuffing:
2 oz (50 g) stale bread, crusts trimmed
1 tablespoon olive oil
1 onion, about 3 oz (100 g), finely chopped
1 clove garlic, finely chopped
salt and freshly ground pepper

❖Place one squid on a work surface. Hold the body with one hand and pull away the tentacles with the other. Discard the insides, except for the ink sac, and the internal quill. Cut the tentacles off the head at the level of the eyes and reserve, discarding the rest of the head. Wash the tentacles and body. Prepare the remaining squid in the same way. Finely chop the tentacles.

❖Prepare the stuffing: grind the bread to coarse crumbs in a blender or food processor. Heat the oil in a nonstick 8-in (20-cm) skillet. Add the chopped onion and garlic and cook over low heat for 5 minutes, stirring, without allowing them to color. Add the chopped tentacles, season with salt and pepper, stir well and cook for 5 minutes. Stir in the breadcrumbs and remove from heat. Stuff the squid bodies with this mixture and secure the opening with a toothpick. Drop the tomatoes into boiling water for 10 seconds. Cool under running water, peel, halve and squeeze out the seeds; finely chop the flesh. Empty the squid ink sacs, straining the liquid through a small sieve into a bowl.

❖Heat the oil in a nonstick 10-in (26-cm) sauté pan. Add the stuffed squid, chopped onion and garlic and cook over low heat for 5 minutes, turning frequently. Pour in the wine and evaporate it over high heat. Add the tomatoes, salt, pepper and cayenne and cook, stirring, until the tomatoes give out no more liquid. Stir in the squid ink and simmer for 30 minutes. Serve hot.

SERVES 4   *Photograph page 69*

Provence

LES BAISERS
Kisses

The Provençal name for these is lei poutoun. *It is the delicious kissing sounds made by the diners as they savor this dish that gives it its name.*

4 lb (2 kg) fresh spinach
1 tablespoon olive oil
1 onion, about 3 oz (100 g), finely chopped
salt

4 lb (2 kg) clams
For the *aïoli*:
1 clove garlic, coarsely chopped
1 egg yolk
2 pinches of salt
3 tablespoons peanut oil
3 tablespoons olive oil

❖Prepare the *aïoli*: combine the garlic, egg yolk and salt in a blender or food processor and mix for 10 seconds. With machine running, pour in the peanut oil and then the olive oil, blending to make a thick emulsion. Set aside.

❖Trim the stalks from the spinach; wash and drain the leaves. Cut the leaves into strips ⅜ in (1 cm) wide.

❖Heat the oil in a large nonstick sauté pan. Add the onion and cook over low heat, stirring, for 3 minutes or until golden. Add the spinach and season with salt. Mix well and cook, covered, for 5 minutes or until the spinach is very soft.

❖Wash the clams in several changes of water; drain. Transfer to a large pot and cook over high heat, turning constantly, until all have opened. Discard any unopened clams. Remove the clams with a slotted spoon and keep warm; discard the shells.

❖Strain the clam cooking liquid into a small saucepan and boil until reduced by half. Blend into the *aïoli*. Turn this mixture into the spinach and stir well. Add the clams, stir and serve immediately.

SERVES 4

Provence

CALMARS AU RIZ
Squid with Rice

The name calmar *comes from the old French* calamar, *an eighteenth-century word for a desk. Like a desk, squid contains all that is necessary for writing: ink and a pen (the name given to its small transparent bone).*

2½ lb (1.2 kg) medium squid
8 oz (250 g) ripe tomatoes
2 onions, about 3 oz (100 g) each, finely chopped
3 cloves garlic, finely chopped
3 tablespoons olive oil
4 pinches of saffron threads
1 teaspoon *herbes de Provence* (see glossary)
1 teaspoon fennel seeds
salt and freshly ground pepper
2 pinches of cayenne pepper
2 cups (10 oz/300 g) Camargue (long-grain) rice
3 cups (24 fl oz/750 ml) water

❖Place one squid on a work surface. Hold the body with one hand and pull away the tentacles with the other. Discard the insides and the internal quill. Cut the tentacles off the head at the level of the eyes and reserve, discarding the rest of the head. Wash the tentacles and body; if the latter contains eggs or roe, leave them, as they have an excellent flavor. Cut both the tentacles and the body into ⅜-in (1-cm) crosswise slices. Prepare the remaining squid in the same way.

❖Drop the tomatoes into boiling water for 10 seconds. Cool under running water, then peel, halve and squeeze out the seeds; chop the flesh finely.

❖Cook the squid in a 6-qt (6-l) enameled pot over low

KISSES (front) AND SQUID WITH RICE (rear), PHOTOGRAPHED IN PROVENCE

heat, stirring with a wooden spoon, until they give out no more liquid. Add the chopped onions and garlic, stir again and cook until no more liquid remains. Add the oil, saffron, herbs, fennel seed, salt, pepper, cayenne and rice and cook, stirring, until everything is lightly browned.

❖Add the tomatoes and water to the pot and bring to boil. Cover and cook until the rice is tender, about 25 minutes. Serve hot, directly from the pot.

SERVES 6

Bretagne/Normandie

CREVETTES AU CIDRE
Shrimp (Prawns) in Cider

This dish is made with small, live shrimp which are caught all year round using a special fine-meshed shrimping net, that is shaped like a pocket about three feet (one meter) deep.

3 cups (24 fl oz/750 ml) dry cider
2 tablespoons coarse sea salt
2 lb (1 kg) small, live shrimp (prawns)
freshly ground pepper
For serving:
whole-grain bread
butter

❖Pour the cider into a large saucepan and bring to boil. Stir in the salt. Add shrimp, return to boil and cook for 1 to 2 minutes.
❖Drain the shrimp and arrange them in a shallow dish. Season with pepper and serve immediately, accompanied by bread and butter.

SERVES 4

Bretagne

LANGOUSTINES DE GUILVINEC
Langoustines, Guilvinec-style

The little port of Guilvinec near Quimper is famous for its fish market. Each day in the late afternoon the fishermen bring in their live catch of fish, shellfish and crustaceans, including tender Norway lobsters of incomparable quality and flavor.

12 langoustines (king prawns or yabbies), just under 3 oz
    (80 g) each
5 oz (150 g) butter
1 tablespoon chopped fresh tarragon
salt and freshly ground pepper
2 pinches of cayenne pepper
4 pinches of sweet paprika
6 tablespoons lemon juice

❖Preheat oven to 450°F (230°C). Halve the langoustines lengthwise and remove the grainy sac from the head. Arrange the halves in a baking dish just large enough to hold them.
❖Melt 1 oz (25 g) butter in a small saucepan over low heat. Remove from heat and add the tarragon, salt, pepper, cayenne and paprika. Drizzle over the langoustines and bake for 5 minutes.
❖Meanwhile, boil the lemon juice in a small non-aluminum saucepan over high heat until reduced by ⅔. Remove from heat and whisk in the remaining butter, cut into small pieces, until the sauce becomes a thick emulsion. Pour into a sauceboat.
❖Arrange the langoustines on four plates and serve immediately with the lemon butter sauce.

SERVES 4

PIERRE HUSSENOT/AGENCE TOP

Limousin

LIMOUSINE D'ÉCREVISSES
Crayfish, Limousin-style

24 live crayfish (small yabbies)
bouquet garni: 1 bay leaf, 1 sprig thyme, 6 sprigs parsley
1 oz (25 g) butter
2 French shallots, finely chopped
salt and freshly ground pepper
2 tablespoons cognac
2 cups (16 fl oz/500 ml) dry white wine
3 tablespoons tomato paste (puree), optional
6 tablespoons heavy (double) cream or crème fraîche
2 egg yolks
2 pinches of cayenne pepper
2 tablespoons chopped fresh tarragon

❖Prepare the crayfish: lift up the central tail fin and twist it to remove the small black vein which runs through the center of the tail. Rinse and drain the crayfish. Tie together the herbs for the bouquet garni.
❖Melt the butter in a nonstick 11-in (28-cm) sauté pan. Add the crayfish, cover and cook for 5 minutes. Add the shallots, season with salt and pepper and cook, stirring, over low heat for 2 minutes. Pour in the cognac and ignite, shaking the pan gently until flames subside. Add the wine, tomato paste and bouquet garni and cook over high heat, stirring, for 2 minutes. Remove the crayfish with a slotted spoon and keep warm.
❖Boil the cooking liquid until syrupy, about 5 minutes. Add half the cream and cook for 2 more minutes. Remove the bouquet garni.
❖Beat the egg yolks with a fork; beat in the remaining cream. Pour into the sauté pan and remove from heat; stir with a wooden spoon until the sauce is smooth and thickened. Add the crayfish and cayenne and reheat, stirring, for 30 seconds.
❖Turn the crayfish and sauce onto a large platter, sprinkle with chopped tarragon and serve immediately.

SERVES 4   *Photograph page 75*

Savoie/Lorraine

GRATIN DE QUEUES D'ÉCREVISSES
Gratin of Crayfish

There are innumerable varieties of this little freshwater crustacean. Of all the types that are cooked and enjoyed throughout France, the best is undoubtedly the "red-footed" river crayfish.

1 onion, about 2 oz (50 g)
2 cloves
2 cloves garlic, peeled and halved
1 carrot, about 2 oz (50 g), peeled and sliced
1 celery stalk
1 sprig thyme
1 bay leaf
4 sprigs parsley
6 peppercorns

2½ qt (2.5 l) water
salt
6 lb (3 kg) live crayfish (yabbies)
8 oz (250 g) mushrooms
1 oz (25 g) butter
freshly ground pepper
1 teaspoon cornstarch (cornflour)
6 tablespoons heavy (double) cream or crème fraîche
2 egg yolks
2 tablespoons dry breadcrumbs
2 tablespoons grated Emmenthaler cheese

❖Peel the onion and stud with cloves. Place the onion, garlic, carrot and celery in a large saucepan with the thyme, bay leaf, parsley and peppercorns. Pour in the water and bring to boil. Season with salt and let simmer 15 minutes.
❖Meanwhile, prepare the crayfish: lift up the central tail fin and twist it to remove the small black vein which runs through the center of the tail. Rinse and drain the crayfish.
❖Add the crayfish to the stock, cover and cook for 5 minutes. Drain, reserving the stock, and let the crayfish cool to lukewarm.
❖Shell the crayfish, setting aside in a bowl the tail meat, the coral and the creamy parts from the heads. Roughly crush the shells and return them to the stock. Cook over high heat for 10 minutes.
❖Meanwhile, trim the mushroom stalks; wash the mushrooms, drain and slice thinly. Melt half the butter in a nonstick 10-in (26-cm) skillet and cook the mushrooms until they no longer exude moisture and are golden. Add to the crayfish.
❖Strain the stock into a saucepan and boil until reduced to about 3 cups (24 fl oz/750 ml). Season with salt and pepper if necessary.
❖Preheat broiler (griller). Combine the cornstarch with half the cream, using a small whisk. Beat the egg yolks with a fork and beat in the remaining cream. Pour the cornstarch mixture into the reduced stock and simmer until thickened, about 3 minutes, stirring constantly with a wooden spoon. Remove from heat and blend in the egg yolk mixture. Keep the sauce warm over low heat without allowing it to boil.
❖With the remaining butter, grease a shallow broilerproof dish just large enough to hold the crayfish, mushrooms and sauce. Spread the crayfish and mushrooms evenly over the base and cover with sauce. Combine the breadcrumbs and cheese and sprinkle over the surface. Broil until crumbs are lightly browned. Serve immediately.

SERVES 6   *Photograph page 75*

Champagne

ÉCREVISSES AU CHAMPAGNE
Crayfish in Champagne

36 live crayfish (small yabbies)
2 oz (50 g) butter
3 French shallots, finely chopped
salt and freshly ground pepper
1 tablespoon *marc de champagne* or cognac
¾ cup (6 fl oz/200 ml) dry champagne
¾ cup (6 fl oz/200 ml) heavy (double) cream or crème fraîche
2 pinches of cayenne pepper
1 tablespoon chopped fresh tarragon

INGREDIENTS FOR CRAYFISH IN CHAMPAGNE

❖Prepare the crayfish: lift up the central tail fin and twist it to remove the small black vein which runs through the center of the tail. Rinse and drain the crayfish.

❖Melt the butter in a 10-in (26-cm) sauté pan. Add the shallots and cook, stirring, for 3 minutes or until softened. Add the crayfish and cook for 5 minutes, stirring constantly. Season with salt and pepper, then pour in the *marc* and ignite, shaking the pan gently until flames subside. Add the champagne, bring to boil, cover and simmer for 5 minutes.

❖Transfer the crayfish to a serving platter with a slotted spoon and keep warm. Boil the cooking liquid over high heat until reduced by half. Stir in the cream and cook over high heat for 2 to 3 minutes or until the sauce is slightly thickened. Season with cayenne pepper and strain over the crayfish. Sprinkle with chopped tarragon and serve immediately.

SERVES 4

Bretagne

PALOURDES FARCIES À LA LORIENTAISE
Stuffed Clams Lorient-style

2 oz (50 g) salted butter
2 onions, about 3 oz (100 g) each, finely chopped
freshly ground pepper
24 clams
coarse sea salt
4 tablespoons dry breadcrumbs

❖Melt the butter in a nonstick 9-in (22-cm) skillet. Add the onions, season with pepper and cook over low heat until soft, about 5 minutes, stirring from time to time with a wooden spoon.

❖Preheat broiler (griller). Wash the clams in several changes of water; drain. Transfer to a large pot, cover with water and cook over high heat, turning constantly, until all have opened. Remove the clams with a slotted spoon and discard any unopened shells. Strain the cooking liquid into the onions, stir, and boil until reduced by half.

❖Pour a layer of coarse sea salt onto each of four individual gratin dishes or snail plates. Arrange 6 clams on each. Sprinkle with some of the onion mixture, then the breadcrumbs.

❖Broil close to the heat source for 3 minutes or until the breadcrumbs are lightly browned. Serve immediately in the same dishes.

SERVES 4   *Photograph page 105*

Pays Basque

SALADE D'ARAIGNÉE
Salad of Spider Crab

In spring and winter the spider crabs are delicious. They have fine, delicate-tasting flesh, a triangular, convex shell and long pitted claws. The females, with their plentiful coral, are the most flavorsome. Spider crabs are abundant in the Atlantic and are also found in the Mediterranean and the English Channel.

bouquet garni: 1 bay leaf, 1 sprig thyme, 6 sprigs parsley
2 tablespoons coarse sea salt
2 tablespoons wine vinegar
4 live spider (Blue Swimmer) crabs, about 1½ lb (800 g) each
4 eggs
1 teaspoon strong mustard
salt and freshly ground pepper
⅔ cup (5 fl oz/150 ml) extra virgin olive oil
2 tablespoons chopped mint
1 teaspoon lemon juice
2 pinches of cayenne pepper

❖In a large pot, bring 3 qt (3 l) water to boil. Tie together the herbs of the bouquet garni and add to the water with the sea salt and vinegar. Plunge in the spider crabs and return to boil, then cook 15 minutes.

❖Drain the cooked crabs and let cool, then shell. Roughly shred and set aside the meat, the coral and the creamy parts from the shells. Scrub the shells under running water; set aside.

❖Place the eggs in a saucepan and cover with cold water. Bring to the boil, then cook for 6 minutes. Shell the eggs and cut in half. Turn the yolks into a bowl, add the mustard, salt and pepper and mix well with a fork. Whisk in the oil in a thin stream until the sauce becomes a thick emulsion. Stir in the mint, lemon juice and cayenne. Cut the egg whites into small dice and add to the bowl.

❖Add the sauce to the crab mixture and toss carefully. Divide among the shells and serve immediately.

SERVES 4

Pays Basque

ARAIGNÉE FARCIE
Stuffed Spider Crab

2 tablespoons coarse sea salt
4 live spider (Blue Swimmer) crabs, about 1½ lb (800 g) each
1 lb (500 g) ripe tomatoes
2 tablespoons vegetable oil
1 onion, about 3 oz (100 g), finely chopped
1 leek, white part only, washed and finely chopped
2 French shallots, finely chopped
1 carrot, about 3 oz (100 g), peeled and finely chopped
1 tender celery stalk with leaves, finely chopped
1 fresh chili pepper, finely chopped
3 tablespoons dry sherry
6 tablespoons chicken stock
salt and freshly ground pepper
1 tablespoon chopped flat-leaf parsley
1 tablespoon dry breadcrumbs
1 tablespoon freshly and finely grated Parmesan cheese

❖In a large pot, bring 3 qt (3 l) water to boil. Add the sea salt, plunge in the spider crabs and return to boil, then cook 15 minutes.

❖Drop the tomatoes into boiling water for 10 seconds, then cool under running water. Peel, halve and squeeze out the seeds; chop the flesh finely.

❖Drain the cooked crabs and let cool, then shell. Roughly shred and set aside the meat, the coral and the creamy parts from the shell. Scrub the shells under running water; set aside.

❖Preheat oven to 450°F (230°C). Heat the oil in a nonstick 10-in (26-cm) sauté pan. Add the chopped vegetables and cook, stirring, over moderate heat for 5 minutes or until golden. Add the sherry and cook until evaporated, stirring constantly. Stir in the tomatoes and chicken stock; season with salt and pepper. Cook over high heat until all liquid is evaporated, about 5 minutes. Add the crab mixture and cook, stirring, for 2 minutes. Remove from heat and stir in the parsley.

❖Divide the filling among the crab shells. Combine the breadcrumbs and cheese and sprinkle over the surface. Bake until lightly browned, about 15 minutes. Serve hot.

SERVES 4

STUFFED SPIDER CRAB (left), SALAD OF SPIDER CRAB (bottom right), AND SQUID COOKED IN THEIR OWN INK (top right, recipe page 70)
PIERRE HUSSENOT/AGENCE TOP

Normandie

CRABE FARCI
Stuffed Crab

These large crabs, or tourteaux, *are caught all along the coasts of Normandie and Bretagne. They have two huge and fleshy pincers, and are also known by other names:* dormeurs *(sleepers),* endormis, pouparts, clos-poing ...

bouquet garni: 1 bay leaf, 1 sprig thyme, 6 sprigs parsley
2 tablespoons coarse sea salt
2 tablespoons wine vinegar
2 large live crabs, about 2 lb (1 kg) each
3 tablespoons milk
3 oz (100 g) fresh bread, crusts trimmed
2 tablespoons calvados
1 tablespoon vegetable oil
1 onion, about 3 oz (100 g), finely chopped
2 French shallots, finely chopped
2 cloves garlic, mashed or pressed
2 tablespoons chopped flat-leaf parsley
salt and freshly ground pepper
2 pinches of cayenne pepper
4 pinches of freshly grated nutmeg
1 tablespoon dry breadcrumbs
1 oz (30 g) butter

❖In a large pot, bring 3 qt (3 l) water to boil. Tie together the herbs of the bouquet garni and add to the water with the salt and vinegar. Plunge the crabs into the boiling liquid and return to boil. Reduce heat and simmer gently for 20 minutes.
❖Bring the milk to boil in a small saucepan. Remove from heat and crumble in the bread. Drain the cooked crabs and let cool, then shell. Set aside the crabmeat, the coral and the creamy parts from the shell. Scrub the shells under running water; set aside. Remove the meat from the claws. Roughly shred the crabmeat, the coral and the creamy parts and add the calvados.
❖Preheat oven to 450°F (230°C). Heat the oil in a nonstick 10-in (26-cm) skillet. Add the chopped onion and shallots and cook over low heat, stirring, for 3 minutes or until golden. Add the garlic and cook, stirring, for 1 minute longer. Remove from heat and add the milk mixture, parsley, salt, pepper, cayenne and nutmeg. Add the crabmeat mixture and mix well.
❖Divide the stuffing evenly between the two shells. Sprinkle with breadcrumbs and dot with butter. Bake until lightly browned, about 15 minutes. Serve hot.

SERVES 2   *Photograph pages 60 – 61*

Ile de France

HOMARD À L'AMERICAINE
Lobster, American-style

There is always some confusion over whether this dish should be called lobster "à l'américaine" or "à l'armoricaine." In 1854 a French cook from Sète, by the name of Pierre Fraisse, after a long career on the other side of the Atlantic opened a restaurant in Paris. The story goes that he named this lobster dish for his American clients, when improvising with a sauce of white wine, champagne and tomatoes reminiscent of his Mediterranean home. The "armoricaine" version of the dish, reputed to have been created by a cook from Bretagne, has not yet been found.

1 live lobster, about 2 lb (1 kg)
3 oz (100 g) butter
12 oz (400 g) ripe tomatoes
1 clove garlic
bouquet garni: 1 bay leaf, 1 sprig thyme, 6 sprigs parsley
1 tablespoon vegetable oil
salt and freshly ground pepper
4 French shallots, finely chopped
1 celery stalk, strings removed, finely chopped
1 carrot, about 3 oz (100 g), peeled and finely chopped
3 tablespoons cognac, preferably *fine champagne*
1¼ cups (10 fl oz/300 ml) dry white wine
2 pinches of cayenne pepper

❖Cook the lobster in boiling water for 3 minutes then cut it in half, separating head from tail and catching the juices in a small saucepan. Split the head in half lengthwise and remove the entrails and stomach; take out the coral and creamy parts and add to the saucepan with half the butter. Cut the tails into medallions according to the natural divisions of the shell.
❖ Drop the tomatoes into boiling water for 10 seconds. Cool under running water, then peel, halve and squeeze out the seeds. Finely chop the flesh and set aside in a colander. Crush the clove of garlic with the side of a cleaver. Tie together the herbs of the bouquet garni.
❖Heat the oil in a nonstick 10-in (26-cm) sauté pan. Add the remaining butter and, when melted, the lobster medallions. Cook over high heat until the lobster turns red, about 3 minutes, turning constantly. Season with salt and pepper. Add the shallots, celery, carrot, bouquet garni and garlic and cook, stirring, over low heat for 3 minutes; do not allow the vegetables to brown. Pour in the cognac and let it evaporate. Transfer the medallions of lobster to a plate. Pour the wine into the pan and let it evaporate. Add the tomatoes and cayenne and mix well to obtain a smooth sauce. Return the lobster to the sauté pan and simmer for 5 minutes.
❖Meanwhile, place the small saucepan of butter, coral and creamy parts over low heat and whisk until the butter is melted and foamy. Remove the bouquet garni from the sauté pan. Add the contents of the small saucepan, stirring with a wooden spoon. Pour the lobster and its sauce into a shallow dish and serve immediately.

SERVES 2

LOBSTER, AMERICAN-STYLE, PHOTOGRAPHED IN PARIS
PIERRE HUSSENOT/AGENCE TOP

THE NORTH, ALSACE, LORRAINE

Solid, rugged, joyful

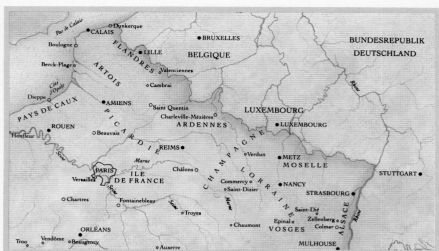

THE NORTH, ALSACE, LORRAINE

Solid, rugged, joyful

The north of France: a cold country, an industrialized country; even in France, people have a wrong impression of the warm-welcoming north, with its stretches of sandy dunes, its fields as green as those of Kent or Sussex in nearby England, its little cottages of red or whitewashed brick with glazed tile roofs, its substantial and copious meals. Who knows that the best cheesemaker in France — Philippe Olivier — lives at Boulogne-sur-Mer, where he ripens not only the best Bries, Comtés, Beauforts, but more than these, the strong cheeses of the north: the *Gris* from Lille, otherwise known as *Vieux Puant* (Old Smelly); the *Boulette* from Cambrai or Avesnes; the *Larron* from Ors and, above all, the Maroilles, reputedly the finest of the strong cheeses. It is the product of the sinuous green Thiérache, a region of woodlands, orchards, cider-apple trees, fresh butter, thick cream and rabbits hopping in the meadows; this Normandy of the north is a fresh, green pastureland that supplies Paris with milk.

But which north are we talking about? In reality, Flanders is divided in two — the French part and the Belgian part. The two capitals, on either side of the border, testify to its splendid treasures: Gothic mansions, brick houses, gabled roofs, the great square and belfry in Lille and in Anvers. The *waterzoï*, a kind of pot-au-feu made either with freshwater fish or with chicken, is common to both regions. So, too, the *potjevfleish* — a "pot of meat" consisting of veal, bacon and rabbit. But the Flemish cuisine is so rich that you would be afraid of leaving out something if you tried to list all the specialties: soups made with beer or with beets, *andouillettes* from Cambrai, *craquelots* from Dun-

LEFT: PARISIAN BRASSERIES ARE UNIQUE: ONE CAN ENJOY A GOOD MEAL OR DRINK AT ANY TIME, DAY OR NIGHT, AND THE WAITERS IN THEIR EFFICIENT MANNER NEVER FORGET AN ORDER.

PREVIOUS PAGES: THE TOWN OF ZELLENBERG IS IN THE HEART OF THE WINE-GROWING AREA OF ALSACE, FAMOUS FOR ITS FRUITY DRY WHITE WINES.

PICKING GRAPES NEAR CHÂTEAU-THIERRY IN THE CHAMPAGNE REGION.

kirk, *flamiche, goyère, carbonnades*. It is a litany that expresses itself in solid dishes.

The northerner is a worker, his climate harsh; he needs foods that will help him resist it, but they do not preclude sophistication. The typical regional drink is beer, which turns up in various dishes — chicken cooked in beer, eel cooked in beer — and accompanies them all, starting with the charcuterie, and the *flamiches* or *flamiques*. These latter vary between Flanders and Picardy — in other words, between the north and the south of the north. In Flanders the *flamiche* is made with the runny Maroilles cheese and in Picardy with leeks, but in both cases it takes the form of a thick, savory tart. The charcuterie products are legion: the traditional *andouillette* of Cambrai, the smoked tongue of Valenciennes, and the country-style sausages, *andouilles* and black puddings that are specialties of the region bounded by Berck-Plage, Calais and Aire-sur-la-Lys (and which have English counterparts on the other side of the Channel). Next to these are the *hochepot*, which is nothing other than a pot-au-feu, and the Flemish *carbonnade*, a dish of beef and chopped onions cooked in beer.

But it must not be forgotten that the north is primarily a maritime region. Sole, eel, salmon, herring, and the fish soup called *caudière* at Berck are the pride of the Artois region and of Flanders. Likewise the seafoods from the shores of Dunkirk: oysters, *tourteaux* (a species of crab), lobsters that are prepared *au gratin* in the same way as scallops.

All blend sagely with the local vegetables: boiled or fried potatoes, beets, red and green cabbages, cauliflowers that are firm and tender at the same time. All are proper precedents to the desserts and sweets of the region: the sugar tarts (*tartes au sucre*), *couques* and, above all, the celebrated *bêtises* of Cambrai. These are nothing more than mint-flavored boiled sweets, slightly puffed and hollow. They are said to have been invented by chance, thanks to a blunder by an apprentice sweetmaker in the firm of Afchin, who simply mixed up his ingredients.

Sweets are the glory of Lorraine, a proud country, by its own wish austere and industrial, which has suffered in all wars. But the wars have also left sweet specialties in each village. The trenches of Verdun, the ossuary of Douaumont, the souvenirs of the Great War: they are here. But right beside these you will discover the famous madeleines of Commercy, the cream-filled puffs of Pont-à-Mousson. *Bergamotes* — pulled candy flavored with bergamot, which has the fragrance of a Sicilian lemon — are the pride of Nancy, the capital, together with the gold-colored wrought iron gates of the Place Stanislas, one of the most harmonious squares in the world.

It was Stanislas Leczinsky, exiled king of Poland, and father-in-law of Louis XV, who brought aid and prosperity to the region. The arts have always flourished around Nancy, which has lent its name to the French school of Art Nouveau. Majorelle (who was responsible for the woodwork of the restaurant Lucas-Carton in Paris), Daum (whose crystal has lost none of its sparkle), Gruber, Gallé . . . all had their beginnings here and all have the right to have their work displayed in the museum. Baccarat crystal, fashioned into some of the most prestigious glasses and carafes in France, is produced only a few kilometers away. Also of nearby origin are a genial local wine, the *Gris de Toul*, and above all a spirit distilled from the mirabelle plum that is the most highly reputed in the whole country. The local orchards are prolific (mirabelle and quetsch plums, cherries); they contour around the inspired hill of Sion-Vaudémont, beloved of Maurice Barrès, the great nationalist writer whose roots were in Lorraine. The Meuse and Moselle rivers still offer carp, pike and trout to be nurtured in ponds.

The local charcuterie is no less prolific. Here pig is king, and jellied suckling pig, a specialty of Metz — the great neighbor and rival of Nancy — is his representative. From the pig come blood puddings, smoked hams and the smoked bacon that gives *tourte* and quiche lorraine their flavor.

Even if one adds to the list of gastronomic riches of Lorraine the macaroons of Nancy, the gingerbread of Remiremont in the Vosges, the kirsch of Fougerolles, the classic *potée lorraine* (a kind of pot-au-feu with cabbage and sausage) — it is still not complete. Lorraine presents itself as hard-working, strict, more discreet than frivolous; and yet it hides in its pocket more than a few treasures to delight the gourmet.

Contrasting with the unknown north and the modest Lorraine is exuberant, exceptionally affluent Alsace. Eating in Alsace is virtually a religious experience; it is impossible to be a well-brought-up Alsatian and not do honor to the table. Helpings in Alsace are two or three times bigger than anywhere else — but the people of Alsace will tell you that these are "normal" size.

If Alsace has a good appetite, it is because — so they say — it has swung between France and Germany for so long and to such an extent that it no longer knows which side it belongs to. Even in Strasbourg, the capital of the region, food holds a royal position: the patisseries and tea salons are monuments, the charcuterie windows are works of art and bistros are institutions.

Besides, they are not really bistros, but rather places where wine is sold — *winstubs*, established long ago by wine merchants who wanted to pass off their surplus production to the citizens of the towns. These *winstubs* are an expression of the gourmet soul of Alsace, marked by conviviality, familiarity and a respect for traditions, and here you discover the simple marvels of the region. First of all, pork, in all forms: jellied (parsleyed brawn, or *presskopf*), smoked shoulder (*wadele*) or fillet (*kasler*), stuffed belly (*saumawen*) or smoked hocks to go with sauerkraut.

Today the snails often come from China, the freshwater crayfish from Yugoslavia, the frogs from Egypt or the Vendée. But traditions persist in spite of the pollution that has decimated the river catches. In Sundgau, the most southerly region of Alsace, right next to the Swiss Jura, fresh lake carp can still be found to be served fried. Along the Rhine, restaurants still offer the *matelote*, a dish that combines perch, pike and eel in a sauce made with cream and the local white wine — even if the fish often come from Holland. The Kockersberg is the region of hops, used for beer, but the hop shoots — asparaguslike in flavor — make a dish for a king. South of Strasbourg, from Geispolsheim to Krautergersheim (literally "Cabbagetown"), stretch fields of cabbages for sauerkraut. This is the territory of the sauerkraut that is so closely identified with Alsace; it is washed and gently stewed, flavored with bacon and eaten with all kinds of local charcuterie, from smoked and fresh sausages to smoked shoulder and black puddings. Never ask someone from Alsace which is the best sauerkraut; they will always reply that it is their mother's.

Another family dish that is emblematic of Alsace is the *baeckeoffe*, a celebrated casserole of three different meats (beef, veal and pork) layered with potato and moistened with white wine. It is placed in the oven before Sunday Mass and is ready to eat, piping hot, when the family returns from the service.

We should not forget that foie gras originated in Alsace, since it was invented by Jean-Pierre Clause, cook to the marshal of Contades, military governor of the town of Strasbourg from 1762 to 1788. Nor that the goose is here a privileged bird and can be paired with the most sublime accompaniments. Nor that the game (roe deer and red

PRACTICING FIDDLE SOLOS ON THE BANKS OF THE RIVER SEINE.

deer, fawns and does, wild boar, pheasants, partridges, mallard ducks) frolic and fly above the prolific forests of the Vosges and the fertile plains along the Rhine, known as the Ried.

Alsatian patisserie? It is one of the best endowed in the world, heiress of the traditions of Vienna and *Mitteleuropa* — and not only for the traditional (and dry) *kugelhopf*, which is served for Sunday breakfast. In Strasbourg, the patisseries are still full of the classic French *mille-feuilles*, *éclairs* and *religieuses*, in addition to German-style Black Forest cake (with chocolate and cherries), cheesecakes, walnut cakes and apple fritters. And the tea salons are legion, their cozy, welcoming, wood-paneled interiors offering, according to the season, plum, cherry or rhubarb tarts.

One could hardly conclude this gourmet's tour of Alsace without listing the wines, sprightly and serious, that the fair province produces, along a ribbon of road that stretches for some one hundred and fifty kilometers from Marlenheim to Thann, with a small enclave in the north at Cleebourg. The fresh Muscat, with its aroma of fresh-picked grapes; the smooth, honest Pinot Blanc; the light, joyous Sylvaner; the elegant, well-bred Riesling; the smoky-flavored Tokay-Pinot Gris, well-made and powerful; the Gewürztraminer, velvety, spicy, rose-scented; the Pinot Noir, which can produce anything from an unpretentious rosé to a classy, oak-aged red. And then the sparkling wine, prepared in the traditional style according to methods practiced in Champagne. And again, the classic spirits: raspberry, plum, pear, elderberry, holly, and wild serviceberry. Not to mention the *marc* distilled from grapes.

Now, after all this, try to tell a gourmand that bountiful Alsace is not the most privileged region!

Provence

GRAND AÏOLI

Aïoli Feast

The word aïoli *is Provençal, derived from* ail *(garlic) and* huile *(oil). The sauce gives its name to this dish which in Provence is traditionally served on Good Friday.*

4 lb (2 kg) salt cod fillets
2 lb (1 kg) shellfish (large sea snails, whelks, clams or cockles)
salt and freshly ground pepper
10 small artichokes
2 lb (1 kg) small carrots, peeled
2 lb (1 kg) small leeks, trimmed
1 lb (500 g) small green beans
10 medium boiling potatoes, peeled
1 cauliflower, separated into small florets
10 eggs

For the *aïoli*:
6 cloves garlic
2 teaspoons strong mustard
3 egg yolks
salt
2 cups (16 fl oz/500 ml) extra virgin olive oil

❖ Soak the salt cod in a large bowl of cold water, skin side up, for 12 hours, changing the water 3 times.
❖ Rinse the shellfish and place in a saucepan. Cover with cold water and bring to boil. Remove the scum during the first 5 minutes of cooking, then season liberally with salt and simmer gently for 45 minutes. Drain the shellfish and either leave them in their shells or remove them and keep warm.
❖ Discard the bruised outside leaves of the artichokes and trim the heart, cutting off the spiky tips. Cook all the vegetables separately in boiling salted water until slightly crisp. Drain and keep warm. Hard-cook the eggs for 10 minutes, then cool and shell.
❖ Drain the salt cod and transfer to a large pot of cold water, skin side down. Bring to boil over low heat, then reduce heat and cook at the barest simmer for 10 minutes. Drain and cool to lukewarm.
❖ Meanwhile, prepare the *aïoli*: force the garlic through a press into a shallow bowl. Add the mustard, egg yolks and salt and stir well. Set aside for 1 minute, then add the oil in a thin stream, whisking until the mixture is quite firm. (The *aïoli* may also be prepared in a food processor.)
❖ Arrange the lukewarm salt cod, shellfish and vegetables on a large platter. Add the hard-cooked eggs, and offer the *aïoli* separately: each diner takes a little *aïoli* and dips the pieces of salt cod, shellfish and vegetables into it before eating them.

SERVES 8–10   *Photograph pages 88 – 89*

Bretagne

SOLE MEUNIÈRE

Sole Meunière

*Before the days of nonstick pans, fish had to be floured before being pan-fried in butter, which accounts for the origin of the name of this dish (*la meunière *is a miller's wife or female owner of a flour mill). The name still applies to any fish cooked in butter.*

4 sole, about 6 oz (200 g) each
salt and freshly ground pepper
5 oz (150 g) salted butter
1 tablespoon fresh lemon juice
For serving:
2 tablespoons chopped flat-leaf parsley

❖ Ask the fishmonger to clean and skin the sole. Rinse them and pat dry. Season with salt and pepper.
❖ Using two nonstick 10-in (26-cm) skillets, melt half the butter and cook the sole for 4 minutes on each side. Transfer them to 4 heated plates. Discard the cooking butter in one of the skillets and add the remaining butter. Add the lemon juice and let the butter melt over very low heat. Pour this sauce over the sole, sprinkle with parsley and serve immediately.

SERVES 4

PETER JOHNSON

SOLE MEUNIÈRE

Normandie

SOLE À LA NORMANDE
Sole with Shrimp and Mushrooms

This dish is thought to have been created in 1838 by Monsieur Langlais, chef of a restaurant called Le Rocher de Cancale in the Les Halles quarter of Paris. Its name derives from the fact that M. Langlais used only ingredients typical of Normandie — cream, shrimp and mussels — and almost certainly cider rather than white wine.

4 sole or gemfish, about 8 oz (250 g) each
salt and freshly ground pepper
bouquet garni: 1 bay leaf, 1 sprig thyme, 6 sprigs parsley
1 carrot, peeled and thinly sliced
1 onion, thinly sliced
2 cloves garlic
¾ cup (6 fl oz/200 ml) dry white wine
2 cups (16 fl oz/500 ml) water
1 tablespoon butter

For the garnish:
2 lb (1 kg) mussels
4 French shallots, finely chopped
6 tablespoons dry white wine
4 oz (125 g) small shrimp (prawns)
5 oz (150 g) small mushrooms
1 tablespoon fresh lemon juice

For the sauce:
2 egg yolks
¾ cup (6 fl oz/200 ml) heavy (double) cream or crème
   fraîche

❖Ask the fishmonger to fillet the fish and to keep the heads and bones. Rinse the fillets and pat dry. Season with salt and pepper. Tie together the herbs for the bouquet garni.
❖Place the heads and bones of the fish in a pot and add the carrot, onion, bouquet garni and whole garlic cloves. Pour in the wine and water and bring to boil. Simmer for 20 minutes to obtain a rich and flavorful stock, or *fumet*.
❖Meanwhile, prepare the garnish. Scrub the mussels under running water and remove the beards. Place them in a large saucepan with the shallots and wine and cook over high heat, turning often, until they open. Discard any unopened shells. Drain and remove the mussels from their shells. Strain the cooking liquid into a saucepan and set aside. Plunge the shrimp into simmering salted water for 1 minute, then drain and shell. Trim the mushrooms, rinse and pat dry; cut into quarters. Place in another saucepan and add the lemon juice. Season with salt and pepper and cook over high heat until the mushrooms give out no more liquid. Combine the mushrooms, mussels and shrimp in one saucepan and keep warm.
❖Preheat oven to 425°F (215°C). Strain the fumet. Using 1 tablespoon butter, grease a baking dish. Lay the fillets of sole in the dish. Pour the fumet over, cover the dish with waxed paper or aluminum foil and bake for 10 minutes.
❖Lift out the fillets with a slotted spoon and arrange on 4 heated plates. Surround with the mixture of mushrooms, shrimp and mussels.
❖Strain the fish cooking liquid into the saucepan of mussel liquid. Boil over high heat until reduced to a syrupy consistency, about 5 minutes. Beat the egg yolks and cream in a

SOLE WITH SHRIMP AND MUSHROOMS

bowl and blend in 2 tablespoons of the hot liquid. Pour the mixture back into the saucepan, remove from heat and beat until the sauce is thick and smooth. Pour over the fish and serve immediately.

SERVES 4

Pays de Loire

BROCHETS GRILLÉS AUX NOIX
Grilled Pike with Walnuts

2 small pike or gemfish, about 1½ lb (800 g) each
salt and freshly ground pepper
4 French shallots, finely chopped
1 sprig thyme, crumbled
1 bay leaf, crumbled
6 sprigs parsley
4 sprigs tarragon
1 tablespoon walnut oil
1 tablespoon fresh lemon juice
24 walnuts
5 oz (150 g) butter

❖Ask the fishmonger to scale and gut the fish; rinse and pat dry. Season with salt and pepper, and lay the fish in a shallow dish.
❖In a small bowl combine the shallots, thyme and bay leaf with salt and pepper. Wash the parsley and tarragon, strip off the leaves and add the bruised stems to the bowl. Mix in the oil and lemon juice and pour over the fish. Marinate in the refrigerator for 6 hours, turning several times.
❖Preheat broiler (griller). Drain the fish, reserving marinade. Broil for 15 minutes, turning once after 7 to 8 minutes and basting frequently with the marinade.
❖Coarsely chop the walnuts in a blender or food processor. Finely chop the parsley and tarragon leaves. Melt the butter in a small saucepan. Add the herbs and walnuts; season with salt and pepper. Pour into a sauceboat. Serve the fish as soon as they are cooked, passing the sauce separately.

SERVES 4

MARINATING INGREDIENTS FOR GRILLED PIKE WITH WALNUTS
PETER JOHNSON

Bretagne/Charentes

MAQUEREAUX MARINÉS

Marinated Mackerel

Caught by the line fishermen from the Gulf of Saint-Malo to the Gulf of Gascogne, the little mackerel used in this recipe are known as lisettes.

12 small mackerel, about 3 oz (100 g) each
salt
1 lemon
bouquet garni: 1 bay leaf, 1 sprig thyme, 6 sprigs parsley
2 cups (16 fl oz/500 ml) dry white wine
1 onion, about 3 oz (100 g), thinly sliced
2 carrots, about 2 oz (50 g) each, peeled and thinly sliced
2½ tablespoons white wine vinegar
2 cloves
1 teaspoon peppercorns
1 dried red chili pepper (bird pepper) or pimento, crumbled

❖Ask the fishmonger to gut the fish; rinse them, pat dry and season with salt. Wash and dry the lemon; cut into thin rounds. Tie together the herbs for the bouquet garni.
❖Pour the wine into a 10-in (26-cm) sauté pan. Add the onion, carrots, lemon, vinegar, bouquet garni, cloves, salt, peppercorns and dried pepper. Bring to boil and simmer for 10 minutes. Add the fish and simmer for 5 minutes.
❖Remove the fish and drain well. Boil the stock until slightly reduced, about 5 more minutes. In a rectangular terrine, alternate the fish with slices of onion, carrot and lemon. Strain the stock; pour over the fish and let cool. Cover the terrine and refrigerate for 12 hours before serving.

SERVES 4

Pays Basque

ANCHOIS AU TXAKOLI

Anchovies in Txakoli Wine

2 lb (1 kg) fresh anchovies
1 chili pepper
2½ oz (75 g) butter
8 oz (500 g) onions, finely chopped
4 cloves garlic, finely chopped
6 tablespoons txakoli (dry white) wine
salt and freshly ground pepper

❖Remove the heads from the anchovies and gut them. Rinse and pat dry with paper towels. Halve the pepper; remove stem and seeds and mince the flesh. Melt the butter in a nonstick 10-in (26-cm) sauté pan. Add the chopped onion, garlic and pepper and cook, stirring, for 2 minutes. Add the anchovies and wine and cook for 10 minutes over high heat, turning the anchovies so that they cook on both sides. Season with salt and pepper. Remove from heat, cover and let rest for 10 minutes before serving.

SERVES 4

PHOTOGRAPHED IN THE PAYS BASQUE:
ANCHOVIES IN TXAKOLI WINE (left), MARINATED MACKEREL (center front),
TTORO (bottom right, recipe page 98) AND CHAUDRÉE (top right, recipe page 98)

PIERRE HUSSENOT/AGENCE TOP

Pays Basque

TTORO
Ttoro

1 pollack or gemfish, about 2 lb (1 kg)
2 rock cod or trevally, about 1 lb (500 g) each
2 red gurnard or white-fleshed fish, about 1 lb (500 g) each
1 lb (500 g) monkfish (anglerfish) or blue-eye cod
8 oz (250 g) mussels
6 uncooked langoustines (Dublin Bay prawns) or yabbies
1 small fresh chili pepper
6 tablespoons extra virgin olive oil
2 cloves garlic, peeled and halved
1 onion, about 3 oz (100 g), thinly sliced
8 oz (250 g) ripe tomatoes, coarsely chopped
1 sprig thyme
1 bay leaf
2 cups (16 fl oz/500 ml) dry white wine
salt and freshly ground pepper

For serving:
croutons
cloves of garlic, halved

❖Ask the fishmonger to scale and gut the fish and remove the heads. Reserve the heads and bones. Cut the monkfish into ¾-in (2-cm) slices, and the others into 1½-in (4-cm) chunks.
❖Scrub the mussels in several changes of water and remove the beards. Drain well. Rinse the langoustines. Halve the chili, remove the seeds and chop the flesh.
❖Heat half the oil in an enameled 4-qt (4-l) pot. Add the fish heads and bones and cook, stirring, over low heat for 5 minutes. Add the garlic, chili and onion and cook, stirring, for 5 minutes or until the vegetables are golden. Add the tomatoes, thyme and bay leaf and cook, stirring, for 1 minute. Pour in the wine and simmer gently for 45 minutes.
❖Strain the liquid into a shallow baking dish.
❖Preheat the oven to 425°F (215°C). Wipe out the pot and pour in the remaining oil. Cook the fish for 3 minutes on each side, then transfer to the baking dish. Add the langoustines and mussels and bake for 5 minutes to reheat the broth and cook the langoustines and mussels.
❖Remove the dish from the oven and serve hot, accompanied by croutons rubbed with garlic.

SERVES 6   *Photograph page 97*

Charentes

CHAUDRÉE
Chaudrée

As popular in Charentes as the bouillabaisse *is in Provence, the* chaudrée *contains one invariable ingredient: the white part of the squid. Sometimes it includes potatoes.*

4 lb (2 kg) mixed fish: skate, sea eel, dogfish (rock salmon), turbot or gemfish, sole, blue-eye cod…
1 lb (500 g) cleaned squid, bodies only
salt and freshly ground pepper
12 oz (400 g) onions, thinly sliced
8 cloves garlic, peeled

2 tablespoons oil
2 cups (16 fl oz/500 ml) dry white wine
2 cups (16 fl oz/500 ml) water
3 oz (100 g) butter

For serving:
croutons

❖Ask the fishmonger to scale and gut the fish and remove the heads. Cut the largest fish into 1½-in (4-cm) chunks and leave the others whole. Wash them and pat dry. Rinse the squid and pat dry; cut into strips ¾ in (2 cm) wide. Season with salt and pepper.
❖Transfer the strips of squid to an enameled 6-qt (6-l) pot and place over low heat. Cook, stirring with a wooden spoon, until the squid have given out all their liquid. Add the onion and garlic and stir until all the liquid is absorbed. Add the oil and cook, stirring, until the squid is lightly browned all over. Pour in the wine and water and bring to simmer.
❖Add the fish to the simmering liquid, beginning with those with the firmest flesh (skate, eel, dogfish), then adding those with softer flesh (sole, turbot) and letting the liquid return to simmer after each addition. Season with salt and pepper and simmer for 15 minutes.
❖Add the butter to the pot and let it melt. Serve the chaudrée immediately, accompanied by croutons.

SERVES 6   *Photograph page 97*

Bretagne

DAURADE AU MUSCADET
Baked Bream in Muscadet

1 bream or carp, about 2 lb (1 kg)
salt and freshly ground pepper
1 lb (500 g) ripe tomatoes
2 lb (1 kg) small new potatoes
2 onions, about 3 oz (100 g) each, thinly sliced
8 cloves garlic, finely chopped
2 cups (16 fl oz/500 ml) Muscadet wine
3 oz (100 g) salted butter

❖Ask the fishmonger to scale and gut the fish. Rinse it and pat dry. Season with salt and pepper.
❖Preheat oven to 450°F (230°C). Drop the tomatoes into boiling water for 10 seconds. Cool under running water, then peel, halve, squeeze out the seeds and coarsely chop the flesh. Peel the potatoes, wash them and pat dry. In a bowl mix together the potatoes, onions, garlic and tomatoes; season with salt and pepper.
❖Lightly butter a baking dish large enough to hold the fish. Place it in the center of the dish and surround it with the tomato mixture. Pour in the wine and dot with butter. Bake for 40 to 45 minutes, turning the potatoes several times and basting the fish frequently with the cooking liquid.
❖By the end of the cooking time there should be very little liquid left. Serve the fish immediately, directly from the dish.

SERVES 4

BAKED BREAM IN MUSCADET (top), MULLET IN RAÏTO (center right, recipe page 100)
AND BOURRIDE OF MONKFISH, SÈTE-STYLE (bottom, recipe page 100)

PETER JOHNSON

BARBUE À L'OSEILLE
Brill with Sorrel

1 brill, Petrale sole, flounder or other flatfish,
    about 3 lb (1.5 kg)
1 onion, about 3 oz (100 g)
2 cloves
bouquet garni: 1 bay leaf, 1 sprig thyme, 6 sprigs parsley
1 carrot, about 3 oz (100 g), peeled and sliced
2 cups (16 fl oz/500 ml) dry cider
2 cups (16 fl oz/500 ml) water
salt and freshly ground pepper
2 lb (1 kg) sorrel
¾ cup (6 fl oz/185 ml) heavy (double) cream or crème
    fraîche

❖Ask the fishmonger to clean and fillet the fish, but keep the head and all the trimmings.
❖Peel the onion and stud with cloves. Tie together the herbs for the bouquet garni. Place the bouquet garni, onion and carrot in a large saucepan and add the fish head and trimmings, cider and water. Bring to boil, season with salt and pepper and simmer gently for 20 minutes.
❖Meanwhile, wash the sorrel, drain it and cut into very fine strips. In a nonstick 10-in (26-cm) sauté pan combine the sorrel, cream, and salt and pepper. Cook over low heat, stirring often, until reduced to a thick sauce, about 5 minutes; keep warm.
❖Rinse and pat dry the fish fillets. Strain the stock, return to the saucepan and bring to simmer over low heat. Add the fish and poach gently for 10 minutes, then drain.
❖Divide the fish among four plates, coat with sauce and serve immediately.

SERVES 4

BROCHET DE L'ILL À LA CRÈME
Pike in Cream Sauce

1 pike or gemfish, about 3½ lb (1.75 kg)
salt and freshly ground pepper
4 oz (125 g) butter
4 French shallots, finely chopped
¾ cup (6 fl oz/185 ml) heavy (double) cream or
    crème fraîche
1 cup (8 fl oz/250 ml) Riesling
1 tablespoon fresh lemon juice

❖Ask the fishmonger to scale and gut the fish, then rinse it and pat dry. Season with salt and pepper.
❖Preheat oven to 450°F (230°C). Using a scant tablespoon of the butter, grease a baking dish large enough to hold the fish. Scatter the chopped shallots over the bottom. Place the fish in the dish and dot with a generous tablespoon of butter. Bake for 15 minutes.
❖Combine the cream and wine in a small bowl and pour over the fish. Bake for 20 minutes longer, basting the fish often with the pan juices.
❖Transfer the cooked fish to a serving platter and keep warm. Add the lemon juice to the sauce and boil over mod-

BRILL WITH SORREL (center left), PIKE IN CREAM SAUCE (top)
AND BRILL IN CIDER (right)

erate heat until thickened, then strain into a small saucepan. Gradually whisk in the remaining butter over low heat to obtain a thick, smooth sauce. Pour the sauce into a sauceboat. Serve the fish hot, accompanied by its sauce.

SERVES 4

BARBUE AU CIDRE
Brill in Cider

1 brill, Petrale sole, flounder or other flatfish,
    about 3 lb (1.5 kg)
salt and freshly ground pepper
2 oz (50 g) butter
3 French shallots, finely chopped
8 oz (250 g) mushrooms, coarsely chopped
6 tablespoons heavy (double) cream or crème fraîche
2 cups (16 fl oz/500 ml) dry cider

❖Ask the fishmonger to clean and prepare the fish, trimming the fins. Rinse it, pat dry and season with salt and pepper.
❖Preheat oven to 425°F (215°C). Using half the butter, grease a baking dish just large enough to hold the fish. Scatter half the chopped shallots and mushrooms over the bottom. Place the fish on top and cover with the remaining shallots and mushrooms.
❖Combine the cream and cider, season with salt and pepper and pour this mixture into the dish. Dot the fish with the remaining butter. Bake for 30 to 35 minutes or until the sauce thickens and coats the fish. Serve hot, directly from the dish.

SERVES 4

Provence

GRATIN DE SARDINES AUX ÉPINARDS

Baked Sardines with Spinach

1¼ lb (600 g) fresh medium sardines
2 lb (1 kg) spinach
salt
1 small egg
1 oz (30 g) freshly and finely grated Emmenthaler or
   Parmesan cheese
¼ cup (2 fl oz/60 ml) extra virgin olive oil
freshly ground pepper
½ teaspoon dried thyme
¼ cup (1 oz/30 g) dried breadcrumbs

❖Scale the sardines and remove the heads; gut and rinse the fish. Split them along the belly and separate the two fillets, removing the row of bones beneath the dorsal fins and tail. Pat the fillets dry using paper towels.
❖Wash and stem the spinach. Cut the leaves, with the water clinging to them, into strips ¾ in (2 cm) wide and place in a large saucepan. Season with salt and cook, covered, over high heat for 5 minutes. Drain the spinach and turn into a bowl. Beat the egg; mix in half the cheese and season with salt and pepper. Blend this mixture into the spinach.
❖Preheat oven to 450°F (230°C). Using some of the olive oil, lightly oil a baking dish just large enough to hold the fillets in a single layer. Spread the spinach mixture over the bottom, then arrange the sardine fillets on top, skin side down. Season with salt and pepper, sprinkle with thyme and pour the remaining oil over. Combine the breadcrumbs with the remaining cheese and sprinkle over the fish. Bake until lightly browned, about 15 minutes. Serve hot, directly from the baking dish.

SERVES 4–5

Provence

SARDINES FARCIES

Stuffed Sardines

2 lb (1 kg) fresh medium sardines
salt and freshly ground pepper
8 oz (250 g) spinach
4 tablespoons extra virgin olive oil
2 green onions (scallions or spring onions), finely chopped
2 cloves garlic, finely chopped
1 egg
8 oz (250 g) ewe's milk cheese, *Brousse de brebis*
   or ricotta
2 tablespoons flat-leaf parsley, chopped
¼ cup (1 oz/30 g) dried breadcrumbs
6 pinches of freshly grated nutmeg

❖Scale the sardines and remove the heads; gut and rinse the fish. Split them along the belly and open out without separating the fillets. Remove the backbone, breaking it off at the tail. Pat the fish dry with paper towels. Season inside and out with salt and pepper.

❖Wash and stem the spinach. Place the leaves, with the water clinging to them, in a saucepan. Season with salt and cook, covered, over high heat for 3 minutes. Drain the spinach and chop finely with a knife.
❖Heat 1 tablespoon oil in a nonstick 10-in (26-cm) skillet. Add the onion and cook, stirring, over low heat for 3 minutes or until golden, then add the garlic and cook for 1 minute longer.
❖Beat the egg in a bowl, add the cheese and mash with a fork. Add the spinach, parsley, the contents of the skillet and half the breadcrumbs. Season with salt, pepper and nutmeg and stir well.
❖Preheat the oven to 450°F (230°C). Using some of the remaining oil, lightly oil a baking dish large enough to hold half the sardines in a single layer. Arrange half the sardines in the dish and spread each one with a spoonful of the stuffing mixture. Cover each sardine with a second one and pour the rest of the oil over. Sprinkle with breadcrumbs and bake for 20 minutes. Serve hot, warm or cold, directly from the baking dish.

SERVES 6

BAKED SARDINES WITH SPINACH (top) AND STUFFED SARDINES

PETER JOHNSON

ESCABÈCHE OF RED MULLET

Bretagne

ANCHOIS GRILLÉS À LA MOUTARDE ET À L'ESTRAGON
Grilled Anchovies with Mustard and Tarragon

24 fresh medium anchovies
salt and freshly ground pepper
6 sprigs tarragon, leaves only
3 oz (100 g) low-salt butter
2 tablespoons strong mustard
½ cup (2 oz/50 g) dry breadcrumbs

❖Remove the heads from the anchovies and gut them. Rinse and split along the ventral fin; open out without separating the fillets. Remove the backbone, breaking it off near the tail. Dry the fish with paper towels and season with salt and pepper. Scatter the tarragon over the fish, then fold the fillets together to enclose the tarragon.
❖Melt the butter in a small saucepan. Add the mustard and stir well, then let cool.
❖Preheat broiler (griller). Arrange the fish on a rack over the broiler pan. Sprinkle with breadcrumbs and spoon half the mustard butter over. Broil for 10 minutes, not too far from the heat source, turning the fish several times and sprinkling with mustard butter.
❖When the anchovies are cooked, arrange them on a serving plate. Sprinkle with the remaining butter and serve.

SERVES 4

GRILLED ANCHOVIES WITH MUSTARD AND TARRAGON (top)
AND STUFFED CLAMS, LORIENT-STYLE (recipe page 78)

PETER JOHNSON

Provence

ROUGETS EN ESCABÈCHE
Escabèche of Red Mullet

Escabèche *is a vinegar marinade of Spanish origin created for preserving little fried fish from which the heads have been removed: hence the name, which comes from* cabeza, *the Spanish word for head. Today, whole fish such as redfish, mackerel and whiting, and cutlets of tuna, bonito, swordfish or hake are also prepared in this manner.*

8 red mullet, about 6 oz (200 g) each
salt and freshly ground pepper
6 tablespoons extra virgin olive oil
6 tablespoons red wine vinegar
3 oz (100 g) fresh mint leaves

❖Ask the fishmonger to scale and gut the fish, leaving the livers intact. Rinse the fish and pat dry; season with salt and pepper.
❖Heat the oil in a nonstick 10-in (26-cm) skillet and cook the fish for 4 minutes on each side. Drain on paper towels and lay in a shallow dish. Transfer 4 tablespoons of the cooking oil to a small saucepan.
❖Pour the vinegar into a second small nonaluminum saucepan and add the mint leaves. Bring to boil, stir and remove from heat. Pour this mixture into the reserved oil and boil for a few seconds, then pour over the fish.
❖Allow the fish to cool. Let stand for at least 4 hours before serving.

SERVES 4

Bretagne

BAR FARCI
Stuffed Sea Bass

1 sea bass, sea bream or snapper, about 3 lb (1.5 kg)
8 oz (250 g) fresh spinach
6 oz (200 g) sorrel
8 oz (250 g) mushrooms
3 oz (100 g) stale bread, crusts trimmed
4 oz (125 g) salted butter
6 French shallots, finely chopped
salt and freshly ground pepper
¾ cup (6 fl oz/185 ml) heavy (double) cream or crème fraîche
6 tablespoons dry white wine

❖ Ask the fishmonger to scale and gut the fish and to open it along the belly, without separating the two fillets, in order to remove the backbone. Rinse and pat dry the opened fish.
❖ Wash and drain the spinach and sorrel; trim the stalks and cut the leaves into very fine strips. Rinse the mushrooms and pat dry, then chop finely. Grind the bread to coarse crumbs in a blender or food processor.
❖ Melt half the butter in a nonstick 10-in (26-cm) sauté pan. Add the shallots and cook, stirring, for 2 minutes over low heat. Add the mushrooms, spinach and sorrel and cook until the vegetables give out no more liquid, about 10 minutes. Season with salt and pepper, mix in the breadcrumbs and remove from heat. Cool to lukewarm.
❖ Preheat oven to 450°F (230°C). Season the inside of the fish with salt and pepper, then fill with the stuffing. Tie the fish together with string. With half the remaining butter, grease a shallow baking dish just large enough to hold the fish; lay the fish in the dish. Combine the cream and wine, season lightly with salt and pepper, and coat the fish with this mixture. Dot with the remaining butter and bake for 45 minutes, turning the fish after 20 to 25 minutes.
❖ Transfer the cooked fish to a serving platter. Boil the sauce until reduced to a thick, creamy consistency and pour over the fish. Serve hot.

SERVES 6

Bretagne

COTRIADE
Cotriade

This soup, based on potatoes, onions and lard, includes a wide variety of fish. It is prepared all along the coast of Bretagne, and there are as many versions as there are fishing ports.

4 lb (2 kg) mixed fish: whiting, mackerel, smelt or red fish, monkfish or blue-eye cod, skate, sole, deep sea bream...
2 lb (1 kg) baking potatoes
⅓ cup (2½ oz/80 g) lard
8 oz (250 g) onions, thinly sliced
salt and freshly ground pepper

For serving:
toasted slices of country bread
red wine vinegar

❖ Ask the fishmonger to scale and gut the fish and remove the heads. Cut the largest fish into 1½-in (4-cm) chunks and leave the others whole; wash and pat dry. Peel the potatoes, wash and cut into 1¼-in (3-cm) cubes.
❖ Melt the lard in an enameled 6-qt (6-l) pot and cook the onions until golden, about 5 minutes, stirring with a wooden spoon. Stir in the potatoes, salt and pepper, then add cold water to cover. Bring to simmer, then cook for 15 minutes.
❖ Add the fish to the simmering liquid, beginning with those with the firmest flesh (skate, monkfish, mackerel), then adding those with softer flesh (bream, sole, whiting, smelt) and letting the liquid return to simmer after each addition. Season with salt and pepper and simmer for 15 minutes.
❖ Remove the cooked fish and potatoes with a slotted spoon and arrange in a shallow dish. Pour a little of the broth over and keep warm. Pour the broth into a tureen and serve immediately, with the toasted slices of country bread. Serve the fish and potatoes dressed with a dash of vinegar.

SERVES 6

Bretagne

MERLANS DE LORIENT
Whiting in Mustard Cream Sauce

4 French shallots, finely chopped
2 tablespoons chopped flat-leaf parsley
salt and freshly ground pepper
2½ oz (80 g) butter
1½ lb (750 g) whiting fillets, skin and bones removed
6 tablespoons Muscadet
1 tablespoon strong mustard
1 tablespoon fresh lemon juice
6 tablespoons heavy (double) cream or crème fraîche

❖ Preheat oven to 425°F (215°C). Mix the shallots and parsley and season with salt and pepper. Using 1 tablespoon of the butter, grease a baking dish just large enough to hold the fillets of fish in a single layer. Spread the shallot mixture over the bottom.
❖ Rinse the fish fillets and pat dry. Season with salt and pepper and arrange in the dish. Blend the wine and mustard and pour over the fish. Dot with 1 tablespoon butter. Bake for 10 minutes.
❖ Transfer the fish fillets to a heatproof serving platter. Pour the cooking liquid into a small saucepan, add the lemon juice and boil until the sauce is reduced to a syrupy consistency. Stir in the cream and boil until thick enough to coat the fish. Remove from heat and whisk in the remaining butter in small pieces.
❖ Preheat broiler. Coat the fish with the sauce, then place under the broiler, close to the heat source, for 2 minutes. Serve immediately.

SERVES 4

WHITING IN MUSTARD CREAM SAUCE (left),
COTRIADE (center) AND STUFFED SEA BASS (right)
PIERRE HUSSENOT/AGENCE TOP

SALT COD WITH BEET GREENS AND CURRANTS (top left),
PUREE OF SALT COD (bottom left) AND SALT COD, BREST-STYLE (right)

Bretagne

MORUE BRESTOISE

Salt Cod, Brest-style

Time was when the fishermen of Bretagne caught the species of fish called gadidae, *and among them fresh cod. When it deserted their coasts, they were obliged to pursue it as far as Terre-Neuve — as they still do today.*

2 lb (1 kg) salt cod fillets
2 lb (1 kg) boiling potatoes
2 oz (60 g) butter
8 oz (250 g) leeks, white parts only, well washed and
    thinly sliced
4 tablespoons water
½ teaspoon arrowroot
2 tablespoons chopped chervil

❖Soak the salt cod fillets in a large bowl of cold water, skin side up, for 12 hours, changing the water 3 times.
❖Drain the cod and transfer it to a large pot of cold water, skin side down. Bring to boil over low heat, then reduce heat and cook at the barest simmer for 10 minutes. Remove from heat and let cool.
❖Place the potatoes in a saucepan of cold salted water and bring to boil. Cook for about 25 minutes or until the potatoes are easily pierced with the point of a knife. Drain, peel and slice into ⅛-in (3-mm) rounds.
❖Melt 1 oz (30 g) butter in a saucepan and cook the leeks until soft and golden, stirring constantly with a wooden spoon. Add 2 tablespoons water. Blend the arrowroot with the remaining 2 tablespoons water and add to the saucepan. Cook over moderate heat, stirring constantly, until the sauce thickens.
❖Preheat oven to 450°F (230°C). Drain and flake the fish.

Using the remaining butter, grease a shallow 9 x 13-in (22 x 32-cm) pan or gratin dish. Arrange the potatoes and cod in layers, finishing with a layer of cod. Sprinkle with chervil, then pour the leek mixture over. Bake until lightly browned, about 10 minutes. Serve hot, directly from the pan.

SERVES 6

Corse

MORUE AUX BLETTES ET AUX RAISINS SECS

Salt Cod with Beet Greens and Currants

2 lb (1 kg) salt cod fillets
2 oz (50 g) dried currants
1 lb (500 g) ripe tomatoes
1 lb (500 g) boiling potatoes
1 lb (500 g) beet greens or Swiss chard
3 tablespoons extra virgin olive oil
1 onion, about 3 oz (100 g), finely chopped
2 cloves garlic, finely chopped
1 bay leaf
salt and freshly ground pepper

❖Soak the salt cod fillets in a large bowl of cold water, skin side up, for 12 hours, changing the water 3 times.
❖Drain the cod and cut it into 1½-in (4-cm) squares. Rinse the currants in hot water and drain. Quarter the tomatoes and puree in a food mill, using the plate with medium-size holes. Peel the potatoes, wash and pat dry; cut into ¾-in (2-cm) cubes.
❖Rinse the beet greens, drain and slice into ¾-in (2-cm) strips. Place in a saucepan with the water clinging to the leaves and cook, covered, over high heat for 4 minutes. Drain.
❖Heat the oil in a nonstick 10-in (26-cm) sauté pan. Cook the chopped onion and garlic, stirring constantly, for 2 minutes or until golden. Add the tomato pulp, bay leaf and potatoes. Season with salt and pepper and cook, covered, over low heat for 15 minutes.
❖Add the cod, greens and currants and cook for 15 minutes, covered, over very low heat. Turn into a shallow dish and serve hot.

SERVES 6

Languedoc

BRANDADE DE MORUE

Puree of Salt Cod

The name of this dish comes from the Provençal word brandar, *to stir. A specialty of the town of Nîmes, it is a puree of cod mixed with olive oil and milk. In Marseille and Toulon it is flavored with crushed garlic and spread on croutons that have been rubbed with more garlic. When a puree of potatoes is added, it becomes a* parmentière de morue.

2 lb (1 kg) salt cod fillets
1 cup (8 fl oz/250 ml) milk

1 cup (8 fl oz/250 ml) extra virgin olive oil
For serving:
croutons

❖Soak the salt cod fillets in a large bowl of cold water, skin side up, for 12 hours, changing the water 3 times.
❖Drain the cod and transfer it to a large pot of cold water, skin side down. Bring to boil over low heat, then reduce heat and cook at the barest simmer for 10 minutes.
❖Meanwhile, heat the milk in a small saucepan. Pour half the oil into a large saucepan.
❖Drain the fish and remove skin and bones. Flake the flesh and add to the oil in the saucepan. Over very low heat, and turning and mashing the mixture with a wooden spoon, gradually add the remaining oil and the hot milk, blending until the mixture is a very smooth puree; this will take about 15 minutes.
❖Turn the *brandade* into a shallow dish and serve immediately, accompanied with croutons.

SERVES 6

QUENELLES

PETER JOHNSON

Lyonnais

QUENELLES
Quenelles

Pike quenelles are a specialty of the Lyonnais region. They are sometimes served coated in Nantua sauce (which originated in the town of the same name), a cream sauce that includes écrevisses (freshwater crayfish) among its ingredients.

1 lb (500 g) pike fillets, skin and bones removed
4 eggs
1¼ cups (10 fl oz/310 ml) heavy (double) cream or crème fraîche
salt and freshly ground pepper
4 pinches of cayenne pepper
4 oz (125 g) butter
For serving:
beurre blanc (page 68) or melted butter

❖Place the fish in a blender or food processor and blend to a fine puree. With the machine running, add the eggs, cream, salt, pepper and cayenne. Add the butter in small pieces, blending until the puree is very smooth. Refrigerate the puree for 12 hours before preparing the quenelles.

❖On a lightly floured work surface, shape large spoonfuls of the mixture into smooth sausage shapes. Half-fill a large saucepan with salted water and bring to simmer. Drop in the quenelles, a few at a time, and simmer for 15 minutes. Drain on a clean cloth, then transfer to a warmed platter. Serve immediately, coated with *beurre blanc* or sprinkled with melted butter.

SERVES 6

Provence

BOURRIDE
Bourride

The link between the bourride de lotte *of Languedoc and the Provençal* bourride *is* aïoli. *But whereas the first is made only with anglerfish and includes a very thick sauce, the second is a true thick soup, containing every variety of white-fleshed fish.*

4 lb (2 kg) mixed white fish: monkfish (anglerfish) or blue-eye cod, sea bass, John Dory, turbot or flounder…
bouquet garni: 1 bay leaf, 1 sprig thyme, 1 sprig dried fennel, 6 sprigs parsley, 1 strip dried orange peel
1 medium carrot, peeled and coarsely chopped
1 onion, about 3 oz (100 g), coarsely chopped
2 leeks, white parts only, well washed and coarsely chopped
6 cloves garlic, peeled
2 cups (16 fl oz/500 ml) dry white wine
3 cups (24 fl oz/750 ml) water
salt and freshly ground pepper
For the sauce:
3 cloves garlic
1 teaspoon strong mustard
2 egg yolks
salt
1 cup (8 fl oz/250 ml) extra virgin olive oil
For serving:
slices of toasted baguette (French bread)
cloves of garlic, halved

❖Ask the fishmonger to scale and gut the fish and remove the heads, reserving the heads and bones. Cut the fish into 1½-in (4-cm) chunks.
❖Tie together the herbs for the bouquet garni. Place the fish heads and bones in a large saucepan. Add the carrot, onion, leeks, garlic, bouquet garni, wine and water and bring to simmer. Season with salt and pepper and simmer for 20 minutes.
❖Meanwhile, prepare the sauce: force the garlic through a press into a shallow bowl. Add the mustard, egg yolk and salt and stir well. Set aside for 1 minute, then add the oil in a thin stream, whisking until the mixture is quite firm; this *aïoli* will thicken the sauce.
❖Strain the broth into another saucepan. Bring to simmer over low heat and add the fish. Simmer, covered, for 10 minutes.
❖Remove the cooked fish from the broth with a slotted spoon and keep warm in a tureen. Blend half the *aïoli* into the broth, off the heat. Pour this sauce over the fish and serve immediately, accompanied by toasted bread rubbed with garlic and spread with the remaining *aïoli*.

SERVES 6   *Photograph page 10*

Provence

BOUILLABAISSE
Bouillabaisse

Bouillabaisse was invented by Mediterranean fishermen who, when they returned from a fishing trip, would cook their more modest fish with a few shellfish in a huge cauldron over a wood fire using olive oil, a piece of dried orange peel and some saffron.

Gradually it became a highlight of the cuisine of the Midi region, each cook adding his or her own individual touch. The common factor in all the recipes is the use of as many white-fleshed rockfish as possible, to which may be added small crabs, mussels, squillfish, and even cuttlefish with their ink.

6 lb (3 kg) of a mixture of fish and crustaceans: rock cod, John Dory, monkfish (anglerfish), blue-eye cod, eel, sea bass, snapper, red mullet, cuttlefish, sole, brill (Petrale sole), small crabs, lobster, crayfish…
¼ cup (2 fl oz/60 ml) extra virgin olive oil
1 lb (500 g) ripe tomatoes, coarsely chopped
2 medium carrots, peeled and thinly sliced
1 leek, well washed and thinly sliced
1 celery stalk, thinly sliced
1 onion, about 3 oz (100 g), thinly sliced
1 sprig dried thyme
1 sprig dried rosemary
1 sprig dried fennel
1 bay leaf
1 strip dried orange peel
10 cloves garlic, peeled
10 sprigs parsley
6 pinches of saffron threads
salt and freshly ground pepper
2 cups (16 fl oz/500 ml) dry white wine

For serving:
slices of toasted baguette (French bread)
cloves of garlic, halved

❖Ask the fishmonger to scale and gut the fish and remove the heads. Reserve the heads, bones and shells. Cut the largest fish into 1½-in (4-cm) chunks and leave the others whole. Wash all the fish and pat dry. If crayfish or lobster is included, cut it in half to separate the head from the tail and remove the grainy sac from the head. Clean the cuttlefish, keeping only the body and tentacles; wash and pat dry.

❖Heat the oil in a 6-qt (6-l) saucepan. Add the heads, bones and shells of the fish and crustaceans and cook over low heat, stirring, for 5 minutes. Add the tomatoes, carrots, leek, celery and onion and cook, stirring, for 5 minutes or until the vegetables are lightly colored. Add the thyme, rosemary, fennel, bay leaf, orange peel, garlic, parsley, saffron, salt and pepper and stir for 1 minute. Add the wine and simmer gently for 45 minutes.

❖Remove the fish trimmings, thyme, rosemary, fennel, bay leaf, orange peel, garlic and parsley. Puree the tomato mixture in a blender or food processor until smooth.

❖Wipe the saucepan and return the pureed mixture to it. Bring to boil over low heat. Add the fish, beginning with those with the firmest flesh (cuttlefish, eel, monkfish, rock cod, red mullet) and later adding those with softer flesh (John Dory, sea bass, sole, brill), letting the mixture return to boil between additions. Finally add the crustaceans. Sim-

mer for 10 minutes, then remove the seafood with a slotted spoon and arrange on a plate. Keep warm.

❖Pour the soup into a tureen and serve hot, over slices of bread rubbed with garlic. Follow with the seafood as a separate course.

SERVES 6 – 8   *Photograph page 10*

Alsace

MATELOTE AU RIESLING
Matelote of Freshwater Fish in Riesling

4 lb (2 kg) mixed river fish: eel, pike, tench or Murray cod, perch or bass, trout…
bouquet garni: 1 sprig thyme, 1 bay leaf, 6 sprigs parsley, 2 sprigs tarragon
2 medium carrots, peeled and sliced
2 leeks, well washed and sliced
2 onions, about 3 oz (100 g) each, sliced
2 cups (16 fl oz/500 ml) Riesling
2 cups (16 fl oz/500 ml) water
4 pinches of freshly grated nutmeg
salt and freshly ground pepper
3 egg yolks
¾ cup (6 fl oz/200 ml) heavy (double) cream or crème fraîche

❖Ask the fishmonger to scale and gut the fish and remove the heads. Reserve the heads and bones. Cut the fish into 1½-in (4-cm) chunks.

❖Tie together the herbs for the bouquet garni. In a large saucepan, combine the carrots, leeks, onions, fish heads and bones, bouquet garni, wine, water, nutmeg, salt and pepper. Bring to simmer, then simmer for 20 minutes.

❖Strain the broth into a clean pot and bring to simmer. Add the fish in the order listed, letting the liquid return to simmer each time before adding the next fish. Simmer for 25 minutes, then remove from heat. Remove the fish with a slotted spoon and keep warm in a shallow dish.

MATELOTE OF FRESHWATER FISH IN RIESLING

❖Boil the cooking liquid until reduced by half. Beat the egg yolks and cream together in a small bowl, using a fork. Beat 2 tablespoons of the broth into the egg yolk mixture. Return this mixture to the broth, off the heat, and whisk until thickened. Pour this sauce over the fish and serve immediately.

SERVES 6

Bourgogne

POCHOUSE

Fish and Onion Stew

4 lb (2 kg) river fish: eel, carp, tench, perch, pike…
5 oz (150 g) lightly salted pork fatback
2½ oz (75 g) butter
25 tiny pickling onions, peeled
salt and freshly ground pepper
3 cups (24 fl oz/750 ml) white Burgundy
6 cloves garlic, peeled
¼ cup (1 oz/25 g) all purpose (plain) flour

For serving:
croutons

❖Ask the fishmonger to scale and gut the fish and remove the heads. Cut the fish into 1½-in (4-cm) chunks, rinse and pat dry.
❖Rinse the fatback. Remove the rind and cut the fat into fine matchsticks. Blanch for 1 minute in boiling water, then drain, rinse and drain again.
❖Melt 1½ oz (50 g) of the butter in a 6-qt (6-l) pot. Add the onions and fatback and cook, stirring, over low heat for 5 minutes or until lightly golden. Season lightly with salt and pepper. Pour in the wine and bring to simmer. Add the garlic and fish and simmer for 20 minutes. Remove the fish and keep warm in a tureen. Discard the garlic.
❖Mix together the flour and the remaining butter in a small bowl to form a soft ball. Blend in 3 tablespoons of the broth, then return the mixture to the pot and cook over low heat, stirring, for 5 minutes or until the sauce thickens to a creamy consistency. Pour over the fish and serve immediately, accompanied by croutons.

SERVES 6

INGREDIENTS FOR FISH AND ONION STEW

TROUT IN RIESLING (top) AND TROUT WITH ALMONDS

Alsace

TRUITES AU RIESLING

Trout in Riesling

4 trout, about 6 oz (200 g) each
salt and freshly ground pepper
2½ oz (75 g) butter
4 French shallots, finely chopped
⅔ cup (5 fl oz/150 ml) Riesling
5 oz (150 g) small mushrooms
6 tablespoons heavy (double) cream or crème fraîche

❖Ask the fishmonger to clean the fish. Rinse them and pat dry; season with salt and pepper.
❖Preheat oven to 425 °F (215 °C). Using 1 tablespoon of the butter, grease a baking dish just large enough to hold the fish. Scatter the chopped shallots over the bottom and lay the fish on top. Pour the wine into the dish and cover with a sheet of waxed paper or aluminum foil. Bake for 20 minutes.
❖Meanwhile, trim the mushroom stems; wash the mushrooms, pat dry and cut into quarters. Melt 1 tablespoon butter in a nonstick 10-in (26-cm) skillet and cook the mushrooms until they are golden and give out no more liquid. Keep warm.
❖Skin the trout and arrange on a serving platter. Surround with mushrooms and keep warm.
❖Strain the trout cooking liquid into a small saucepan and boil over high heat until reduced to a syrupy consistency. Add the cream and cook until the sauce is thick and creamy. Briskly stir in the remaining butter with a wooden spoon. Coat the fish and mushrooms with the sauce and serve immediately.

SERVES 4

PETER JOHNSON

Champagne

TRUITES AUX AMANDES

Trout with Almonds

4 trout, about 6 oz (200 g) each
salt and freshly ground pepper
5 oz (150 g) butter
4 oz (120 g) flaked almonds

❖Ask the fishmonger to clean the fish. Rinse them and pat dry; season with salt and pepper.
❖Melt half the butter in a nonstick 10-in (26-cm) skillet and cook the trout for 6 minutes each side. Transfer to a serving platter and keep warm.
❖Discard the butter from the skillet and wipe out the pan. Add the almonds and toast lightly over low heat, stirring often. Add the remaining butter and let it melt over low heat. Pour over the trout and serve immediately.

SERVES 4

Bourgogne

CARPE FARCIE

Stuffed Carp

1 carp, about 3 lb (1.5 kg)
5 oz (150 g) stale bread, crusts trimmed
3 oz (100 g) thinly sliced streaky bacon
2 tablespoons butter
1 clove garlic, finely chopped

PETER JOHNSON

3 French shallots, finely chopped
salt and freshly ground pepper
1 tablespoon chopped flat-leaf parsley
1 egg
6 tablespoons (100 ml) dry white wine
¾ cup (6 fl oz/185 ml) heavy (double) cream or
 crème fraîche

❖Ask the fishmonger to scale and gut the fish and to open it along the belly, without separating the two fillets, in order to remove the backbone. If the fish contains any roe, set this aside and chop coarsely. Rinse the fish and pat dry on all surfaces.

❖Grind the bread into coarse crumbs in a blender or food processor. Trim the rind from the bacon and finely chop the meat with a knife.

❖Melt 1 tablespoon butter in a nonstick 10-in (26-cm) sauté pan. Add the chopped garlic and shallots and cook over low heat, stirring, for 2 minutes. Add the bacon and cook, stirring, for 2 more minutes. Season with salt and pepper. Stir in the roe, parsley and breadcrumbs, then remove from heat. Mix in the egg and let cool.

❖Preheat oven to 450°F (230°C). Season the inside of the fish with salt and pepper and spread with the stuffing. Fold the fillets together and tie the fish at intervals.

❖Use the remaining butter to grease a baking dish large enough to hold the fish; lay the fish in the dish. Add the wine and bake for 45 minutes, basting often with the cooking juices.

❖Transfer the cooked fish to a serving platter. Boil the sauce until reduced to a syrupy consistency. Add the cream and cook, stirring, until it thickens, about 2 more minutes. Pour sauce over the fish and serve.

SERVES 6

STUFFED CARP

EELS IN GREEN SAUCE

Picardie

ANGUILLES AU VERT

Eels in Green Sauce

2 lb (1 kg) medium eels
salt and freshly ground pepper
3 oz (100 g) sorrel
3 oz (100 g) fresh spinach
10 sprigs flat-leaf parsley
4 sprigs chervil
4 sprigs sage
2 sprigs tarragon
1 sprig mint
1½ oz (40 g) butter
3 French shallots, finely chopped
6 tablespoons dry white wine
2 sprigs thyme
1 bay leaf
2 egg yolks
6 tablespoons heavy (double) cream or crème fraîche

❖Skin and gut the eels, wash them and slice into chunks 1½ in (4 cm) thick. Pat dry with paper towels and season with salt and pepper.

❖Remove the stalks from the sorrel, spinach, parsley, chervil, sage, tarragon and mint. Wash, pat dry and chop the leaves.

❖Melt the butter in a nonstick 10-in (26-cm) sauté pan. Add the chunks of eel and the shallots and cook over low heat, stirring, for 5 minutes or until the eel is just lightly browned. Discard the butter from the pan and stir in the wine. Add thyme and bay leaf and bring to boil. Cover and simmer for 5 minutes over low heat.

❖Remove the thyme and bay leaf and add the remaining herbs, sorrel and spinach. Mix well and simmer, covered, for 5 minutes.

❖Meanwhile, beat the egg yolks and cream with a fork in a small bowl. Stir in 2 tablespoons of the cooking liquid, then return the mixture to the sauté pan. Remove from heat and stir until the sauce thickens and coats the chunks of eel. Turn into a shallow dish and serve immediately.

SERVES 4

PETER JOHNSON

FROM FRANCHE-COMTÉ TO DAUPHINÉ

From one mountain to another

LEO MEIER

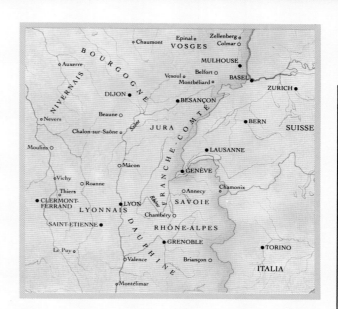

FROM FRANCHE-COMTÉ TO DAUPHINÉ

From one mountain to another

The appearance of Franche-Comté's landscape provides its name — the *reculées*, or recesses, as one plateau comes after the other, then withdraws behind the valley. The Jura mountains have many of these. This gentle, soft, green mountain range, rarely exceeding 1000 meters in height, shoulder to shoulder with Switzerland, belongs entirely to the free county that was for so long disputed between the Kings of Spain and the Dukes of Burgundy. It was once the land of the *gaude*, but this thick gruel, enriched with fresh butter, is now hardly ever made. Nor is the *bresi*, salted beef dried by the hearth.

This is the kingdom of small mountains, of fresh air, of pure wines — light, fruity reds from Poulsard and Trousseau grapes, whites from the Chardonnay and, especially, the distinctively colored Savagnin, rosy-tinged and golden yellow. The wine from this grape, left in barrels for six years during which time one-third of its volume is lost through evaporation, becomes *vin jaune*, or yellow wine. The real treasure of the region, it takes its flavor and scent from walnuts, resin and dried flowers, delicately mixed.

The reason for insisting on the particular quality of the Jura wines, the best of which are found between Arbois — the city of Pasteur — and the belvedere of Château-Chalon, is that they marry admirably with the dishes of the Franche-Comté: sausages, *côti du Sauguais* (the smoked pork chop that is a standard dish of Arbois), chicken with *vin jaune* and morels, veal sweetbreads with cream and wine sauce, walnut cakes and, naturally, the cheeses of the region.

There are the Comté and the Morbier of the local dairies, the Vacherin from Mont d'Or and

LEFT: GRAPEVINES ADORN THIS FARMHOUSE NEAR CHALON-SUR-SAÔNE IN BOURGOGNE, A REGION PROUD OF ITS RED WINES.

PREVIOUS PAGES: SHROUDED IN MIST, MONT BLANC IS THE HIGHEST MOUNTAIN IN EUROPE, BREATHTAKINGLY BEAUTIFUL AND DESERVEDLY FAMOUS.
LEO MEIER

again, but more commercial, the Cancoillotte from Besançon or Haute-Saône, a runny cheese made from skim milk. The Comté, which bears the name of its province, is a splendid Gruyère-type cheese made from unpasteurized cow's milk, with an aroma of grassy meadows. It demonstrates that the Franche-Comté, so aptly named, has in no way abdicated its characteristic frankness, nor the natural qualities of the pastures of its plateaus.

At the foot of the plateaus, the beautiful valley of the Loue produces the kirsch of La Marsotte. The valley has hardly changed since the time when Gustave Courbet, a native of Ornans — the town has established a museum in his studio — painted it from the viewpoint of a wide-eyed observer. Brook trout and river fish are still plentiful in the clear waters that abound in the vicinity of Lods and Mouthier-Haute-Pierre.

Right next door is Burgundy — another wine region, and famous in a different way. From Dijon to Chagny, an expanse of vineyard: the Côtes de Nuits from Fixin to Corgoloin, the Côtes de Beaune from Ladoix to Cheilley-les-Maranges. Here are found some of the world's most celebrated wine appellations: Clos Vougeot, Chambertin, Vosne-Romanée, Pommard, Meursault, Montrachet. A region of fine wines, exquisite fare and joyous revelry.

Henri Vincenot, the incomparable Burgundian writer, used to tell the story of the "three-man wine," the *vin de trois* — which, it seems, needed three people to appreciate it: "an obliging taster and two men to carry him." Burgundian humor.

There is no other region more serious, however, about the art of dining. Old traditions persist in spite of the increasing rarity of old-fashioned ingredients — the snails of Burgundy, known as *gros gris* or "large greys"; the *pochouse verdunoise*, a fricassée of freshwater fish cooked in white wine. Wine has always played an important part in the cuisine: *civet* with red wine, marinades based on white wine or, again, "verjuice" from freshly crushed grapes.

There are other festive products as well, and all seem to converge at Dijon, the splendid capital of the former duchy — a town of old dwellings, historic churches and cobbled streets where the old palace of Charles the Bold now houses a magnificent art museum. Dijon is the home of mustard; its gingerbread, or *pain d'épices*, is equally famous. Blackcurrant liqueur — *crème de cassis* — made from the tiny berries picked around Arcenant, a sleepy village high above the Côtes de Nuits, has known an illustrious career thanks to Canon Kir, mayor of Dijon, who mixed it with white wine to create the drink which now bears his name.

Mushrooms, pike, freshwater crayfish and *sauce nantua*, prepared with a puree of the same crayfish, belong to the shared assets of Burgundy and the Franche-Comté, the destinies of which were once intertwined. But Burgundy, which at the height of its glory was greater than the kingdom of France,

LIKE MOST ALPINE RESORTS, CHAMONIX REMAINS AN OLD-FASHIONED MOUNTAIN TOWN, WITH CHARMING CHALETS LIKE THIS ONE THAT ATTRACT A SOPHISTICATED INTERNATIONAL CLIENTELE.

THE BORDER TOWN OF CHAMONIX, HIGH IN THE FRENCH ALPS, IS A POPULAR TOURIST RESORT ALL YEAR ROUND.

a trump hand when it comes to attracting the gourmet: pears from the Rhône valley, nougat from Montélimar, the wines of Hermitage, Condrieu, Cornas, Château-Grillet and Saint-Joseph; more wines from the Côte-Rôtie, violet-scented reds made from the Syrah grape, the amiable red and white wines of Mâcon, the great Pouilly-Fuissés, the seductive Saint-Verans; the modest wines from Crozes-Hermitage. And then the Beaujolais, which is a whole saga in itself. "Lyons," wrote Léon Daudet, "is watered by three rivers: the Rhône, the Saône and the Beaujolais."

More than just a city of good living, Lyons is a symbol. It is the great gastronomic crossroads where all routes meet: a bridge to the Côte d'Azur from Paris, a link with Switzerland and eastern Europe, touching the Charolais, Bresse and Auvergne region, making the most of its important strategic situation and benefiting from the unsurpassed reputation it has enjoyed since it was known by the Romans as Lugdunum.

It used to be said that Lyons is a city that makes you hungry. At one time it was the women, the *mères*, who set the gastronomic standards. Mère Charles, Mère Guy, Mère Blanc and the most famous of all, Mère Brazier, have now been replaced by men who do not always have descendants. So is Lyons stagnating, resting on the good fortune of its location? No: in truth, Lyons is still a capital of good eating and good living, even if it is left to Paris, or indeed to the other provinces, to set the styles.

There are plenty of good charcutiers, those kings of the *rosette*, the preserved sausage, the *andouillette*, the *sabodet*, the boiling sausage, the tripe known as *gras double* and the little bundles of pork rind. They provide the superb products on which is based the popular cuisine of Lyons, the cuisine served in the *bouchons* — familiar little bistros where the wine comes in jugs — and in the most characteristic of the large restaurants of the town, Léon de Lyons. Here, too, you can eat poached sausage accompanied by potatoes cooked in oil; or *tablier de sapeur* (the fireman's apron), made from beef mesentery that is cut into pieces, then crumbed and fried; or perhaps brains cooked with capers.

The cheese called *cervelle de canut* owes its name to the silk weavers from the mills of Lyons, the *canuts*. It is a blend of fresh cheese beaten until smooth with salt and pepper, finely chopped shallot and fresh herbs, white wine and a dash of oil, and it epitomizes the honest, simple character of the food of Lyons. Other typical dishes? Spit-roasted chickens, served simply with cardoons (a vegetable of the same family as the artichoke) or a gratin of macaroni; veal liver fried with onions and vinegar; pike quenelles cooked in beef fat; *andouillette*, prepared from pork and veal mesentery and pan-fried with onions and white wine or vinegar, sometimes with mustard as well; chicken with slices of truffle slipped under the skin, said

has been able to appropriate the riches of its smaller neighbors: the Charolais, renowned for its beef; the Morvan, for its ham; the Bresse, for its highly esteemed white poultry. Thus dishes such as ham in cream sauce, chicken in white wine, *coq au vin*, Burgundian beef and slow-simmered stews, are all evidence of the enormous wealth of the province.

The cheeses of Epoisses and Chambertin, both strong, soft and made from cow's milk, are perfect mates for the powerful, well-structured red wines of the Côte de Nuits. *Oeufs en meurette* (eggs poached in red wine), *gougères* (little cheese puffs, traditionally served at the start of a meal) and various charcuterie products, like parsleyed ham set in a clear, wine-flavored jelly enlivened with fresh thyme, chervil and tarragon: these add the finishing touch to a festive spread.

Lyons could easily pass for the natural daughter, or elder sister, of Burgundy. For years writers have overflowed with praise for this ex-capital of ancient Gaul — the "capital of fine food" — claiming it to be, in the words of Curnonsky, "world capital of gastronomy." Or as Henri Clos-Jouve put it, "Lyons is a larder."

In fact, Lyons and its surrounding regions hold

to be *en demi-deuil* (in half-mourning); or chicken poached in a pig's bladder filled with vegetable stock, with cream added later; chicken flavored with vinegar; the savory tart (called *tartre*) of Les Allymes; the sugar-topped *galette*, or cake, from Pérouges; the *bugnes*, or fritters, from Bresse — all these are just as much part of the repertoire of Lyons, which makes the most of all the resources of the orchards, the valleys, the lakes, the pastures and the vineyards that surround it.

The mountains encircling Lyons bring a breath of fresh air from their intoxicating heights, and are hardly mean with their riches. *Gratin dauphinois*, so popular in Lyons but also throughout the whole of France, consists of layers of thinly sliced potatoes, cooked in the oven with cream. The *ravioles* of Romans, in the Drôme, are small pasta shapes stuffed with goat cheese. The sharp, satisfying flavor of Saint-Marcellin cheese — soft, medium-sized, made with cow's milk — makes a pleasant ending to a cozy dinner. The various charcuterie items — which rejoice in such names as *boudins farçons*, *mursons*, *caillettes* (small pâtés of liver combined with spinach) — are some of the assets of the Dauphiné, although they are also found on the other side of the Rhône, on the rugged slopes of the Ardèche.

Savoy, with its expansive mountainside pastures, its wooded farms, its flower-bedecked chalets, its huge barns, its forest fruits and its dairy traditions, offers unexpected wealth; even the French have little idea of the diversity of its products. The lakes of Bourget, Annecy and Léman produce magnificent fish: trout, perch, carp, eel and a local specialty, the *féra*, but best of all the superb, rosy-fleshed *omble-chevalier*, which is cooked simply *à la meunière* or served with foaming butter.

The local cheeses, which must be included among the finest in France, are often seen at their best in the modern market of Lyons at La Part-Dieu. They include the Reblochon, produced in the region between Thônes and the Grand-Bornand from unpasteurized, unfermented milk, its rind washed frequently during two weeks of aging in a cool cellar; the Beaufort, pride of the Beaufortin region, a land of steeples, *clochers à bulbe* and undulating pastures — the "prince of Gruyères," according to Brillat-Savarin, made only during a period of 100 days in summer when cows graze on the mountain pastures, from warm milk that smells of both grass and curds; the Tamié, which is a strong-flavored, Reblochon-type cheese, made by monks in the abbey of the same name; the Tomme des Bauges, with its rich, powdery white

THE TRANQUIL BARRAGE DE ROSELAND,
ONE OF MANY ALPINE DAMS, WILL TURN TO ICE IN THE WEEKS TO COME.

LEO MEIER

VEGETABLE GARDENS SURROUND THE TINY SHINGLE-TOPPED HOMES OF
ST-PIERRE-DE-CHARTREUSE IN DAUPHINÉ.

rind; the *Persillé* cheese, made from slowly heated goat's milk that takes on a musty flavor: are these not enough to demonstrate the great wealth of cheeses from Savoy? More significantly, many of the traditional dishes of the region rely on this variety of cheeses — like the *pela des Aravis*, which is a simple dish of melted cheese on boiled potatoes, or the renowned *fondue* based on melted Gruyère, with white wine and sometimes kirsch and nutmeg.

Are these traditional dishes tending to disappear for reasons of health and diet? On the farms between Megève and Chamonix they still prepare the *farcement savoyard* (a cake made with grated raw potato to which are added prunes, dried pears, raisins, eggs and flour), the *farçon* (a potato puree enriched with eggs and chopped herbs), and the *caïon*, a dish of pork cooked in red wine, which is accompanied by polenta. And you still find — not only in Savoy — the *matafan* or *mate-faim*, a thick, substantial potato pancake which in Burgundy and the Jura is made with apples and sugar. The pastries here — like the sponge known as *biscuit de Savoie*, whose basic ingredients are eggs and sugar — are as delicate as snow. Another find is the brioche of Saint-Genix, originally from the Pâtisserie Debeauve at Yenne: a hand-shaped brioche, filled with praline and covered with brown sugar.

Savoy wines include the Roussette and the Chignin, made from Roussette grapes (smooth, elegant, distinctive); the Bergeron, from the Roussane (full-bodied and structured); and the Apremont or Abymes, from the Jacquère grape (lighter, more diuretic); it is all too easy to think of them as uncomplicated, après-ski wines, but the two first mentioned improve greatly with age. The most typical local red comes from the Mondeuse, a grape brought to the region long ago by the Allobroges. The wine has a heady perfume of mountain fruit and a considerable aging potential.

From local fruits and berries are made jams, jellies, syrups and spirits. *Génépi*, which results from the distillation of an indigenous Savoy plant, is the local digestive *par excellence*. But how many know that it was in Chambéry that French vermouth was born, in 1821, at the Routin distillery? The recipe calls for macerating whole plants, roots, bark and mountain flowers in the local dry white wine. Here, too, *Chambéry fraise* was launched, to become a favorite apéritif for Americans in France in the postwar years: a simple beverage, made from alpine strawberries and white wine.

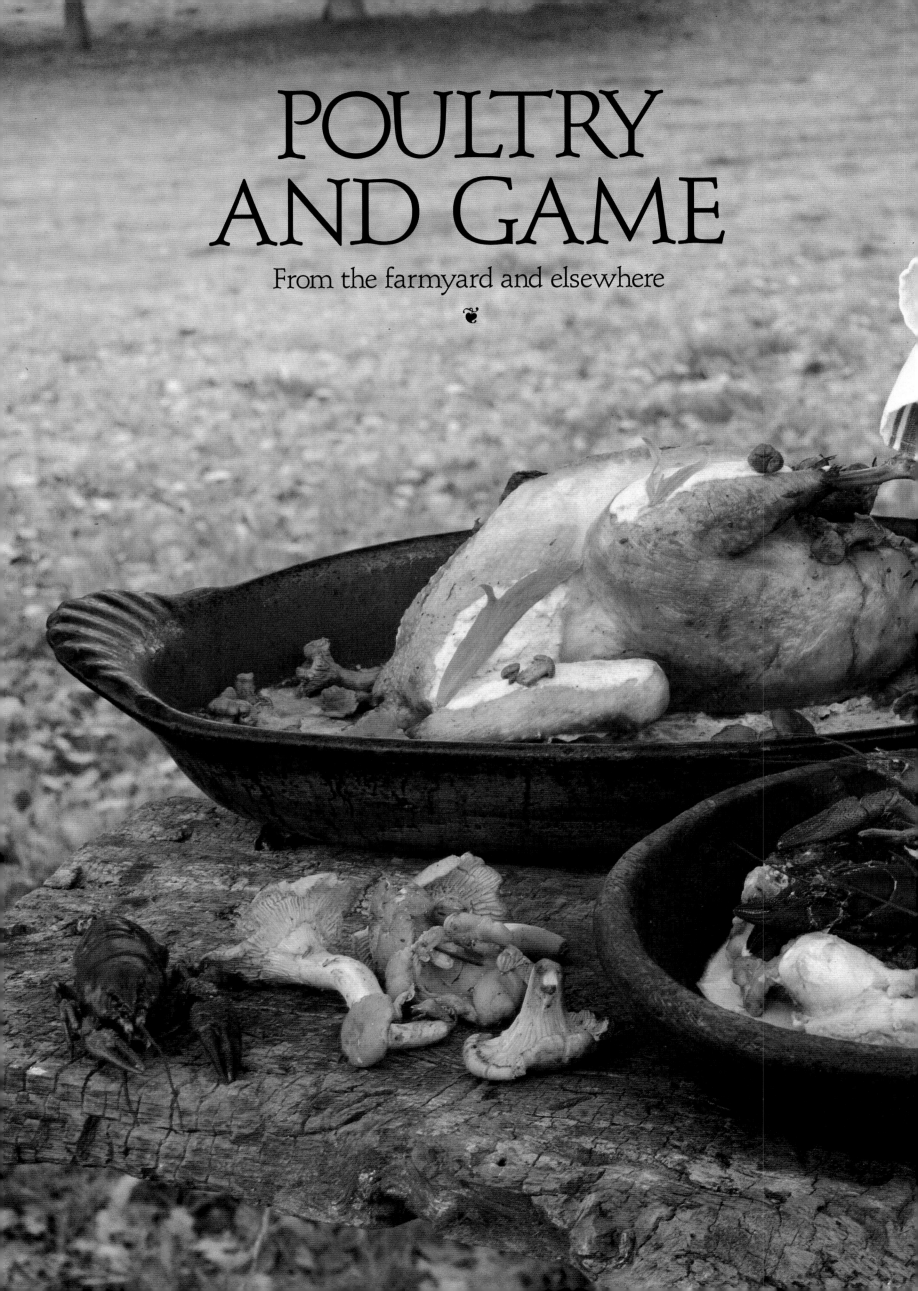

POULTRY
AND GAME

From the farmyard and elsewhere

FOIE GRAS, THE ENLARGED LIVER OF A FORCE-FED DUCK OR GOOSE, IS ONE OF THE MOST ANCIENT FRENCH DELICACIES. THE BEST *FOIE GRAS* COMES FROM ALSACE AND PÉRIGORD, AND IS PRODUCED BETWEEN OCTOBER AND APRIL.

POULTRY AND GAME

From the farmyard and elsewhere

It all began with the Sunday *poule au pot* which Henri IV, much-beloved king of France, wished to provide as festive fare for all his subjects. Over five centuries, many changes have taken place: chicken has become an economical dish, even an everyday one. So much for the exceptional, the special-occasion dish; the so-called "battery" chicken is mass-produced.

As a reaction against the raising of poultry not in farmyards but in closed, cramped quarters, practitioners of the traditional system have grouped together to defend their "label," granted in accordance with the extent of the pasture area and of the liberty allowed the bird. The finest of all, the greatest luxury, is the Bresse chicken: white-feathered, blue-clawed, allowed 10 square meters space each, fed on grain. The poultry is superb, with tender, juicy and tasty flesh, the gentle and soothing reflection of a fertile earth. In Bresse, chickens are treated like children.

The chickens of Loué, in the Landes of Chalosse, are also of top quality, raised in the open air and fed on grain. The best way of eating them? Spit-roasted, or gently pot-roasted, or cooked *en vessie*, in a pig's bladder. Their fatty skin becomes deliciously crisp when cooked, the feet — grilled — are eaten in a salad, and the tender, delicate white meat can be made into scallops or marinated.

If the truth be known, poultry appeals to all palates, lends itself to all kinds of preparations and all vegetables, adapts to all traditions. With cream, with tarragon, with vinegar, with wild mushrooms from the forest, with rich *vin jaune*, with freshwater crayfish (*écrevisses*), with garlic, with cider, with butter, with mustard, stuffed, poached in stock, cooked with rice, with a cream sauce known as *suprême*, with peppers, with truffles, with beer, with champagne, with Riesling: every region has its own recipe. Indeed, poultry is the lowest common denominator of the French.

The *coq*, or rooster (typically a bird at least one year of age, its reproductive duties already past), which is traditionally cooked *au vin*, either red, white or *jaune*, in order to tenderize its somewhat tough flesh, is becoming rare. The situation is similar for the hen. Both are being profitably replaced by year-old chickens. The *ne plus ultra* is the capon, a specialty of Bresse and of the Landes of Upper

PREVIOUS PAGES: GUINEA FOWL STUFFED WITH GIROLLES (top left, recipe page 130), SADDLE OF HARE IN CREAM SAUCE (top right, recipe page 128), CHICKEN WITH CRAYFISH (bottom left, recipe page 131), AND CHICKEN WITH VINEGAR (bottom right, recipe page 127), PHOTOGRAPHED IN LYONNAIS.
PIERRE HUSSENOT/AGENCE TOP

LEO MEIER

THE FRENCH HAVE LONG BEEN KEEN HUNTERS. IN EARLY FALL THE HUNTING SEASON BEGINS, AND THIS FARMER WASTES NO TIME TRAMPING THROUGH HIS FIELDS OF LETTUCE IN SEARCH OF HARE OR PHEASANT.

MANY OF THE HALF-TIMBERED HOUSES IN DINAN, BRETAGNE, ARE OCCUPIED BY ARTISANS. THIS ONE IN THE *CENTRE VILLE* IS A RESTAURANT WHERE THE POULTRY AND GAME DISHES ARE SURE TO BE SUPERB.

LEO MEIER

Gascony: male chickens are castrated at six weeks, fattened from the age of six months, and weigh four to five kilos by the time they are killed and sold for Christmas. This plump and succulent bird, with meltingly tender flesh, is a real delight; as a festive treat, it is unsurpassable.

Among poultry one must also include the guinea fowl; the turkey, which is eaten with chestnuts at Christmas in what has become an international tradition, and which also, in the form of breaded slices or *escalopes*, is beginning to replace veal; and the pheasant, which might come from either the poultry farm or the wild. Certain birds that used to exist only in the wild state have now been domesticated.

Amongst the many forests of the Sologne, partridge, quail and mallard ducks are bred and released at the start of the hunting season. But domestic pigeons, fattened on grain, are not to be confused with the wood pigeon (*pigeon ramier*), of darker, denser flesh and flavor. From the lakes to the copses, from the forests to the thickets, there is still fine game to be found in France.

As for the duck, it is one of those ingredients

125

that give rise to some of the great French dishes. Its special quality is a firm, substantial flesh, which can be cooked rare like steak and which lends itself to sweet-sour combinations, to the flavor of the orange, to sauces enriched with liver, or foie gras, and other offal, and with the juices extracted from the carcass by means of a silver duck press. The finest breed is the Challans, from the region of Nantes. The *Mulard* breed produces excellent foie gras. The Barbary duck, however, is equally appreciated and rather more common.

More and more often, the fillets of the fattened duck, called *magrets* or *maigrets*, are cooked rare, following a fashion initiated in the Gers by the chef of Auch, André Daguin. In effect, they are duck "steaks." The tradition of preserving the duck in *confits*, by cooking it in its fat and storing the product in earthenware pots, goes back to the Moors, who passed through the southwest of France. The method is equally applicable to the more stringy meat of the goose, which is highly appreciated in Alsace, especially among the Jewish community.

The rabbit, for many years disregarded and relegated to everyday fare, has made a triumphant return to the table. But regional traditions never abandoned the rabbit, accompanying it with prunes, mustard or cider and inviting gourmets to partake of its plump thighs and also its saddle (the meaty part from the end of the ribs to the tail), which might be pan-fried, roasted, cooked *en gibelotte* or *en civet*, or stuffed. It can truly be considered part of the *grande cuisine*, as long as it is not overcooked to the extent that it becomes insipid. The best rabbits often come from the Gâtinais, the flat region around Orléans to the south of Paris. If you cross the Loire, you come to the Sologne with its forests and its hunting lands, where you can still find the hare (a type of wild rabbit). Its dark meat retains the flavor of the forests, the moss and the heather that it brushes aside as it flees the hunter. As a *civet* or *à la royale*, stuffed with foie gras and served with a sauce flavored with its offal, with pan-fried fruits such as quinces and pears, with a chestnut puree or with fresh pasta, it represents the tastiest of autumn fare.

AN OLD BRETAGNE BARN HAS AN AIR OF PEACEFUL RUSTICITY, CHARACTERISTIC OF THE MONT-ST-MICHEL REGION.

LEO MEIER

Lyonnais

POULET AU VINAIGRE

Chicken with Vinegar

2 ripe medium tomatoes
1 chicken, about 3 lb (1.5 kg), cut into 8 serving pieces
salt and freshly ground pepper
1 tablespoon vegetable oil
1 oz (25 g) butter
6 cloves garlic, peeled
6 tablespoons tarragon vinegar
⅔ cup (5 fl oz/150 ml) dry white wine
2 pinches of sugar
⅔ cup (5 fl oz/150 ml) heavy (double) cream or crème fraîche
1 teaspoon strong mustard

❖Drop the tomatoes into boiling water for 10 seconds. Cool under running water, peel, halve and squeeze out the seeds; finely chop the flesh.

❖Season the chicken with salt and pepper. Heat the oil in a nonstick 10-in (26-cm) sauté pan and add the butter. As soon as it has melted, add the chicken pieces and garlic cloves and cook until golden brown, about 10 minutes. Pour in the vinegar and let it evaporate. Stir in the wine and tomatoes and season with salt, pepper and sugar. Cook for 45 minutes, stirring from time to time.

❖While the chicken is cooking, combine the cream and mustard in a small bowl. Remove the cooked chicken from the pan and keep warm. Strain the cooking juices through a fine sieve into a saucepan, crushing the garlic to a paste. Boil over high heat until syrupy, about 5 minutes. Add the mustard mixture and boil over high heat for 2 minutes to produce a thick, creamy sauce. Pour over the chicken pieces and serve immediately.

SERVES 4 – 6   *Photograph pages 122 – 123*

Auvergne/Bourgogne

COQ AU VIN

Chicken Casserole

This dish was originally made with Chanturgues, a red wine from Auvergne. This has become rare and is now replaced by red wine from Bourgogne. However, every province in France claims to have invented the dish, and indeed similar preparations based on red or white wine are found almost everywhere.

1 chicken, about 4 lb (2 kg), cut into 10 serving pieces
salt and freshly ground pepper
6 tablespoons all purpose (plain) flour
bouquet garni: 1 bay leaf, 1 sprig thyme, 1 sprig rosemary,
    8 sprigs parsley
1 slice streaky bacon, about 3 oz (100 g)
24 small (button) mushrooms
1 tablespoon vegetable oil
2 oz (50 g) butter
24 small pickling onions, peeled
2 tablespoons cognac
3 cups (24 fl oz/750 ml) red Burgundy, such as Chambertin
3 cloves garlic, peeled

CHICKEN CASSEROLE

PETER JOHNSON

4 pinches of freshly grated nutmeg
1 teaspoon sugar
For serving:
croutons

❖Season the chicken with salt and pepper. Spread the flour on a plate and roll the chicken pieces in it, shaking off excess.

❖Tie together the herbs for the bouquet garni. Cut the bacon into fine matchsticks, removing the rind. Trim the mushrooms, wash and pat dry.

❖Heat the oil in a 6-qt (6-l) pot and add the butter. Cook the onions, bacon and mushrooms until softened, then remove and set aside. Brown the chicken pieces on all sides for about 10 minutes. Sprinkle in the cognac and ignite, shaking the pot gently until flames subside. Pour in the wine and stir in the bouquet garni, garlic, salt, pepper, nutmeg and sugar. Bring to simmer and cook for 1 hour, stirring from time to time.

❖Add the mushroom mixture and cook for 30 minutes longer.

❖Remove the cooked chicken pieces from the pot and arrange on a serving platter. Remove the bouquet garni and let the sauce boil over high heat for 2 minutes or until thickened. Pour over the chicken and serve immediately, accompanied by croutons.

SERVES 6

Franche-Comté

RABLE DE LIÈVRE À LA CRÈME

Saddle of Hare in Cream Sauce

This dish is also popular in Alsace, where it is served with spätzele *(noodles) and sautéed wild mushrooms.*

2 saddles of hare, halved crosswise
salt and freshly ground pepper
2 tablespoons cognac
¾ cup (6 fl oz/200 ml) chicken stock (recipe page 34)
1 tablespoon vegetable oil
1 onion, about 3 oz (100 g), sliced
1 carrot, peeled and sliced
2 cloves garlic, peeled and quartered
1 sprig thyme
1 bay leaf
6 sprigs parsley
⅔ cup (5 fl oz/150 ml) heavy (double) cream or crème fraîche

❖Rinse the meat and pat dry; season with salt and pepper. Pour the cognac, stock and oil into a bowl. Add the onion, carrot, garlic, thyme, bay leaf and parsley, crushing the herbs between the fingers. Place the pieces of hare in this marinade, turn them to coat and marinate in the refrigerator for 12 hours, turning several times.
❖Remove the pieces of hare and pat dry. Strain the marinade, discarding herbs and flavorings.
❖Preheat oven to 450°F (230°C). Place the pieces of hare in a baking dish just large enough to hold them. Brown the hare in the oven for 10 minutes on each side, then roast for 30 minutes longer, frequently pouring a little of the marinade into the bottom of the dish and basting the hare with the pan juices.
❖Transfer the hare pieces to a plate and keep warm. Pour the pan juices into a small saucepan and skim the fat from the surface. Boil until reduced to a syrupy consistency, about 2 minutes. Add the cream and boil until the sauce is thick and creamy, 3 to 4 minutes longer. Pour the sauce over the hare and serve immediately.

SERVES 4 *Photograph pages 122 – 123*

Provence

POULET AUX QUARANTE GOUSSES D'AIL

Chicken with Forty Cloves of Garlic

In Provence, where it is called the poor man's truffle, garlic is the basis of the local cuisine. Braised en chemise *("in a shirt" — in other words, unpeeled), the garlic cloves become soft and creamy, making a delicious puree that enhances the flavor of poultry.*

1 chicken, about 3½ lb (1.75 kg)
salt
2 sprigs fresh thyme
2 sprigs fresh rosemary
2 sprigs fresh sage
2 tender celery stalks, with their leaves
2 sprigs flat-leaf parsley

40 cloves of fresh, young garlic, unpeeled
3 tablespoons olive oil
freshly ground pepper
For serving:
toasted slices of country bread

❖Preheat oven to 400°F (200°C). Sprinkle the chicken with salt inside and out. Stuff the chicken with half the thyme, rosemary, sage and celery; add the parsley and 4 cloves of garlic. Place the remaining herbs and celery in an oval earthenware or enameled pot just large enough to hold the chicken. Add the oil, salt, pepper and remaining garlic cloves. Roll the chicken in the oil to coat on all sides. Cover the pot and bake for 1¾ hours.
❖Transfer the cooked chicken to a serving platter and surround it with the cloves of garlic. Skim the fat from the cooking juices and pour into a sauceboat. Serve the chicken hot, accompanied by its sauce and toasted slices of bread. Each diner crushes the garlic slightly to remove the skin and spreads the wonderful fragrent puree that is left onto a slice of bread.

SERVES 5 – 6

Provence

LAPIN EN PAQUETS

Rabbit Parcels

It is the method of preparation that gives this dish its name: each piece of rabbit is enclosed in a "packet" of bacon. Rabbit is cooked this way throughout Provence, and sometimes fried eggplant (aubergine) slices are used instead of the tomatoes.

8 oz (250 g) ripe tomatoes
2 tablespoons olive oil
salt and freshly ground pepper
2 pinches of sugar
1 rabbit, about 3¼ lb (1.6 kg), cut into 8 serving pieces
8 very thin slices streaky bacon
8 small sprigs thyme
2 cloves garlic, peeled and finely slivered

❖Preheat oven to 400°F (200°C). Drop the tomatoes into boiling water for 10 seconds. Cool under running water, then peel, halve, squeeze out the seeds and coarsely chop the flesh. Combine the tomatoes and 1 tablespoon olive oil in a nonstick 10-in (26-cm) sauté pan. Add salt, pepper and sugar and cook over high heat, stirring constantly, until reduced to a thick puree.
❖Using the remaining oil, grease a shallow baking dish large enough to hold the rabbit pieces in a single layer. Pour in the tomato puree.
❖Rinse the rabbit and pat dry; season with salt and pepper. Place one piece of rabbit in the center of a slice of bacon. Season with a sprig of thyme and a few slivers of garlic. Wrap the bacon around the rabbit and secure with a toothpick. Repeat with the remaining ingredients.
❖Arrange the rabbit "parcels" on the tomato puree and bake for 1 hour, turning the parcels after 30 minutes.
❖Remove the toothpicks and arrange the rabbit parcels on a serving platter. Cover with the tomato sauce and serve immediately.

SERVES 4

RABBIT PARCELS (left) AND CHICKEN WITH FORTY CLOVES OF GARLIC (right), PHOTOGRAPHED IN PROVENCE.
PIERRE HUSSENOT/AGENCE TOP

PETER JOHNSON

BOILED CHICKEN, TOULOUSE STYLE

Languedoc

POULE AU POT À LA TOULOUSAINE

Boiled Chicken, Toulouse-style

1 chicken, about 4 lb (2 kg), with liver, gizzard, heart and
    neck
salt and freshly ground pepper
3 tablespoons milk
3 oz (100 g) fresh bread, crusts trimmed
4 cloves garlic
6 oz (200 g) prosciutto or other raw ham
2 eggs
1 tablespoon chopped flat-leaf parsley
4 pinches of freshly grated nutmeg
2 onions, about 3 oz (100 g) each
4 cloves
bouquet garni: 1 bay leaf, 1 sprig thyme, 6 sprigs parsley
2 medium carrots, peeled and thickly sliced
2 tender celery stalks, cut into large chunks
10 peppercorns, white and black mixed
For serving:
slices of toasted bread

❖Season the chicken inside and out with salt and pepper.
❖Heat the milk in a small saucepan and crumble in the
bread. Mix to a smooth paste, then remove from heat and
let cool.
❖Finely chop 2 cloves of garlic. Chop the ham and chicken
liver finely in a food processor.
❖Break the eggs into a bowl and beat with a fork to blend.
Add the garlic, chopped ham and liver, soaked bread,

parsley, salt, pepper and nutmeg and mix with a wooden
spoon until smooth. Stuff the chicken with this mixture
and sew the opening with kitchen thread.
❖Peel the onions and stud with cloves. Tie together the
herbs for the bouquet garni. Pour 3 qt (3 l) water into a pot
large enough to easily hold the chicken. Add the chicken
innards and neck, onions, carrots, celery, remaining 2 cloves
of garlic, peppercorns and bouquet garni. Bring to boil and
add the chicken. Season with salt. Cover and simmer
gently for 3 hours.
❖Remove the chicken, carve, sprinkle with a little stock
and keep warm. Strain the cooking liquid into a tureen.
Serve the soup with toasted bread, followed by the chicken
and its stuffing.

SERVES 8

Savoie

PINTADE FARCIE AUX GIROLLES

Guinea Fowl Stuffed with Girolles

1 guinea fowl, about 2½ lb (1.2 kg), with liver
salt and freshly ground pepper
1 lb (500 g) fresh *girolles* or 1 oz (30 g) dried mushrooms,
    soaked in tepid water for 10 minutes
2 oz (50 g) chicken livers
1 tablespoon chopped fresh parsley
2 tablespoons chopped fresh tarragon
2 oz (50 g) butter
2 French shallots, finely chopped
2 tablespoons port
6 tablespoons heavy (double) cream or crème fraîche

❖Season the guinea fowl inside and out with salt and pepper.
❖Prepare the stuffing: wash 6 oz (200 g) *girolles* and pat dry
(or pat dry a little less than half the soaked dried mushrooms). Chop finely. Rinse the chicken livers and the guinea
fowl liver, pat dry and chop finely. Combine the mushrooms,
livers and herbs in a bowl. Melt half the butter, season with
salt and pepper and cool to lukewarm. Add to the liver mixture and blend well. Fill the cavity of the guinea fowl with
the stuffing and secure the opening with kitchen thread.
❖Preheat oven to 425°F (215°C). Melt the remaining butter
in a pot large enough to hold the guinea fowl. Brown it on
all sides over low heat, then remove it and discard the butter.
Lightly brown the shallots in the same pot, stirring constantly. Return the guinea fowl to the pot, cover and bake
for 45 minutes.
❖Meanwhile, wash the remaining mushrooms and pat
dry. After 35 minutes cooking, scatter them around the
guinea fowl and cook for 10 minutes, stirring after 5
minutes. When both guinea fowl and mushrooms are
cooked, arrange them in a serving dish and keep warm.
Boil the cooking liquid until reduced to a syrupy consistency. Add the port and cream and boil until the sauce is
thick, about 2 minutes longer, then stir in the remaining
tarragon and pour into a sauceboat.
❖To serve, carve the guinea fowl into portions; surround
with slices of stuffing and mushrooms. Pass the sauce separately.

SERVES 4–6   *Photograph pages 122–123*

Lyonnais

POULET AUX ÉCREVISSES
Chicken with Crayfish

24 crayfish
8 oz (250 g) ripe tomatoes
1 chicken, about 3 lb (1.5 kg), cut into 8 serving pieces
salt and freshly ground pepper
3 tablespoons vegetable oil
2 oz (50 g) butter
1 cup (8 fl oz/250 ml) dry white wine
2 cloves garlic, quartered
1 carrot, peeled and thinly sliced
1 onion, about 2 oz (50 g), chopped
2 French shallots, chopped
2 pinches of dried thyme
2 tablespoons cognac
6 tablespoons heavy (double) cream or crème fraîche

❖To prepare the crayfish, twist and pull the central tail fin to remove the black vein. Rinse and drain the crayfish. Drop the tomatoes into boiling water for 10 seconds. Cool under running water, peel, halve and squeeze out the seeds.

❖Season the chicken with salt and pepper. Heat the oil in a nonstick 10-in (26-cm) sauté pan with half the butter. Lightly brown the chicken pieces on all sides. Pour in half the wine and let it evaporate over high heat. Stir in the tomatoes and garlic, season with salt and pepper and cook over low heat for 45 minutes.

❖Meanwhile, melt the remaining butter in a 9-in (22-cm) sauté pan. Add the carrot, onion, shallots, thyme and crayfish and cook for 3 minutes, turning the crayfish constantly. Sprinkle in the cognac and let it evaporate. Add the remaining wine and mix well over high heat. Cook for 5 minutes longer, then remove the crayfish from the pan and let cool. Shell the crayfish, reserving 6 as a garnish; set aside.

❖Transfer the cooked chicken from the sauté pan to a serving dish. Pour the contents of the crayfish cooking pan into the chicken cooking pan and cook over high heat for 5 minutes or until the sauce is syrupy. Add the cream and boil until the sauce is thick and creamy, 3 to 4 more minutes. Strain it through a fine sieve, pressing down on the vegetables to extract all their flavor.

❖Return the sauce to the larger sauté pan. Add the chicken and crayfish and reheat for 1 minute. Arrange the chicken and crayfish on a platter, garnish with the reserved whole crayfish and serve immediately.

SERVES 4 – 6   *Photograph pages 122 – 123*

Pays Basque

POULET BASQUAISE
Basque Chicken

4 small green peppers (capsicums)
1 lb (500 g) ripe tomatoes
1 chicken, about 3 lb (1.5 kg), cut into 8 serving pieces
salt and freshly ground pepper
3 tablespoons vegetable oil
2 onions, about 3 oz (100 g) each, finely chopped

CHICKEN WITH RICE (top, recipe page 132), BASQUE CHICKEN (bottom left) AND CHICKEN WITH COMTÉ CHEESE (bottom right, recipe page 132)

3 cloves garlic, finely chopped
1 slice prosciutto or Bayonne ham, about 5 oz (150 g), cut into small cubes
1 fresh chili pepper, seeded and finely chopped
⅔ cup (5 fl oz/150 ml) dry white wine

❖Cut the green peppers in half and remove the stems, seeds and white ribs. Cut the flesh into fine strips. Drop the tomatoes into boiling water for 10 seconds. Cool under running water, peel, halve and squeeze out the seeds; finely chop the flesh.

❖Season the chicken with salt and pepper. Heat the oil in a nonstick 10-in (26-cm) sauté pan and lightly brown the chicken pieces on all sides. Remove from the pan. Add the onions and garlic and stir for 1 minute. Add the ham, peppers and chili and cook over low heat, stirring, for 5 minutes or until the vegetables soften and are lightly browned.

❖Return the chicken pieces to the pan, pour in the wine and let it evaporate over high heat. Add the tomatoes and season with salt and pepper. Cover and cook over low heat for 45 minutes, stirring from time to time.

❖Transfer the chicken to a shallow dish. Boil the cooking liquid over high heat until thick. Pour over the chicken and serve immediately.

SERVES 4 – 6

Savoie

POULET AU COMTÉ
Chicken with Comté Cheese

This delicious dish is equally good whether it is made in Savoie, in Franche-Comté or in the Lyonnais region, where it is simply called poulet au fromage. *Sometimes half the Comté cheese is replaced by Emmenthaler.*

1 chicken, about 3¼ lb (1.6 kg), cut into 8 serving pieces
salt and freshly ground pepper
1 tablespoon vegetable oil
¾ cup (6 fl oz/200 ml) dry white wine, preferably from Savoie
2 tablespoons strong mustard
3 oz (100 g) finely and freshly grated Comté cheese

❖Preheat oven to 425°F (215°C). Season the chicken with salt and pepper. Heat the oil in a nonstick 10-in (26-cm) sauté pan and lightly brown the chicken pieces on all sides. Remove the chicken from the pan and discard the oil. Pour in the wine and deglaze the pan, using a wooden spoon to scrape up the browned bits. Blend the mustard into the wine.
❖Arrange the chicken pieces in a baking dish large enough to hold them in a single layer. Pour over the sauce from the pan. Bake for 40 minutes, turning the chicken from time to time.
❖Sprinkle the chicken with grated cheese and cook for 5 minutes longer or until the cheese melts and starts to brown. Serve hot, directly from the dish.

SERVES 6   *Photograph page 131*

Bourgogne

POULE AU RIZ
Chicken with Rice

This simple, invigorating family dish is prepared in every French home. Sometimes the rice is sprinkled with finely grated Emmenthaler.

1 chicken, about 4 lb (2 kg), with liver, gizzard, heart and neck
salt and freshly ground pepper
8 oz (250 g) carrots
bouquet garni: 1 bay leaf, 1 sprig thyme, 6 sprigs parsley
1 tablespoon vegetable oil
1 oz (25 g) butter
8 oz (250 g) onions, finely chopped
2 cups (16 fl oz/500 ml) white Burgundy
1¼ cups (10 fl oz/300 ml) water
2 cups (11 oz/350 g) long-grain rice

❖Season the chicken inside and out with salt and pepper. Peel the carrots and quarter them lengthwise, then cut into ¼-in (.5-cm) fan-shaped slices. Tie together the herbs for the bouquet garni.
❖Heat the oil in a 4-qt (4-l) pot and lightly brown the chicken on all sides. Remove from the pot and discard the oil. Place the butter, carrots and onions in the pot and soften over low heat, stirring constantly with a wooden spoon. Add the chicken liver, gizzard, heart and neck and cook

for a further minute. Return the chicken to the pot, add the wine and water and bring to simmer. Add the bouquet garni, salt and pepper. Turn the chicken onto its side, cover the pot and cook over very gentle heat for 1 hour.
❖Turn the chicken over to its other side and simmer gently for a further hour.
❖Place the chicken on its back and sprinkle the rice around it. Cover and cook for 30 minutes longer over low heat, without stirring.
❖Remove the chicken and place it on a serving platter. Discard the chicken innards and neck and the bouquet garni; stir the rice with a fork. Surround the chicken with the rice and serve.

SERVES 6   *Photograph page 131*

Normandie

POULET VALLÉE D'AUGE
Chicken with Mushroom Sauce

This recipe takes its name from the Vallée d'Auge in Normandie, which is renowned for its apples. It includes butter, cream and calvados, all basic ingredients of the cuisine of Normandie.

1 chicken, about 3 lb (1.5 kg), cut into 8 serving pieces
salt and freshly ground pepper
1 tart apple
1 tablespoon vegetable oil
2 oz (50 g) butter
2 tablespoons calvados
1 tablespoon water
1 lb (500 g) mushrooms
⅔ cup (5 fl oz/150 ml) heavy (double) cream or crème fraîche

❖Season the chicken with salt and pepper. Peel and core the apple and cut into ½-in (1-cm) cubes.
❖Heat the oil in a nonstick 10-in (26-cm) sauté pan. Add half the butter and, as soon as it has melted, lightly brown the chicken pieces on all sides, turning them with a wooden spoon. Add the apple and mix for 1 minute. Pour in the calvados and ignite, shaking the pan gently until flames subside. Stir in the water, cover and cook over very low heat for 45 minutes.
❖Meanwhile, trim the mushrooms, rinse and pat dry. Slice thinly. Melt the remaining butter in a nonstick 10-in (26-cm) skillet and cook the mushrooms over high heat until they are golden and give out no more liquid.
❖Remove the cooked chicken pieces from the pan and keep warm on a platter. Boil the cooking liquid until reduced to a syrupy consistency. Add the cream and boil over high heat for about 2 minutes, stirring with a wooden spoon, until the sauce is thick and smooth. Add the mushrooms and stir for 1 minute. Pour the sauce over the chicken pieces and serve immediately.

SERVES 4–6

RABBIT IN CIDER (top left, recipe page 140), CHICKEN WITH MUSHROOM SAUCE (top right), AND CHICKEN WITH CREAM AND TARRAGON (bottom, recipe page 134), PHOTOGRAPHED IN NORMANDIE.
PIERRE HUSSENOT/AGENCE TOP

Normandie

POULET À LA CRÈME À L'ESTRAGON

Chicken with Cream and Tarragon

1 chicken, about 3½ lb (1.75 kg)
salt
10 sprigs fresh tarragon
1 oz (25 g) butter
¾ cup (6 fl oz/200 ml) chicken stock
¾ cup (6 fl oz/200 ml) heavy (double) cream or crème
    fraîche

❖Season the chicken inside and out with salt. Place 8 sprigs of tarragon inside the cavity of the chicken.

❖Melt the butter in a pot just large enough to hold the chicken. Brown the chicken on all sides for about 10 minutes. Remove from the pot and discard the butter. Pour in the stock and deglaze the pot, scraping up browned bits with a wooden spoon. Return the chicken to the pot, cover and cook over low heat for 1 hour and 20 minutes.

❖Meanwhile, strip the leaves from the reserved tarragon and chop finely. Remove the cooked chicken from the pot and keep warm. Boil the cooking juices until reduced to a syrupy consistency, then add the cream and boil for 2 minutes longer. Stir in the chopped tarragon and remove from heat.

❖Carve the chicken into portions and arrange on a serving plate. Pour the cream sauce over and serve immediately.

SERVES 4 – 6 *Photograph page 133*

Alsace

FAISAN EN CHARTREUSE

Pheasant Carthusian

The term en chartreuse *refers to a combination of meat (generally game birds) and vegetables which are layered in a round or oval mold. At one time it consisted only of vegetables, and the name referred to the vegetarian diet of the Carthusian monks.*

1 pheasant, about 3 lb (1.5 kg)
salt and freshly ground pepper
3 oz (100 g) butter
5 oz (150 g) carrots, peeled
5 oz (150 g) turnips, peeled
5 oz (150 g) small green beans
1 green cabbage, heart only
6 tablespoons chicken stock
2 tablespoons madeira
3 oz (100 g) ground (minced) veal
1 egg white
⅔ cup (6 fl oz/150 ml) heavy (double) cream or crème fraîche

❖Season the pheasant inside and out with salt and pepper. Melt half the butter in a pot large enough to hold the pheasant. Brown it on all sides for about 15 minutes, then cover and cook over low heat for 30 minutes.

❖Meanwhile, cut the carrots and turnips into strips about the same size as the beans. Cook each of the three vegetables separately in boiling salted water until slightly crisp.

PHEASANT CARTHUSIAN

Drain. Core the cabbage heart; cut into quarters, then into ½-in (1-cm) strips. Melt 1 oz (25 g) butter in a nonstick 10-in (26-cm) sauté pan and cook the cabbage strips for 1 minute, stirring constantly. Add the stock, season with salt and cook, covered, over low heat until the cabbage is very tender, about 20 minutes.

❖Remove the pheasant from the pot and set aside; discard the butter. Add the madeira and boil for 1 minute, then transfer to a bowl and set aside.

❖Remove the meat from the pheasant. Cut the thigh and breast meat into neat strips and set aside; finely chop all remaining meat, including the parts very close to the bone. Mix the finely chopped meat with the veal. Beat the egg white in a bowl until foamy. Add the meat mixture, cream, salt and pepper and blend until smooth. Refrigerate until needed.

❖Preheat oven to 400°F (200°C). Set aside a small amount of butter; use the rest to grease a 2-qt (2-l) soufflé dish. Arrange the carrot and turnip sticks and the beans on the bottom and around the sides, alternating colors. Cover with a layer of half the meat mixture, then half the cabbage. Arrange the strips of pheasant on the cabbage. Cover with the remaining cabbage, then with a smooth layer of the remaining meat mixture. Coat a sheet of waxed paper with the reserved butter and use it to cover the dish, buttered side down. Place the soufflé dish in a shallow pan of simmering water and bake for 40 minutes.

❖Remove the *chartreuse* from the oven and let rest for 10 minutes. Unmold it onto a serving plate. Reheat the reserved cooking juices and pour around the *chartreuse*. Serve immediately.

SERVES 4 – 6

Languedoc

CANARD AUX NAVETS DU PARDAILHAN
Duck with Glazed Turnips

This extraordinary turnip grows on the Minervois plateau. It is elongated in shape, snow white with a covering of black skin, and firm-textured with a slightly pungent taste.

1 duck, about 3 lb (1.5 kg)
2 oz (50 g) goose fat or butter
2 tablespoons cognac
1 tablespoon juniper berries
6 tablespoons dry white wine
2 lb (1 kg) long, slender turnips, peeled
salt and freshly ground pepper
1 tablespoon sugar

❖Season the duck inside and out with salt and pepper. Melt half the goose fat in an oval pot large enough to hold the duck and brown it on all sides for 15 minutes. Sprinkle with cognac, scatter around the juniper berries and pour in the wine. Bring to boil, then cover and simmer for 45 minutes.

❖Meanwhile, cut the turnips into 1½ x ½-in (4 x 1-cm) sticks. Melt the remaining goose fat in a nonstick 10-in (26-cm) sauté

DUCK WITH GLAZED TURNIPS

pan and lightly brown the turnips, turning them over in the hot fat for about 5 minutes. Sprinkle with sugar and salt, season lightly with pepper and turn carefully until the turnips are covered with a sticky, caramelized glaze. Cover and cook the turnips until just tender, about 8-10 minutes. Keep warm.

❖Remove the cooked duck from the pot and keep warm. Skim the fat from the cooking juices. Boil the juices until syrupy, about 2 minutes. Add the turnips to the pot and turn them in the hot liquid for 1 minute.

❖Carve the duck and arrange on a serving dish. Surround with turnips and serve immediately.

SERVES 4

Languedoc

MAGRETS GRILLÉS SAUCE AILLADE
Breast of Duck with Garlic Sauce

Sauce aillade, *which is particularly appreciated in Toulouse, may be made using equal amounts of olive oil and walnut oil. Breast of duck served with this fragrant sauce is excellent accompanied with sautéed cèpes.*

2 cloves garlic, coarsely chopped
3 tablespoons armagnac
1 sprig thyme, crumbled
salt and freshly ground pepper
2 fresh duck breasts, 12 oz (350 g) each
24 fresh walnuts, shelled and peeled
3 cloves garlic, peeled and halved
2 tablespoons water
6 tablespoons extra virgin olive oil

❖Combine the chopped garlic, armagnac and thyme in a bowl and season with salt and pepper. Add the duck breasts and turn to coat. Let marinate at room temperature for 1 hour, turning often.

❖Combine the walnuts, halved garlic cloves and water in a food processor and blend to a thick paste. Season with salt and pepper. With the machine running, pour in the oil in a thin stream to produce an emulsified sauce. Transfer to a sauceboat and set aside.

❖Drain the duck breasts, reserving marinade. Pat them dry and wipe off the garlic. Heat an enameled 4-qt (4-l) pot over moderate heat and lay the duck breasts on the bottom, skin side down. Cook for 8 minutes, basting the meat with the fat given out during cooking. Discard the fat, turn the breasts over and cook for 5 minutes longer, pricking the skin with a fork to allow some of the fat to escape. Remove the duck from the pot and discard all fat. Strain the reserved marinade into the pot and boil for 1 minute, then remove from heat. Return the duck breasts to the pot skin side down, cover and let rest for 15 minutes.

❖Remove the duck from the pot and slice thinly. Divide slices among four heated plates. Add to the pot any juices that have escaped during slicing. Pour this sauce over the duck and serve immediately, accompanied by the garlic sauce.

SERVES 4   *Photograph pages 12 – 13*

Orléanais

CANARD À L'ORANGE
Duck with Orange

1 duck, about 3 lb (1.5 kg)
salt and freshly ground pepper
1 tablespoon vegetable oil
6 medium oranges
1 lemon
¼ cup (2½ oz/75 g) sugar
2 tablespoons water
3 tablespoons red wine vinegar
6 tablespoons dry white wine
1 teaspoon arrowroot
3 tablespoons curaçao
1 tablespoon red currant jelly

❖Preheat oven to 425°F (215°C). Season the duck inside and out with salt and pepper. Place the duck in a greased roasting pan and roast for 1 hour, basting regularly with the pan juices.

❖Meanwhile, prepare the fruits: wash and dry the oranges and lemon. Carefully remove the zest from the lemon and two of the oranges with a zester. Squeeze the juice of these three fruits into a bowl. Peel the remaining oranges so that no trace of white pith is left, collecting any juice in the bowl. Separate the oranges into segments.

❖Heat the sugar and water in a saucepan over low heat until the sugar caramelizes to a light golden color. Add the vinegar and citrus juices and boil for 1 minute.

❖Remove the cooked duck from the oven, tilting it so that any juices inside the bird will run into the pan. Keep warm on a plate.

❖Skim the fat from the roasting juices. Add the wine and deglaze the pan over high heat, scraping up browned bits with a wooden spoon. Boil until the liquid is reduced by half. Transfer to a small saucepan and return to boil. Blend the arrowroot and curaçao in a small bowl, then pour into the boiling sauce with the red currant jelly. Boil, stirring constantly, until the sauce thickens, about 2 minutes. Stir in the zest and the orange segments and remove from heat.

❖Carve the duck and arrange it on a serving plate. Remove some of the orange segments from the sauce with a slotted spoon and arrange around the duck. Pour the sauce into a sauceboat and serve immediately.

SERVES 4

Île de France

CANARD MONTMORENCY
Duck with Cherries

Montmorency is the name of a variety of small cherry — a bitter-sweet morello that is excellent for cooking. It is used in a number of dishes, both savory and sweet.

1 duck, about 3 lb (1.5 kg)
salt and freshly ground pepper
1 lb (500 g) Montmorency cherries
⅔ cup (5 fl oz/150 ml) dry white wine
1 teaspoon sugar
1 teaspoon arrowroot
3 tablespoons cherry brandy

❖Preheat oven to 425°F (215°C). Season the duck inside and out with salt and pepper. Place in roasting pan and roast for 1 hour, basting frequently with the cooking juices. Meanwhile, pit the cherries, catching all juices.

❖Remove the cooked duck from the oven, tilting it so that any juices inside the bird will run into the pan. Transfer to a plate and keep warm. Skim the fat from the juices in the roasting pan. Place the pan over high heat, pour in the wine and deglaze the pan, scraping up browned bits with a wooden spoon. Boil until the liquid is reduced by half. Transfer to a small saucepan and add the cherry juice and sugar.

❖Bring the contents of the saucepan to boil. Blend together the arrowroot and cherry brandy and pour into the boiling sauce. Boil, stirring constantly, until the sauce thickens, about 2 minutes. Add the cherries and remove from heat.

❖Carve the duck and arrange on a serving plate. Surround it with a few cherries. Pour the remaining sauce and cherries into a sauceboat and serve immediately.

SERVES 4

PETER JOHNSON

DUCK WITH CHERRIES

DUCK WITH ORANGE
PIERRE HUSSENOT/AGENCE TOP

PETER JOHNSON

PRESERVED DUCK

Languedoc

CONFIT DE CANARD
Preserved Duck

Confits of goose or duck are made all over Languedoc. Every family has its terrines or special wide-mouthed jars in which the homemade confit is kept, ready for an impromptu feast.

1 duck, about 3 lb (1.5 kg), cut into 6 pieces
2 cloves garlic, peeled and halved
2 sprigs dried thyme
¼ cup (2 oz/60 g) coarse sea salt
2 tablespoons coarsely ground pepper
2½ lb (1.2 kg) duck or goose fat, or more

❖Rub the pieces of duck all over with garlic. Crumble the thyme into a shallow dish; mix with the coarse salt and pepper. Roll the duck pieces in this mixture, then place in a bowl. Cover and refrigerate for 12 hours.
❖Pat the duck dry. Melt the fat in a large pot over low heat. Add the duck pieces and turn them over in the fat. Make sure they are well covered; if necessary, add more fat. Cover the pot and cook for 2 hours over very low heat; the fat should barely simmer.
❖Remove the duck pieces from the pot. Cool the fat to lukewarm, then strain. Pour the melted fat into a terrine to a depth of ½ in (1 cm). Arrange the pieces of duck on top. Cover with the remaining fat and let cool. Cover the terrine and store in the refrigerator, where it will keep for several months.
❖To serve, remove the duck pieces from the fat and either grill or cook in a nonstick skillet to remove as much fat as possible. They may be served hot, accompanied by fried potatoes or mushrooms. When cool, the duck is excellent with a salad of chicory or dandelion, dressed with walnut oil and served on garlic-flavored croutons.

SERVES 6 – 8

Languedoc

CANARD AUX OLIVES
Duck with Olives

The classic recipe for duck with olives used all over France contains only green olives. Languedoc cooks mix black and green olives, which gives an unexpected and richer flavor.

10 oz (300 g) green olives in brine, pitted
1 duck, about 2½ lb (1.2 kg)
salt and freshly ground pepper
1 tablespoon vegetable oil
3 tablespoons white vermouth
1 cup (8 fl oz/250 ml) chicken stock
3 oz (100 g) black olives in olive oil, pitted

❖Rinse the green olives in warm water, then soak them for 1 hour in warm water to cover, changing the water once.
❖Season the duck inside and out with salt and pepper. Heat the oil in a round or oval pot just large enough to hold the duck. Brown on all sides for about 15 minutes, then discard the fat. Sprinkle the duck with vermouth, then turn it over in the pot and allow the vermouth to evaporate. Pour in the stock and bring to boil. Cover and simmer for 45 minutes, turning the duck two or three times.
❖Remove the duck from the pot and keep warm. Skim the fat from the pan juices, then boil the juices for 2 minutes or until syrupy. Drain the green olives and add them to the pot with the black olives; simmer for 1 minute.
❖Carve the duck and arrange it on a serving platter. Surround it with the olives. Pour the sauce into a sauceboat and serve immediately.

SERVES 4 *Photograph pages 12 – 13*

Lorraine

CANARD À TOUTES LES HERBES
Duck with Herbs

5 oz (150 g) sorrel
5 oz (150 g) fresh spinach
5 oz (150 g) small leeks, white and tender green parts only
1 lettuce heart
3 tender celery stalks, with leaves
4 sprigs flat-leaf parsley
3 sprigs tarragon
3 sprigs chervil
2 sprigs mint
1 duck, about 4 lb (2 kg), cut into 10 serving pieces
salt and freshly ground pepper
1 oz (25 g) lard
1 tablespoon all purpose (plain) flour
¾ cup (6 fl oz/200 ml) dry white wine
1 bunch chives, chopped
6 tablespoons heavy (double) cream or crème fraîche

❖Wash, dry and stem the sorrel and spinach. Cut the leeks, lettuce and celery into ½-in (1-cm) strips. Strip the leaves from the parsley, tarragon, chervil and mint and chop finely.
❖Season the duck with salt and pepper. Melt the lard in a

INGREDIENTS FOR DUCK WITH HERBS

4-qt (4-l) round or oval pot and brown the pieces of duck on all sides for about 10 minutes. Discard the cooking fat. Sprinkle the duck pieces with flour and stir for 1 minute. Pour in the wine and bring to boil. Add the vegetables and herbs and mix well. Cover and cook over low heat for 1 hour, stirring from time to time.

❖Stir in the cream and cook for 30 minutes longer, again stirring from time to time. When the duck is cooked, it will be surrounded by a thick, aromatic green sauce. Turn it into a shallow dish and serve immediately.

SERVES 6

Languedoc

FOIE GRAS FRAIS AUX RAISINS
Fresh Foie Gras with Grapes

This version of the classic dish in the grand tradition of French cuisine has been simplified so that only the true taste of the fresh foie gras comes through.

5 oz (150 g) white muscat grapes
4 slices fresh duck foie gras, about 3 oz (80 g) each and ½ in (1 cm) thick, chilled
salt and freshly ground pepper
1 tablespoon armagnac

❖Peel the grapes and remove the seeds, working over a plate to catch the juice.
❖Heat a nonstick skillet over moderate heat. Season the slices of foie gras with salt and pepper. Cook them for 40 seconds on each side or until a crusty surface forms. Arrange them on 2 heated plates.
❖Discard the fat in the pan and pour in the armagnac and grape juice. Boil the liquid until reduced by half. Add the grapes to the pan and mix for 30 seconds. Surround the slices of foie gras with grapes, pour the sauce over and serve immediately.

SERVES 2   *Photograph pages 12 – 13*

Quercy/Périgord

LAPIN AUX PRUNEAUX
Rabbit with Prunes

The delicious Enthe plum, dried to become a prune, is used in as many savory dishes as sweet ones.

¾ cup (6 fl oz/200 ml) red wine
1 tablespoon sugar
16 "Agen" prunes
1 rabbit, about 3¼ lb (1.6 kg), cut into 8 serving pieces
salt and freshly ground pepper
2 tablespoons vegetable oil
1 sprig fresh thyme
1 onion, about 3 oz (100 g), finely chopped
2 cloves garlic, finely chopped
2 French shallots, finely chopped
2 tablespoons armagnac
⅔ cup (5 fl oz/150 ml) heavy (double) cream or crème fraîche

❖Combine the wine and sugar in a saucepan and bring to boil. Stir until the sugar has dissolved. Add the prunes and simmer for 10 minutes, stirring. Remove from heat, cover and let stand for 10 minutes, then strain off and reserve the liquid, leaving the prunes in the saucepan.
❖Rinse the rabbit and pat dry; season with salt and pepper. Heat the oil in a nonstick 11-in (28-cm) sauté pan and lightly brown the rabbit pieces on all sides for about 10 minutes. Crumble in the thyme and add the onion, garlic and shallots. Cook, stirring, until the rabbit pieces are well browned, about 5 minutes longer.
❖Pour in the armagnac and ignite, shaking the pan gently until flames subside. Stir in the wine reserved from the prunes and bring to boil. Cover and simmer for 40 minutes.

RABBIT WITH PRUNES

❖Remove the rabbit pieces to a heated plate and keep warm. Boil the liquid in the pan over high heat until reduced to a syrupy consistency. Add the cream and boil until the sauce is smooth, about 3 minutes. Return the rabbit to the pan, add the prunes and reheat for 2 minutes, stirring.
❖Arrange the rabbit and prunes in a shallow dish. Coat with sauce and serve immediately.

SERVES 4

Bretagne/Normandie

LAPIN AU CIDRE
Rabbit in Cider

1 rabbit, about 3¼ lb (1.6 kg), cut into 9 pieces (reserve liver)
salt and freshly ground pepper
1 slice streaky bacon, about 3 oz (100 g)
3 oz (100 g) small fresh cèpes (*porcini* mushrooms)
1 tablespoon vegetable oil
1 oz (25 g) butter
4 French shallots, finely chopped
2 tablespoons calvados
1 cup (8 fl oz/250 ml) dry cider
1 egg yolk
1 tablespoon strong mustard
6 tablespoons heavy (double) cream or crème fraîche

❖Rinse the rabbit and pat dry; season with salt and pepper. Cut the bacon into small strips, removing the rind. Trim, wash, dry and quarter the mushrooms. Heat the oil in a nonstick 11-in (28-cm) sauté pan. Add the butter and gently cook the shallots, bacon and mushrooms, stirring constantly with a wooden spoon. Scrape this mixture from the pan, add the rabbit pieces and brown on all sides for 10 minutes. Pour in the calvados and let it evaporate. Stir in the cider and bring to boil, then cover and cook over low heat for 30 minutes, turning two or three times. After 30 minutes, return the bacon, mushrooms and shallots to the pan and simmer for 15 minutes longer.

❖In a bowl beat the egg yolk, mustard and cream. Add the uncooked rabbit liver, pushing it through a sieve, and mix well.

❖Remove the cooked rabbit from the sauté pan with a slotted spoon and arrange in a serving dish with the mushrooms and bacon. Boil the cooking liquid over high heat until reduced to a syrupy consistency. Pour the mustard mixture into the pan and stir for 30 seconds, then remove from heat. Whisk the sauce until smooth and creamy. Pour it over the rabbit and serve immediately.

SERVES 4 *Photograph page 133*

Alsace

Civet de Lièvre aux Spätzele

Hare in Red Wine with Egg Noodles

The word civet *in France is indicative of the culinary procedure whereby game, furred or feathered, is simmered in red wine and served with a sauce cooked with the animal or bird's blood.*

3 cups (24 fl oz/750 ml) red wine
3 tablespoons cognac
1 onion, about 3 oz (100 g), sliced
1 medium carrot, peeled and sliced
2 cloves garlic, peeled and quartered
1 sprig thyme
1 bay leaf
1 sprig rosemary
1 teaspoon coarsely ground pepper
1 hare, about 4 lb (2 kg), cut into 9 serving pieces,
   (reserve liver)
8 oz (250 g) streaky bacon
3 tablespoons vegetable oil
18 small pickling onions, peeled
1 tablespoon all purpose (plain) flour
salt and freshly ground pepper
8 oz (250 g) small (button) mushrooms
For the noodles:
2¾ cups (11 oz/350 g) all purpose (plain) flour
3 eggs
3 tablespoons cold water
salt and freshly ground pepper
4 pinches of freshly grated nutmeg
2 oz (50 g) butter

❖Pour the wine and cognac into a bowl. Add the onion, carrot, garlic, thyme, bay leaf and rosemary, crumbling the herbs between the fingers, and the pepper. Add the pieces of hare to this marinade, turn them to coat and marinate for 12 hours in the refrigerator, turning several times.

❖Remove the pieces of hare from the marinade and pat dry. Strain the marinade, discarding the herbs and flavorings. Cut the bacon into matchsticks, removing the rind.

❖Heat the oil in a heavy 4-qt (4-l) pot and lightly brown the pieces of hare on all sides for about 10 minutes. Add the bacon and pickling onions and cook, stirring, until the pieces of hare are well browned, about 5 minutes. Sprinkle with flour and stir for 1 minute longer. Pour the marinade into the pot and bring to boil, then cover and cook for 2 hours over very low heat, stirring occasionally. Season with salt and pepper.

❖Meanwhile, trim the mushrooms; wash, pat dry and cut into quarters. Add them to the pot after the 2 hours' cooking time; stir and cook for 30 minutes longer.

❖While the hare is cooking, prepare the egg noodles: sift the flour into a bowl. Beat the eggs in a separate bowl with the water, salt, pepper and nutmeg. Pour this mixture into the flour and mix vigorously with a wooden spoon to make a soft, smooth dough which comes away from the sides of the bowl. Roll out the dough on a wooden board, in several separate batches.

❖Bring a large saucepan of salted water to boil. Using a moistened palette knife, cut off small strips of the dough and drop them into the boiling water. As soon as they come to the surface, lift them out with a slotted spoon and transfer them to a dish of cold water. Repeat this process until all the dough is cooked.

❖Melt the butter in a nonstick 10-in (26-cm) skillet and add the noodles. Turn them over in the hot butter for 5 minutes, keeping them moving constantly. Keep warm.

❖Remove the pieces of hare with a slotted spoon and arrange on a shallow dish. Press the raw hare liver through a sieve into a bowl and mix in ¼ cup (2 fl oz/60 ml) of the sauce from the hare. Return the mixture to the pot and stir for 30 seconds over low heat, without allowing the liver to cook. Pour this sauce over the pieces of hare and serve immediately with the noodles.

SERVES 6

HARE IN RED WINE WITH EGG NOODLES

STUFFED HARE

Périgord

LIÈVRE EN CABESSAL
Stuffed Hare

Cabessal is the name of a napkin tied into a crown shape, which women used to place on their heads so they could carry heavy weights. The hare bound into a ring shape suggests the cabessal.

6 tablespoons chicken stock
3 oz (100 g) stale bread, crusts trimmed
10 oz (300 g) veal, knuckle or shoulder, boned
3 oz (100 g) *pancetta*, fresh pork belly or rindless streaky bacon
3 oz (100 g) prosciutto or other unsmoked ham
2 cloves garlic, finely chopped
2 French shallots, finely chopped
1 tablespoon chopped parsley
salt and freshly ground pepper
6 pinches of freshly grated nutmeg
1 sprig thyme
1 egg
1 hare, about 4 lb (2 kg)
6 oz (200 g) fresh pork rind
1 onion, about 3 oz (100 g), finely chopped
3 cups (24 fl oz/750 ml) dry red wine, such as Cahors
3 tablespoons armagnac

❖Heat the chicken stock in a small saucepan and crumble in the bread. Stir, remove from heat and leave the bread to absorb the stock. Using a food processor, grind (mince) together the veal, pork and ham.
❖In a bowl mix together the meats, garlic, shallots, parsley, bread, salt, pepper, nutmeg and the thyme, crumbled between the fingers. Add the egg and mix well.
❖Season the hare with salt and pepper. Spread the stuffing mixture inside the hare and sew up the opening with kitchen thread. Bend the hare into a circle by bringing the front and hind legs together and tying them with kitchen thread.
❖Oil a round or oval pot just large enough to hold the hare. Rinse the pork rind, roll it into a cylinder and secure with string. Drop it into boiling water for 1 minute; rinse and drain. Slice the roll into strips ½ in (1 cm) wide and spread these on the bottom of the pot, together with the onion. Place the hare on top.

❖Cook the hare for 15 minutes over moderate heat, then turn and cook for 15 minutes on the other side. Pour in the wine and armagnac and bring to simmer. Cover and cook over very low heat for 5 hours, without disturbing it.
❖Carefully transfer the hare to a serving plate. Boil the cooking liquid until reduced to a syrupy consistency. Pour into a sauceboat and serve immediately. The hare is very tender and the meat falls away from the bones; it is traditionally "carved" with a spoon.

SERVES 6

Corse

LAPIN À L'ISTRETTU
Rabbit, Corsican-style

1 rabbit, about 3¼ lb (1.6 kg), cut into 9 serving pieces (reserve the liver)
salt and freshly ground pepper
14 black olives in brine
2 tablespoons olive oil
1 sprig dried thyme
1 sprig dried rosemary
1 bay leaf
6 cloves garlic, peeled and halved
8 oz (250 g) onions, thinly sliced
⅔ cup (5 fl oz/150 ml) dry white wine
3 tablespoons tomato paste (puree)
2 tablespoons capers, drained

❖Rinse the rabbit pieces and pat dry; season with salt and pepper. Rinse the olives and pat dry. Slice thickly, discarding the pits.
❖Heat the oil in a nonstick 11-in (28-cm) sauté pan and lightly brown the rabbit pieces on all sides for about 10 minutes. Crumble in the thyme and rosemary. Add the bay leaf, the halved cloves of garlic and the onions and cook, stirring, until the rabbit pieces are well browned, about 5 minutes longer. Stir in the wine and tomato paste and bring to boil, then cover and cook for 30 minutes over low heat.
❖Add the rabbit liver, olives and capers and simmer, stirring often, until the sauce thickens and coats the rabbit pieces, about 15 more minutes.
❖Turn the rabbit into a shallow dish and serve immediately.

SERVES 4

Bourgogne

LAPIN À LA MOUTARDE
Rabbit with Mustard Sauce

1 rabbit, about 3 lb (1.5 kg)
salt and freshly ground pepper
1 tablespoon vegetable oil
4 tablespoons strong mustard
1 sprig fresh thyme
1 oz (25 g) butter
6 tablespoons dry white wine
⅔ cup (5 fl oz 150 ml) heavy (double) cream or crème fraîche

RABBIT, CORSICAN STYLE (top) AND RABBIT WITH
MUSTARD SAUCE (bottom)

❖Preheat oven to 425°F (215°C). Rinse the rabbit and pat dry; season with salt and pepper. Oil a shallow oval baking dish large enough to hold the rabbit. Spread the entire surface of the rabbit with 3 tablespoons mustard and place it in the dish. Strip the thyme leaves from the stalk and sprinkle over the rabbit. Dot with thin slivers of butter. Bake for 50 minutes, basting the rabbit regularly with the pan juices and wine.

❖Arrange the cooked rabbit on a serving platter and keep warm. Pour the cream and the remaining mustard into the baking dish and scrape up browned bits with a wooden spoon. Pour this mixture into a saucepan and boil for 2 to 3 minutes.

❖Coat the rabbit with the sauce and serve immediately.

SERVES 4

143

PROVENCE, CORSE, LANGUEDOC-ROUSSILLON

Sun-drenched dishes

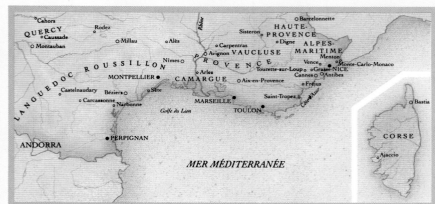

PROVENCE, CORSE, LANGUEDOC-ROUSSILLON

Sun-drenched dishes

The road threads inland, sidles in between the plateaus, changes sides as it follows the dry banks of the Durance, forgets the Luberon to the left, and at last enters a totally new country. It is not yet the mountains, but a foretaste of their heights, which here reach to around five hundred meters. At Forcalquier, a belvedere dominates the highest part of the village, indicating the directions to Vienna, St. Petersburg and Constantinople. In other words, the region is far-seeing, and has been for a very long time. The eagle's aerie of Lurs, patiently undergoing renovation, has a stations-of-the-Cross path that takes in the whole horizon: on one side the Lure mountain, a remnant of snow still on its highest peaks; on the other, the plateau of Valensole, from where one's gaze drops to the lavender-colored fields below.

Everything here seems to be built to man's proportions. Reach the high priory of Ganagobie, with its panoramic view, and Haute-Provence is spread before you, still an Eldorado. Here men protect their crops, replant, kill weeds and honor the vine; they also produce lavender honey and almond nougat, breed the best lambs in the world (those known as *Sisteron*), uphold the tradition of the Banon cheeses made from goat's milk, harvest wild mushrooms and truffles, crush splendid black olives for oil. Their links: the products of the soil.

Further towards the south and west are the Alpilles: a mountainous mass which scoffs at geography, turns away on one peak and playfully meets the desert mass of La Crau. At the handsome village of Les Baux, the wind blows so strongly one might think it would run out of breath. Vineyards squeeze themselves between

LEFT: EARLY MORNING SUNLIGHT FILTERS THROUGH THE NARROW STREETS OF NICE AS LOCAL RESIDENTS GO ABOUT THEIR DAILY BUSINESS.

PREVIOUS PAGES: IN THE HILLS BEHIND NICE, TOURETTE-SUR-LOUP PERCHES HIGH UP ON THE CRAGGY CLIFFS WHICH HAVE BEEN PAINSTAKINGLY TERRACED TO ALLOW SPACE FOR HOME GARDENS AND PATHWAYS INTO THE VALLEY.

LEO MEIER

TUCKED AWAY BEHIND THE BUSY MARKET STALLS IN DIGNE, HAUTE-PROVENCE, A SMALL BOY PLAYS WITH HIS TWO-MONTH-OLD KITTEN WHILE WAITING FOR A SYMPATHETIC PASSER-BY TO OFFER IT A HOME.

cooked, then the fish themselves: wrasse, *rascasse* or red rock cod, gurnard, weaver, *blavier*, anglerfish or *baudroie*, tiny cuttlefish, bream. Then, too, bass (called *loup* in the Mediterranean) is paired with fennel — although the infidels, chasing the custom of tourists, also add pastis, and even go so far as to flame it. The crayfish that is said to be Mediterranean often comes from somewhere else. But the soup made from *favouilles* — little crabs found along the coast — is a real treat, and tiny *supions*, or baby cuttlefish, are an absolute delicacy.

Provence is a store of fine products, tempting aromas and good dishes, and the Côte d'Azur is its display window. Here is sold what is produced elsewhere. The local cuisine is more economical, less luxurious: fish, properly prepared, and the local vegetables, spiced and seasoned, that make up *ratatouille*. Light and fresh, they are the kings of the kitchen in summer: zucchini, red and green peppers, eggplant, cucumbers.

Does "niçoise" salad really belong to Nice? With its tomatoes, broad beans, cucumbers, baby artichokes, green peppers, onions, hard-cooked eggs, anchovies, tuna and black olives, it is the very image of the region — although now it seems to be reserved for the visiting foreigner, for it is hardly ever found in the bistros of old Nice.

Here a Mediterranean gastronomy dominates, recalling the history of the county of Nice, for many years Italian territory. The ravioli filled with silverbeet, the stuffed sardines, the stockfish or *stoficado* (a stew of dried cod), the pizza and the *pissaladière* (the former garnished with tomato, the latter with onion marinated in olive oil, both with bases of bread dough), the hearty beef stew called *daube* or *estouffade*, the preparations of tripe: all these, as aromatic as the flowers in the market on the Cours Saleya, already have a faintly trans-alpine flavor. Likewise the *panisse* or *socca*, a gruel of chickpea flour boiled in salted water, spooned into dishes to set, then unmolded, cut into smaller pieces and fried. These are the "chips" of the southerners!

The real Provence is the one that protects her hinterland — its herbs, its markets, its lamb, for example, which is the best in the world. Which lamb has the juiciest meat, the most succulent flavor, the least fat? That of Sisteron. Its origins: the lower Alps. Its diet: aromatic thyme, rosemary, sage and savory. The Sisteron lamb lives its life in the fresh air; it is a *broutard*, a lamb that browses in the meadows, and is fattened on corn — not a milk-fed lamb. "In the lamb, everything is good," declares the enthusiastic Robert Lombard, known as "Bichette," a butcher in Château-Arnoux in Haute-Provence. The rack of lamb, with its combination of fat and lean, is the tastiest. But the leg, the shoulder and the cheeks all have their own particular qualities. A traditional dish of the region is the *pieds paquets*, little parcels made from the stomach of the lamb, stuffed with finely chopped mesentery with ham, tomatoes and herbs.

the two villages of Saint-Etienne-du-Grès and Eygalières. The olive reigns supreme. Lambs frolic in liberty, feeding on the pastures, as do the goats which seem to make the most of the blue sky.

All sing the praises of the landscape of Provence, with its clear blue skies, its old houses of yellowed stone, and its holy trinity of lamb, goat and olive tree. Alpilles and Haute-Provence: two faces of the same land, where the cuisine always has a hint of garlic and a scent of sunshine. It is undoubtedly for this reason that it best symbolizes the oft-envied French subtlety.

In every village, between Aix and Apt, Manosque and Carpentras, from Sorgues to Saint-Didier, from the top of Provence to the bottom, the markets are gardens of fragrance. The stalls are redolent of herbs — thyme, lavender and rosemary, tarragon and mint, chervil, savory and chives. They burst with wild asparagus, purple artichokes, *roquette* with its hazelnutlike flavor; with *cébettes*, the local onion; with *mesclun*, with *trévise*, with chicory and endive. Not to mention the squashes that become *petits farcis provençaux* (stuffed vegetables) and the tasty zucchini flowers that are cooked as fritters.

For the fish which accord so comfortably with the olive oil of the region, one must look further afield — to Cannes, for example, which has the finest market of its kind, at Forville, where are arrayed all Mediterranean products that go into a bouillabaisse. This dish, which has become largely identified with Marseilles, is also found at Cap d'Antibes and Golfe Juan. It is always served as two courses, first the broth in which the fish were

The other treasure of the region is its olives — black, almost dry, without any trace of bitterness. The secret? It is simply a matter of letting them suffer the cold in order to sweeten the flavor, then gently frying them in a little oil and cooling them before they are eaten. The local oil is also a miracle of freshness and clarity. The authentic olive oil of Provence, such as that produced at Maussane-des-Alpilles, is the result of the first cold pressing. There is nothing but the oil and aroma of the fruit — no grinding, which crushes the kernel inside the stone and so contributes a bitter tinge, and no "criminal" centrifuge.

The third of the progeny of Provence: the goat cheese called Banon, after a village of the same name. But the appellation refers chiefly to a method: the cheese is dried, brushed with water, dipped in *marc*, then wrapped in a chestnut leaf and tied with raffia. In this form, it can be aged in a cool cellar until it has developed its characteristically strong flavor, and it can be kept for a long period of time.

Garlic is always a part of Provençal cuisine — above all, in that most characteristic sauce, *aïoli*, a garlic mayonnaise which accompanies cold poached fish, hard-cooked eggs or meats. The name *grand aïoli* designates a festive dish for which boiled meat, poached cod, hard-cooked eggs, snails and cooked vegetables are arrayed around the sacred sauce: a kind of *pot-au-feu* in the Provençal style.

Bread in Provence takes on a particular appearance, and is prepared in a particular way. The prime example is *fougasse*; it is a bread of irregular shape cooked *à la volée*, speedily, in an open oven and therefore in a dry atmosphere. The bakers may choose to flavor it with garlic, or anchovies, or orangeflower water. It should not be forgotten that Provence also has a sweet tooth and makes magnificent glacé fruits, nor that it is a lover of the almond, so essential to the famous *calissons* of Aix-en-Provence, made with almond paste and glacé fruits. The special sweetmeat which has become the glory of Montélimar is its nougat, which needs only sugar syrup, honey, almonds and pistachio nuts. The *nougat noir*, or black nougat, contains lavender honey, caramelized sugar and Provençal almonds — although Spanish almonds, supposedly coarser in flavor, are creeping into the kitchens of almost all the craftsmen-confectioners.

THE ARCHEOLOGICAL SITE OF FILITOSA, SOUTH OF AJACCIO IN CORSE, WHERE HUGE STONE MONOLITHS CARVED WITH HUMAN FACES GAZE OUT TO SEA.

STEFAN AGGI/AGENCE TOP

THE ATTRACTIVE COASTAL TOWN OF MENTON WAS, UNTIL 1914, THE HOME OF A LARGE BRITISH COLONY. APART FROM BEING A POPULAR BEACH RESORT, IT IS ALSO FAMOUS FOR ITS CONSTANTLY FLOWERING AND FRUIT-BEARING LEMON TREES.

Corsica is solitary, high-minded and readily censorious. Austere? Yes, a little. It struggled for its independence for a long time before deciding to become French. Its gastronomy might appear unworldly and even fairly insignificant, but it has the merit of remaining original, rooted in the soil, defining its territory.

Corsica's traditions are those of an island, but one very much attached to the soil. In the first place, they reflect its mountainous nature: the kid, which is usually spit-roasted; the *brousse* or *bruccio*, a fresh goat cheese which might be sprinkled with *grappa* and which accompanies the local desserts, such as *fiadone* cake, or fritters known as *fritelle*.

Italy's proximity is seen in the cannelloni, ravioli and lasagne made by the local *mammas*. Charcuterie reigns supreme, whether it depends on tripe and offal (blood pudding or *sangue*, pork liver sausages or *figatelle*), or is based on game (blackbird pâté), or borrows from transalpine traditions (*coppa*, raw ham).

The local fruits come from the forests: chestnuts, figs, *arbousiers* (strawberry trees), olives. The principal Corsican fish are mountain trout, but there are also those from the sea, in the vicinity of Bonifacio, Bastia or Cargèse — bream, mullet, red mullet, red rock cod. All go well with the local vintages, the fiery red wine from Toraccia or the softer, sweeter types like the muscat from Saint-Florent or from Patrimonio.

An amphitheater, its cultivated terraces opening wide onto the Mediterranean: this is the traditional image of the Languedoc. This vast southwestern part of the Midi has an undeniable accent, a result of its intermediate position between the olive groves of Provence and the Landes of Gascony, between garlic and foie gras, adopting certain dishes of the one and of the other.

The coast is close by — which means fish. And at Bouzigues are found oysters, mussels, scallops and clams that are eaten with chopped garlic, shallots and parsley. The *bourride* of Sète is made with anglerfish; it is the sister of the Provençal bouillabaisse, with its broth strained at the end of cooking and thickened with *aïoli*. The *brandade* of Nîmes, a puree combining salt cod with a mixture of oil and milk, is almost the little sister of similar dishes belonging to Marseilles and Toulon, where crushed garlic is also added.

But crossing the Gard and heading towards Montpellier, the cuisine of the Languedoc quickly turns to the southwest. The little pies (*petits pâtes*) of Pézenas and Béziers are made with mutton and mutton fat, raisins, brown sugar and grated lemon rind, which already gives a hint of Gascony. This is confirmed by the *cassoulet*, of which three versions are known.

The first, the most simple and pure, from Castelnaudary, is of course made with white haricot beans, but also with pork in varied guises

150

(hock, ham, loin, fat, rind, sausage) and a little pre-served goose. More subtle, perhaps, is that of Car-cassonne, which adds leg of mutton and also, in the hunting season, partridges. Finally, the most urbane *cassoulet*, from the great city of Toulouse, includes preserved goose or duck, mutton, Toulouse sausage, plus the ingredients already listed for the Castelnaudary version, although in smaller quantities.

The Languedoc cares for its traditions. This is not a region where fats are frowned on. Olive oil, walnut oil, pork fat and the fatty liver are generally preferred to butter. Pâtés of foie gras, of game, of wild rabbit, of thrush — tiny birds cooked with a dash of port — and of ortolans, which are eaten whole, head and bones included, while one pulls a napkin over one's head in order to enjoy the tan-talizing aromas to the full: these are what unite the Gascon southwest and the Périgord.

But Spain is not far away. You think you have caught a glimpse of it between the rocky vine-yards of Corbières, the Minervois, Maury; and the terraces of Banyuls already give a foretaste of Catalonia. The vines cling to the sturdy, mountain-ous ravines, yielding a wine that is almost black, with an aroma of chocolate and roasted coffee — you would swear that it is almost a French port.

This rich, generous Banyuls, which comes from the area around the picturesque port of Collioure and near Cerbère, next to Spain, demonstrates that the borders here have been unstable. The people are dark-skinned, black-haired. Crayfish *civet*, anglerfish in the Catalan style, anchovy pâtés, cod cooked in a spicy mixture of eggplant, peppers and tomato: this is the Roussillon, which has been French only since the time of Richelieu. Shoulder of mutton *en pistache*, garnished with whole cloves of garlic, or pigeon cooked in *rancio* (a sweet, aged, fortified wine): these are some more of the robustly flavored dishes which turn up on the other side of the frontier. And come to think of it, this deep red wine from Collioure, with its hints of purple, goes quite well with a paella ... but that takes us into another country.

THE DUSKY PINK HUES AND CASCADING FLOWER BOXES TYPIFY THE ROMANTIC BEAUTY OF GRASSE, A TOWN WHICH HAS INSPIRED MANY ARTISTS, AND IN PARTICULAR, JEAN-HONORÉ FRAGONARD OR "LE PETIT FRAGO".

MEATS
Gang of four

A SELECTION OF LOCALLY PRODUCED SALAMIS FROM DIGNE IN THE
ALPES-DE-HAUTE-PROVENCE TEMPTS SHOPPERS AT THE MARKET.

MEATS

Gang of four

The French adore meat. They may well claim to have a passion for fish, reputedly lighter, more healthy and more sympathetic to the chef's culinary fantasies, but as soon as they venture into a foreign country, they cannot stop thinking about good old *steack-frites* — steak and fries — which have been all around the world. But there is steak, and there is steak.

Let's start with beef. Beef comes from a bovine animal, castrated, raised and fattened for the production of meat. The French herd numbers about 25 million, spread among various breeds: Limousin, Salers, Aubrac, Maine Anjou, Blonde Aquitaine, and above all the Charolais, whose reputation is the most acclaimed.

Beef is said to be "marbled" when it has fine white threads between the muscle fibers, indicating an optimum degree of fattening. This is the meat, nicely fat and flavorful, that is most prized by beef lovers. As a rule it should not be eaten too fresh, but rather aged in a cool room for at least two to three weeks. In this way the meat develops its full flavor and acquires a good texture: it becomes perfectly matured.

But there is, as I have noted, steak and steak. The best cuts for an authentic *bifteck* come from the loin, the rump, the flank, the sirloin and the fillet, which is the most tender but least flavorful part of the animal, and which furnishes the thick cut known as chateaubriand. The sirloin is highly suitable for *tournedos*.

Braised, boiled or pan-fried, beef is robust and handsome. The entrecôte, tender and with a nice cover of fat, is a cut worthy of a king, much appreciated when pan-fried and served with a sauce based on shallots and red wine (known as Bercy or *marchand de vin* sauce). Red wine and beef also combine in Burgundian-style beef, in the *daube* or with beef cooked as a *civet*. Or the beef might be braised (*estouffade*), or cooked in a consommé, lowered into the liquid and taken out by means of a string (*ficelle*) — hence the name *boeuf à la ficelle*. When all is said and done, there is nothing more adaptable nor more varied than magnificent beef.

Veal comes from a young, unweaned calf — that is, one that has been nourished solely on milk, natural or reconstituted, then slaughtered at between one and four months. The best and the worst coexist under this name: the milk-fed calf, raised by its mother, with tasty, tender, succulent flesh, and hormone-added veal for which the calves are fed a chemical diet and raised in a small enclosure, to produce a tough meat which shrinks and

PREVIOUS PAGES: BEEF BRAISED WITH CALVADOS (bottom right, recipe 165), VEAL POT ROAST, ANJOU-STYLE (top, recipe page 173) AND VEAL MARENGO (bottom left, recipe page 176), PHOTOGRAPHED IN THE PAYS DE LOIRE.
PIERRE HUSSENOT/AGENCE TOP

THE ROMANS DEVELOPED THE ART OF PORK BUTCHERY AND INTRODUCED IT TO THE FRENCH WHO PRESERVED THE TRADITION DURING THE MIDDLE AGES. IN 1476 CHARCUTERIES WERE GRANTED THE MONOPOLY OF SELLING PORK MEAT.

BRETAGNE IS RENOWNED FOR ITS FLAVORSOME PRE-SALÉ LAMB; YOUNG LAMBS THAT HAVE BEEN RAISED ON THE SALTY MARSHLANDS SURROUNDING MONT-ST-MICHEL.

exudes moisture during cooking. The former is prized; the latter can only be condemned. Fortunately, it seems that the situation is changing as veterinary controls are now in force.

Racks of veal cut between the ninth and thirteenth rib make the tender, juicy cutlets that, like their sister the *escalope* (often replaced by more economical turkey in everyday French cuisine), are gently pan-fried, simmered in their juices with cream and mushrooms, or breaded. The family-style *blanquette de veau*, which calls for tender cuts from the breast, shoulder and neck, is customarily accompanied by rice. It is the perfect example of a bourgeois dish.

But the most prized parts of the animal — excluding the offal (superb liver, or *foie de veau*, sliced thickly and cooked until just pink, along with kidneys which, preferably, are served whole and still red at the center) — are the *grenadins* or slices of fillet, perhaps the most delicate cut but not necessarily the most tasty. Veal is still a luxury, but there are certain economical and tasty cuts — such as the knuckle, which will happily simmer in a thousand different ways, marrying equally well with fried potatoes as with Belgian endive. Aromatic and savory, it's enough to make you remember the fine veal of yesteryear.

LEO MEIER

A COW HERD LEADS HIS COWS TO PASTURE AT A LEISURELY PACE ALONG THE
HEAVILY WOODED ALPINE ROADS.

AN ABUNDANCE OF GOOD-QUALITY PRODUCE HAS LED TO THE
CREATION OF NUMEROUS REGIONAL SPECIALTIES IN PROVENCE SUCH AS
GAYETTES, A SAUSAGE PATTY MADE WITH PIG'S LIVER, AND *SOU-FRASSAM*,
MEAT-STUFFED CABBAGE SIMMERED IN STOCK WITH VEGETABLES.

And how about lamb as the queen of meats?
Aged from one to six months and weighing
between 30 and 50 lb (15 and 25 kg), lamb provides
meat that is more tender and delicate than that of
older sheep. The most highly ranked, preferred by
gourmets, is that from Sisteron, in Upper Provence; its flavor reflects the animal's diet of wild
thyme, rosemary, savory and sage. Thus a "simple" Provençal roast of lamb, which might be studded with garlic, scents the air with the perfume of
the land where it lived.

Milk-fed lamb, six weeks old, is valued more for
its tenderness than for its flavor. The leg, or *gigot*,
makes the most agreeable of dishes; it is a favorite
among the French, often served on Sundays
accompanied by flageolet beans. *Pré salé* lamb,
which has grazed on the salty pastures around the
peninsula of Mont-Saint-Michel, is also highly
regarded. But there is excellent lamb from other
regions as well: from the Texel breed in the Ardennes and Ile de France, from the Berrichonne breed
in the Cher, the Vendée and the Pyrenees.

Every cut of lamb is flavorful: chops, rack, neck,
saddle, shoulder (often neglected, and cheaper
than the leg) and breast, which may be simply
grilled. Whether a slow-simmered dish in a *daube*
or *navarin*, or simply spit-roasted, lamb remains a

LEO MEIER

royal dish — one of the few things about which the French always seem to agree.

Pork has a bad reputation. Said to be vulgar, blamed for illnesses resulting from tapeworms, pork — more commonly called *le cochon*, "the pig," — is, however, a well-flavored meat. Prized by the people of eastern France, it goes very well with beer and cabbage, is the starting point for charcuterie (ham, terrines, pâtés), and indeed is the natural accompaniment (in the form of sausages, salted shoulder or knuckle) of the traditional sauerkraut. The tender *échine* or shoulder cut, the suckling pig slaughtered in its youth, the *travers* or chops which are salted, the salted and smoked belly, or again the tender *filet mignon*, not to mention the royal suckling pig, roasted on the spit: here are a thousand reasons to come to terms with the pig.

In Alsace, in the north, in Lorraine, the marriage of the gourmet and the pig has always been celebrated in traditional dishes. In the Loire Valley, as in the southwest and in Picardy, *noisettes* of pork are often paired with prunes. The trotters, the tongue, grilled pig's ears, smoked bacon: these make for brasserie-style dishes called *canailles*, because they offer a good excuse to the Parisian bourgeois to *s'encanailler* — to mix with the lower classes, to change his style of food at after-theater suppers. Glass or mug in hand, the pig thus regains his pedigree on both the plate and the palate of the most civilized gourmet.

THE SPARSE ROCKY TERRAINE OF HAUTE-PROVENCE IS UTILIZED AS GRAZING GROUNDS FOR GOATS AND SHEEP. THE GOATS' MILK IS USED IN A VARIETY OF LOCAL CHEESES AND THE SHEEPS' MEAT IS PREPARED FOR REGIONAL DISHES SUCH AS *GIGOT FARCI* (STUFFED LEG OF LAMB).

A COOK'S PALETTE OF SPICES ON DISPLAY AT A LOCAL MARKET IN TROYES, ONCE THE CAPITAL OF CHAMPAGNE. MORE THAN OTHER REGIONS, CHAMPAGNE IS AN AREA WHERE MEAT IS PARTICULARLY POPULAR, ESPECIALLY LAMB, AND THE CENTURY-OLD PENCHANT FOR SPICES FEATURES IN NUMEROUS REGIONAL SPECIALTIES FROM FLEMISH GINGER WAFERS TO BREADS, POULTRY AND OF COURSE MEAT.

Ile de France

POT-AU-FEU ET MIROTON
Boiled Beef and Miroton

The principle of a pot-au-feu *is always the same, but the ingredients vary from one region to another. In Auvergne, for example, stuffed cabbage leaves are added; in Bourgogne, oxtail; in Champagne, chicken and rabbit; in Provence, veal knuckle, and so on.* Miroton *or* mironton *is one of the many ways of preparing the leftovers of meat cooked in the* pot-au-feu.

For the *pot-au-feu:*
bouquet garni: 1 bay leaf, 1 sprig thyme, 6 sprigs parsley,
    2 celery stalks with leaves
1 small onion, about 2 oz (50 g)
3 cloves
4 lb (2 kg) beef, such as chuck, neck, topside or brisket
1 large carrot, peeled and cut into 4 chunks
2 teaspoons coarse sea salt
1 teaspoon mixed peppercorns (black and white)
3 cloves garlic, peeled
For the vegetables:
18 small carrots, peeled
12 small turnips, peeled
12 leeks, white parts only, washed
12 small potatoes, peeled
3 celery hearts
For the *miroton:*
1 lb (500 g) boiled beef, left over from the *pot-au-feu*
1 oz (25 g) butter
8 oz (250 g) onions, finely chopped
salt and freshly ground pepper
1 tablespoon red wine vinegar
6 tablespoons stock from the *pot-au-feu*
2 tablespoons dried breadcrumbs

❖Prepare the *pot-au-feu:* tie together the herbs of the bouquet garni. Peel the onion and stud it with the cloves. Place the meat in a large pot. Add the carrot, onion, bouquet garni, salt, peppercorns and garlic cloves. Pour in cold water to cover generously. Bring slowly to boil, then cook at the barest simmer for 4 to 5 hours or until the meat is very tender, skimming the liquid for the first half hour.

❖Remove the meat, vegetables and flavorings and let the stock cool for about 30 minutes, then remove the layer of fat from the surface with a spoon. If you have time, allow the stock to cool for several hours; all the fat will rise to the surface and all particles will settle to the bottom, leaving a perfectly clear stock.

❖Prepare the vegetables: bring a large saucepan of water to boil. Add the vegetables and cook for 10 minutes, then drain. Transfer to a nonstick 11-in (28-cm) sauté pan and half-cover with degreased stock. Cover and cook over low heat until the vegetables are tender and no more liquid is left in the sauté pan, about 15 to 20 minutes. Reheat the stock and meat. Serve the broth in cups and the meat on a platter, carved into slices and surrounded by vegetables, reserving ¼ of the meat for the *miroton.*

❖Prepare the *miroton:* preheat oven to 450°F (230°C). Finely crumble the meat from the *pot-au-feu.* Melt the butter in a nonstick 10-in (26-cm) sauté pan and stir the onions over low heat until golden, about 10 minutes. Season with salt and pepper. Add the meat and cook, stirring, for 5 minutes

BOILED BEEF AND MIROTON

or until the meat is lightly browned. Sprinkle with vinegar and allow the vinegar to evaporate over high heat. Add the stock and simmer uncovered, stirring from time to time, for 10 minutes or until the stock evaporates.

❖Spread the mixture in a baking dish in a layer ¾ in (2 cm) thick. Sprinkle with breadcrumbs and bake for 5 minutes or until the surface of the *miroton* is lightly browned. Serve immediately.

SERVES 6

Ile de France

BOEUF À LA FICELLE
Poached Beef on a String

The name of this dish undoubtedly comes from the phrase pelican à la ficelle. *The pelican is an atrophied muscle on the heart side of the animal which the butchers kept for themselves.*

When their work was finished they would go to a restaurant in the Villette quarter of Paris and cook this piece of meat in a large pot of boiling salted water. In order to recognize his piece, each butcher would attach it to a length of string carrying his number. This pelican was eaten with coarse salt as soon as it was cooked.

4 pieces of beef, rump, fillet or tenderloin, each about 5 oz
    (150 g) and 1¼ in (3 cm) thick
salt and freshly ground pepper
3 qt (3 l) beef stock (from Pot-au-Feu, recipe this page)
For serving:
coarse salt
a variety of mustards
cornichons (small French sour pickles or gherkins)

❖Tie the pieces of beef with string as you would a parcel, leaving a loop 2½ in (6 cm) long at the center. Season with salt and pepper.

❖Pour the stock into a 4-qt (4-l) pot and bring to boil. Slip the handle of a wooden spoon under the string loops so that the pieces of meat are suspended from it. Rest the spoon on the sides of the pot. Poach 4 minutes for steaks that will be pink at the center, or more or less to taste. Remove the meat from the stock and place one piece on each of 4 warmed plates. Serve immediately, accompanied by coarse salt, mustards and cornichons.

SERVES 4

POACHED BEEF ON A STRING (top), LAMB WITH SPRING VEGETABLES (bottom right, recipe page 172) AND VEAL IN WHITE SAUCE (bottom left, recipe page 174), PHOTOGRAPHED IN THE ILE DE FRANCE.
PIERRE HUSSENOT/AGENCE TOP

PROVENÇAL BRAISED BEEF

Provence

BOEUF À LA GORDIENNE
Provençal Braised Beef

1 lb 10 oz (1.8 kg) beef suitable for braising, such as topside, neck or chuck steak
1 onion, about 3 oz (100 g)
2 cloves
bouquet garni: 1 sprig thyme, 1 sprig sage, 1 bay leaf, 2 celery stalks, 2 strips orange rind
3 cups (24 fl oz/750 ml) red wine, such as Côtes du Rhône
3 tablespoons red wine vinegar
4 cloves garlic, peeled and quartered
5 oz (150 g) fresh pork rind, trimmed of all fat
3 tablespoons olive oil
8 oz (250 g) medium carrots, peeled and cut into ¼-in (.5-cm) slices
salt and freshly ground pepper
4 pinches of freshly grated nutmeg
7 oz (200 g) bacon

❖Cut the meat into 2-in (5-cm) cubes. Peel the onion and stud with cloves. Tie together the ingredients for the bouquet garni. Place the cubes of meat in a large bowl and cover with the wine and vinegar. Add the bouquet garni, garlic and onion, cover and refrigerate for 12 hours.

❖Preheat oven to 350°F (180°C). Cut the pork rind into ¾-in (2-cm) squares. Drop into boiling water for 2 minutes, then drain. Scatter ⅔ cup of the squares over the bottom of a 4-qt (4-l) enameled pot.

❖Heat the oil in a nonstick 11-in (28-cm) sauté pan. Add the carrots and cook over high heat until lightly browned and caramelized, 7 to 8 minutes. Sprinkle with salt, pepper and nutmeg. Remove with a slotted spoon and set aside.

❖Drain the cubes of meat and pat dry. Cut the bacon into thin matchsticks. Lightly brown the meat and the bacon in the same pan used for the carrots, for about 5 minutes.

❖Place the meat and bacon in the pot and surround with carrots. Cover the meat with the remaining squares of pork rind and pour the marinade over. Add the bouquet garni, garlic and onion. Season with salt and pepper. Cover the pot with a sheet of oiled waxed paper or parchment paper and place the lid on top. Bake for 5 hours.

❖Remove the onion, garlic and bouquet garni from the pot. If desired, boil the cooking juices over high heat for several minutes to reduce to a syrupy consistency. Serve the meat with the carrots, bacon, pork rind and sauce.

SERVES 6

Ile de France

BOEUF MODE
Aromatic Braised Beef with Vegetables

4 lb (2 kg) beef (round steak, neck, topside, chuck, etc.) in one piece, larded and tied by the butcher
salt and freshly ground pepper
½ teaspoon *quatre-épices* (see glossary)
6 tablespoons cognac
3 cups (24 fl oz/750 ml) dry white wine
2 calf's feet, halved
3 oz (100 g) fresh pork rind, trimmed of all fat
1 large onion
3 cloves
bouquet garni: 1 bay leaf, 1 sprig thyme, 6 sprigs parsley
3 tablespoons vegetable oil
1 oz (25 g) butter
1 large carrot, peeled and sliced
3 cloves garlic, peeled
30 small pickling onions
10 small carrots

❖Wipe the meat. Combine salt, pepper and *quatre-épices* and sprinkle over the meat. Place in a deep bowl just wide enough to hold it and pour the cognac and wine over; the meat should be completely immersed. Cover and refrigerate for 12 hours, turning the meat from time to time.

❖Remove the meat from the marinade and pat dry; reserve the marinade. Bring a large saucepan of water to boil. Drop in the calf's feet and pork rind and boil for 5 minutes. Drain them and cool under running water. Cut the rind into large squares. Peel the large onion and stud with cloves. Tie together the herbs for the bouquet garni.

❖Heat 2 tablespoons oil and the butter in an oval flameproof casserole large enough to hold the meat. Brown the meat on all sides for about 10 minutes. Add the sliced carrot and cook, stirring, for 2 minutes. Add the calf's feet, pork rind, bouquet garni, onion studded with cloves, and the whole cloves of garlic. Pour in the wine; the meat should be covered, but if not, add more wine, water or beef stock. Season with salt and pepper and bring to simmer. Simmer very gently for 5 hours.

❖Meanwhile, peel the small onions and the small carrots. Cut the carrots into ¼-in (1-cm) slices. Heat the remaining oil in a nonstick 11-in (28-cm) sauté pan and add the butter. When it is melted, lightly brown the onions and carrots for about 5 minutes, stirring constantly with a wooden spoon. Add salt and pepper and cook, stirring, for 2 minutes longer, until the vegetables caramelize. Add 6 fl oz (200 ml) stock from the beef and cook for 20 minutes over low heat, until tender.

❖When the meat has cooked for 5 hours, remove the pot from the heat. Remove the meat from the bones of the calf's feet and cut into ¼-in (1-cm) squares. Similarly cut

AROMATIC BRAISED BEEF WITH VEGETABLES

PETER JOHNSON

the pork rind into small squares. Transfer the meat from the pot to a serving platter. Surround it with the veal, pork rind, glazed carrots and onions. Keep hot.

❖Strain the cooking liquid — it will be reduced, highly aromatic and syrupy — and pour it into a sauceboat. Serve immediately; each diner takes a slice of beef, a few cubes of the veal and pork rind, and some glazed vegetables and pours over some of the reduced sauce.

SERVES 8–10

Provence

ALOUETTES SANS TÊTES

Beef Rolls

The shape of these little meat rolls is reminiscent of tiny birds with the heads removed: hence the name of the recipe (literally "larks without heads").

3 lb 10 oz (1.8 kg) rump steak, cut into ⅜-in (1-cm) slices
18 slices prosciutto, each weighing about ½ oz (15 g)
2 oz (60 g) soft white bread, crusts trimmed
2 cloves garlic, finely chopped
4 tablespoons chopped flat-leaf parsley
6 pinches of freshly grated nutmeg
freshly ground pepper
3 tablespoons olive oil
1 oz (25 g) butter
3 oz (100 g) carrots, peeled and finely chopped
5 oz (150 g) onions, finely chopped
2 tender celery stalks, chopped
¾ cup (6 fl oz/200 ml) red wine
8 cups (2 qt/2 l) tomato puree
salt
½ teaspoon sugar

❖Cut each slice of meat into rectangles weighing about 3 oz (100 g). Cut the slices of prosciutto in half crosswise. Using a food processor, grind the bread to crumbs. Combine the crumbs with the garlic, parsley and nutmeg; season well with pepper.

❖Place a rectangle of meat on a work surface and cover with two half-slices of prosciutto. Spread a portion of the bread-crumb mixture to within ⅜ in (1 cm) of the edge. Starting at a narrow end, roll the meat and secure by tying with kitchen thread. Repeat with the remaining ingredients to form about 18 rolls.

❖Heat the oil in a 6-qt (6-l) pot. In two or three batches, quickly sear the rolls, turning them with two wooden spoons, but do not allow them to brown all over. Remove and set aside.

❖Add the butter to the pot and let melt. Stir in the carrots, onions and celery, cover and cook over very low heat until very soft but not browned, about 10 minutes. Return the beef rolls to the pot and pour the wine over. Boil until the liquid is reduced to a syrupy consistency, about 15 minutes. Add the tomato puree; if the beef rolls are not completely covered, add water to cover. Season with salt, pepper and sugar. Cover and cook over very low heat for 3 hours, stirring several times.

❖Transfer the beef rolls to a shallow dish and keep warm. Boil the sauce over moderate heat until smooth and thickened, about 10 minutes.

❖Meanwhile, remove the thread from the beef rolls. Reheat them for 5 minutes in the sauce, then return rolls and sauce to the dish and serve.

SERVES 8

BEEF ROLLS

PETER JOHNSON

Flandres

CARBONNADES FLAMANDES
Beef Braised in Beer

In Flandres most meats are served with fried potatoes, and carbonnades are no exception — but you could also serve them with steamed or mashed potatoes.

3 lb 10 oz (1.8 kg) beef suitable for braising, such as round
    steak, brisket, neck or chuck steak
salt and freshly ground pepper
bouquet garni: 1 sprig thyme, 1 bay leaf, 6 sprigs parsley
1 slice whole-grain country-style bread, about 3 oz (100 g)
2 tablespoons strong mustard
1 tablespoon vegetable oil
1 oz (25 g) butter
12 oz (400 g) onions, thinly sliced
1 tablespoon firmly packed brown sugar
2 tablespoons red wine vinegar
16 fl oz (500 ml) dark beer

❖ Ask your butcher to cut the meat into slices ½ in (1 cm) thick and then into 2 x 2½-in (5 x 6-cm) rectangles. Season with salt and pepper. Tie together the herbs of the bouquet garni. Cut the crusts from the slice of bread and spread it with the mustard.

❖ Preheat oven to 350°F (180°C). Heat the oil in a nonstick 10-in (26-cm) sauté pan and quickly seal the slices of meat over high heat for 2 minutes each side. Set aside. Melt the butter in the sauté pan. Add the onions and cook, stirring, for 5 minutes or until golden brown. Add the brown sugar and cook until the onions are lightly caramelized. Pour in the vinegar and evaporate it over high heat.

❖ Arrange alternating layers of meat and onions in an oven-proof 4-qt (4-l) casserole, inserting the slice of bread and the bouquet garni in the middle. Pour the beer into the sauté pan and heat it over high heat. Transfer it to the casserole, adding more if necessary to just cover the meat. Cover and braise in the oven for 4 hours without disturbing.

❖ Transfer the meat to a shallow dish and keep warm. Puree the bread, onions and cooking juices through the fine holes of a food mill or in a food processor to make a smooth sauce. Reheat the sauce over high heat, then pour over the meat. Serve immediately.

SERVES 6

Corse

STUFATU
Corsican Stew with Pasta

Stufatu is the Corsican word for stew. The term is applied to numerous dishes cooked by simmering.

2½ lb (1.25 kg) beef suitable for braising, such as neck or
    chuck
8 oz (250 g) raw smoked ham
bouquet garni: 1 bay leaf, 1 sprig thyme, 1 sprig rosemary,
    6 sprigs parsley

1 lb (500 g) ripe tomatoes
¼ cup (2 fl oz/60 ml) olive oil
8 oz (250 g) onions, thinly sliced
6 cloves garlic, finely chopped
1 cup (8 fl oz/250 ml) dry white wine
salt and freshly ground pepper
4 pinches of freshly grated nutmeg
1 oz (30 g) dried cèpes (*porcini* mushrooms)
For serving:
12 oz (375 g) fresh pasta, or 10 oz (315 g) dried pasta
2 oz (50 g) butter
4 oz (100 g) freshly grated Corsican sheep's milk cheese or
    Parmesan

❖ Cut the beef and the ham into ¾-in (2-cm) cubes. Tie together the herbs for the bouquet garni. Drop the tomatoes into boiling water for 10 seconds. Cool under running water, peel, halve and squeeze out the seeds; coarsely chop the flesh.

❖ Heat the oil in a 4-qt (4-l) pot and cook the meat, ham, onions and garlic for 5 minutes, stirring constantly with a wooden spoon. Add the tomatoes, wine and bouquet garni and mix well. Season with salt, pepper and nutmeg and bring to simmer. Cover and simmer for 1 hour.

❖ Meanwhile, place the mushrooms in a bowl, cover with 2 cups warm water and leave them to swell.

❖ Add the mushrooms to the pot with the strained soaking liquid and simmer for 2 hours longer.

❖ Prepare the pasta: drop the pasta into a large pot of boiling salted water and cook until *al dente*. Drain, place in a shallow dish and toss with the butter. Pour over half the sauce from the meat and mix well. Season with pepper and serve immediately, the meat in its sauce accompanied by pasta; pass the grated cheese separately.

SERVES 6

Languedoc

BROUFADO
Braised Beef with Anchovies

3 lb 10 oz (1.8 kg) rump steak
¼ cup (2 fl oz/60 ml) olive oil
¼ cup (2 fl oz/60 ml) red wine vinegar
2 cups (16 fl oz/500 ml) dry white wine
3 tablespoons cognac
2 onions, 3 oz (100 g) each, thinly sliced
bouquet garni: 1 sprig thyme, 1 bay leaf, 6 sprigs parsley
2 cloves garlic, halved
salt and freshly ground pepper
3 anchovies preserved in salt
3 tablespoons capers, rinsed and dried
4 cornichons (small French sour pickles or gherkins), thinly
    sliced
1 teaspoon arrowroot
2 tablespoons cold water

❖ Cut the meat into 2-in (5-cm) cubes. Pour 2 tablespoons oil, the vinegar, wine and cognac into a large bowl. Add the onions and meat and combine. Cover and refrigerate for 12 hours.

PETER JOHNSON

CORSICAN STEW WITH PASTA (bottom), BRAISED BEEF WITH
ANCHOVIES (center) AND BEEF BRAISED IN BEER (top)

❖Preheat oven to 350°F (180°C). Tie together the herbs for
the bouquet garni. Pour the contents of the bowl into a 4-qt
(4-l) pot. Add the garlic, bouquet garni, salt and pepper and
bring to simmer. Cover and braise in the oven for 4 hours.
❖Rub the salt off the anchovies under cold running water.
Lift off the fillets and cut in fourths. Add the capers and
cornichons to the pot and braise for 1 hour longer.

❖Transfer the pieces of meat to a warmed plate using a
slotted spoon. Blend the arrowroot with the cold water and
pour into the sauce. Boil until the mixture thickens, about
2 minutes. Stir in the anchovies, then return the meat to the
pot and simmer for 5 minutes. Serve directly from the pot.

SERVES 6

Bourgogne

BOEUF BOURGUIGNON

Burgundy Beef

8 oz (250 g) pork belly
1 tablespoon vegetable oil
2 oz (50 g) butter
36 small pickling onions, peeled
3 lb 10 oz (1.8 kg) beef suitable for braising, such as round,
    topside or chuck steak
3 tablespoons *marc de Bourgogne* or brandy
3 cups (24 fl oz/750 ml) red Burgundy
36 small (button) mushrooms
1 tablespoon fresh lemon juice
salt and freshly ground pepper
2 teaspoons arrowroot
2 tablespoons cold water

❖Rinse the pork belly under running water, then cut into thin strips. Drop into boiling water and blanch for 5 minutes; drain and rinse.

❖Heat the oil in a 6-qt (6-l) pot and cook the strips of pork belly over low heat until golden brown, about 5 minutes, stirring constantly. Remove from the pot with a slotted spoon and set aside.

❖Add a little less than half the butter to the pot and cook the onions over very low heat until golden, turning frequently, about 10 minutes. Remove with a slotted spoon and add to the pork.

❖Cut the meat into 2-in (5-cm) cubes. Cook in the pot in batches until lightly browned, about 5 minutes, turning frequently. Set aside.

❖Discard the fat from the pot. Add the *marc* and, 1 minute later, the wine, scraping up browned bits with a wooden spoon. Ignite the wine and wait until flames subside. Return the meat to the pot and bring to simmer. Cover and cook over very low heat for 3 hours.

❖Meanwhile, trim the mushroom stems, rinse the mushrooms and pat dry. Melt the remaining butter in a nonstick 10-in (26-cm) sauté pan. Add the mushrooms and lemon juice, season with salt and pepper, and cook the mushrooms until they are golden and have stopped giving out any liquid.

❖Add the pork, onions and mushrooms to the pot and cook over low heat, covered, for 1 hour longer.

❖Remove the meat, pork, onions and mushrooms with a slotted spoon and set aside. Bring the sauce to boil. Blend the arrowroot and cold water, add to the boiling sauce and boil over high heat for 1½ minutes or until the sauce is thickened and smooth. Return the meat and other ingredients to the pot and reheat for 2 minutes. Transfer to a shallow dish and serve.

SERVES 8

BURGUNDY BEEF

PETER JOHNSON

Maine

POTHINE DE BOEUF
Beef Braised with Calvados

Pothines of meat are typical of Maine. The pothine, *or* pothin, *is the heavy cast-iron casserole in which the meats are simmered, either over an open fire or on the edge of the stove.*

3 lb 10 oz (1.8 kg) beef, such as round, neck, topside or chuck
   steak, in one piece
3 oz (100 g) raw smoked ham
3 oz (100 g) *pancetta* or fresh pork belly
bouquet garni: 1 sprig thyme, 1 bay leaf, 6 sprigs parsley
1 onion, about 3 oz (100 g)
2 cloves
1 calf's foot, halved
3 oz (100 g) fresh pork rind, trimmed of all fat
2 tablespoons vegetable oil
2 cloves garlic, halved
1 cup (8 fl oz/250 ml) beef stock
6 tablespoons calvados
1 cup (8 fl oz/250 ml) dry white wine
salt and freshly ground pepper

❖Ask the butcher to lard the piece of meat with the ham and pork belly and to tie it securely. Tie together the herbs for the bouquet garni. Peel the onion and stud with cloves.
❖Bring a large saucepan of water to boil. Add the calf's foot and pork rind and boil for 5 minutes. Drain and refresh under running water, then cut the rind into large squares.
❖Preheat oven to 350°F (180°C). Heat the oil in an oval pot large enough to hold the meat, and brown the meat on all sides. Add the calf's foot, pork rind, bouquet garni, onion and garlic. Pour in the stock, calvados and wine; the meat should be completely covered, but if not, add more wine or stock. Season with salt and pepper, cover and bring to simmer. Braise in the preheated oven for 5 hours.
❖Extract the meat from the calf's foot and cut it into ½-in (1-cm) squares. Cut the pork rind into similar squares. Remove the beef with a slotted spoon and transfer to a serving platter. Surround with the squares of veal and pork rind and keep warm.
❖If necessary, boil the cooking liquid over high heat until aromatic and syrupy in consistency. Pour into a sauceboat and serve.

SERVES 8   *Photograph pages 152 – 153*

Lyonnais

GRILLADE DES MARINIERS
Boatman's Grill

This dish is called a grillade *because the meat is thinly cut — as it would be for a grill. As for the boatmen, this is a reference to the bargemen who plied the Rhône, and who would carry this dish with them already prepared so they had only to heat it when they were ready to eat.*

3 lb 10 oz (1.8 kg) rump steak
5 tablespoons olive oil
2 tablespoons red wine vinegar

PETER JOHNSON

BOATMAN'S GRILL

1 bay leaf, crumbled
1 strip orange rind, about 2 in (5 cm) long
2 cloves
salt and freshly ground pepper
4 pinches of freshly grated nutmeg
4 cloves garlic, peeled
2 lb (1 kg) onions, thinly sliced
4 anchovies preserved in salt

❖Ask the butcher to cut the meat into slices about ¼ in (.5 cm) thick and weighing about 3 oz (100 g).
❖In a bowl combine 3 tablespoons of the oil, the vinegar, bay leaf, orange rind, cloves, salt, pepper and nutmeg. Whisk with a fork until well blended, then add the meat and stir to coat well. Cover and refrigerate for 12 hours.
❖Preheat oven to 350°F (180°C). Crush 3 cloves of garlic through a garlic press into another bowl. Add the onions, season with salt and pepper and mix well.
❖Oil a 4-qt (4-l) casserole or baking dish with a lid, using 1 tablespoon oil. Spread a layer of onion mixture over the bottom. Cover with a layer of meat. Continue to alternate the ingredients, finishing with a layer of onions. Discard the orange rind, then pour the marinade over the onions and meat. Cover and braise in the oven for 4 hours.
❖Wash the anchovies under cold running water, rubbing off the salt. Lift off the fillets and place them in a food processor. Add the remaining clove of garlic, the last tablespoon of oil and ¼ cup (2 fl oz/60 ml) of the liquid from the baking dish and blend to a smooth paste. Pour this paste into the baking dish, stir carefully and simmer for 3 minutes. Serve immediately, straight from the baking dish.

SERVES 6

Bretagne

KIG-HA-FARZ

Buckwheat Pudding with Meat and Vegetables

This traditional Breton dish was once served at family celebrations. The woman of the house carefully kept the white linen bags in which the farz was enclosed, boiling and drying them in the sun after each use. They were then put away in the linen cupboard until the next occasion.

3 lb (1.5 kg) beef suitable for braising, such as top round (topside), neck or chuck
bouquet garni: 1 bay leaf, 1 sprig thyme, 6 sprigs parsley, 3 celery stalks
1 onion
3 cloves
1 lb (500 g) fresh pork belly
1 tablespoon coarse sea salt
1 teaspoon mixed black and white peppercorns
½ teaspoon coriander seeds
3 leeks
1 green cabbage
6 carrots, peeled
6 turnips, peeled
1 celery heart
1 oz (30 g) butter
salt and freshly ground pepper
For the *farz:*
2 oz (60 g) butter
2 cups (8 oz/250 g) buckwheat flour
6 tablespoons milk
6 tablespoons heavy (double) cream or crème fraîche
1 egg
1 teaspoon superfine (caster) sugar
3 oz (100 g) raisins

❖Pour 4 qt (4 l) water into a large pot and bring to boil. Add the piece of beef and simmer gently for 15 minutes, skimming the surface regularly. Tie together the herbs of the bouquet garni. Peel the onion and stud with cloves. Add the pork belly, bouquet garni, onion, coarse salt, peppercorns and coriander to the pot, cover and simmer gently for 2 hours.
❖Trim off the deep green parts of the leeks. Wash the leeks and halve crosswise, separating the white part from the tender green part; tie together in two bundles. Quarter and core the cabbage.
❖Prepare the *farz*: transfer ¾ cup (200 ml) of the cooking liquid from the pot to a small saucepan. Add 2 oz (60 g) butter and allow it to melt. Sift the flour into a bowl. Add the butter mixture, milk, cream, egg and sugar and mix to a smooth paste using a wooden spoon. Blend in the raisins. Wrap the mixture in a square of white cotton cloth and tie the two ends with kitchen thread, taking care not to compress the *farz* too much.
❖Add the leeks, carrots, turnips and celery to the pot and return to boil. Add the *farz* and simmer gently for another 1½ hours.
❖Meanwhile, parboil the cabbage in water to cover for 5 minutes. Drain and transfer to a nonstick 10-in (26-cm) sauté pan with the butter. Season with salt and pepper. Cover and cook over very low heat for 1 hour or until very

tender. Keep warm. Remove the cooked vegetables, meats and *farz* from the pot and strain the stock into a soup tureen. Slice the meats and arrange on a plate; surround with vegetables. Remove the *farz* from its cloth covering and coarsely crumble it around the vegetables. Have guests help themselves to some of each, pouring a little of the stock over before eating.

SERVES 6

Ile de France

STEAK AU POIVRE

Pepper Steak

Invented around 1920 in the kitchens of the Trianon Palace at Versailles, steak au poivre *has become one of the classic dishes of French cuisine. In order to give a lift to some very tender but rather tasteless beef from Argentina, the chef, Emile Lerch, had the idea of covering it with crushed peppercorns before cooking it.*

Today, mignonette *or coarse ground pepper is also referred to as* poivre à steak.

1 porterhouse or rump steak, about 13 oz (400 g) and 1 in (3 cm) thick
salt
1 tablespoon cracked peppercorns
2 oz (60 g) butter
2 tablespoons cognac
3 tablespoons heavy (double) cream or crème fraîche

❖Ask the butcher to trim the meat and to cut it into two equal-size steaks. Pat dry and season with salt. Spread the peppercorns on a plate and roll the steaks over them to coat each side lightly.
❖Melt half the butter in a 10-in (26-cm) skillet. Cook the steaks over high heat for 2 to 3 minutes on each side, according to taste. Pour the cognac over and ignite. When the flames subside, remove the steaks from the pan and keep warm on a plate.
❖Discard the butter from the pan and add the cream. Boil for 1 minute over high heat, then whisk in the remaining butter.
❖Pour this sauce over the steaks and serve immediately.

SERVES 2

PEPPER STEAK

PETER JOHNSON

OPPOSITE PAGE: BUCKWHEAT PUDDING WITH MEAT AND VEGETABLES (top left) AND LEG OF LAMB, BRITTANY-STYLE (bottom right, recipe page 170), PHOTOGRAPHED IN BRETAGNE
PIERRE HUSSENOT/AGENCE TOP

Flandres

HOCHEPOT
Oxtail Stew

The word pot *indicates that different meats and vegetables are cooked together in the same pot. Sometimes this Flandres pot-au-feu is enriched by the addition of some pig's tail and bacon.*

2 lb (1 kg) oxtail
1½ lb (750 g) beef spareribs (flank)
1½ lb (750 g) lamb shoulder
8 oz (250 g) lightly salted pork belly
1 pig's ear
8 leeks
1 onion, about 3 oz (100 g)
3 cloves
2 cloves garlic
bouquet garni: 2 bay leaves, 1 sprig thyme, 10 sprigs parsley
8 small carrots, peeled
8 small turnips, peeled
1 celeriac (celery root), peeled
1 bunch celery, washed
10 juniper berries
10 peppercorns, black and white mixed
8 medium-size boiling potatoes
1 green cabbage
salt
1 unsmoked kielbasa (boiling sausage)
For serving (optional):
toasted bread
grated Emmenthaler cheese

❖Ask the butcher to cut the oxtail into 1½-in (4-cm) sections. Rinse the meats and pat dry. Place the oxtail, spareribs, lamb shoulder, pork belly and pig's ear in a large pot and cover with plenty of cold water. Bring to boil and cook for 5 minutes, then drain the meats, discarding the liquid. Return the meats to the pot and cover again with plenty of cold water. Bring to boil over low heat.
❖Clean the leeks and tie together in 2 bunches. Peel the onion and stud with cloves. Peel the cloves of garlic and crush them with the hand or the side of a cleaver. Tie together the herbs for the bouquet garni.
❖Add the carrots, turnips, celeriac, celery, leeks, garlic, bouquet garni, juniper berries and peppercorns to the pot and simmer gently for 2 hours.
❖Meanwhile, peel and wash the potatoes. Core and quarter the cabbage. Blanch the cabbage in boiling water to cover for 5 minutes, then transfer to a nonstick 10-in (26-cm) sauté pan with the potatoes. Season with salt. Add 6 tablespoons stock from the meat and cook over low heat, covered, for 20 minutes, or until cabbage and potatoes are tender, adding more liquid from time to time as necessary.
❖About 45 minutes before the end of the cooking time, prick the sausage with a fork and add to the pot with the meats.
❖Drain the meats and carve into ¾-in (2-cm) slices. Arrange on a platter and surround with the boiled vegetables, cabbage and potatoes, moistening them with a little stock. Strain the remaining stock into a soup tureen. Serve the broth hot, either as is or with toasted bread and grated cheese, followed by the meats and vegetables.

SERVES 8   *Photograph pages 6 – 7*

Ile de France

ENTRECÔTES BERCY, POMMES FRITES
Rib Steaks, Bercy-style, with French Fries

The Bercy quarter of Paris, which for a long time was home to the most important wine market of Europe, gave its name to a method of cooking with wine and shallots that was fashionable in Parisian restaurants around 1820.

This was also the era of the traveling marchands de frites *or* friteurs *who operated around the Pont-Neuf selling potatoes fried in sizzling hot oil called* pommes Pont-Neuf.

Gradually these merchants spread all over Paris and their fried potatoes became known simply as frites *or* pommes frites.

2 lb (1 kg) boiling potatoes
about 2 qt (2 l) peanut (groundnut) oil
2 entrecôtes, rib steaks or Scotch fillets, 1¼ lb (600 g) each, trimmed
salt and freshly ground pepper
3 oz (100 g) beef marrow
1 tablespoon vegetable oil
3 oz (100 g) butter
4 French shallots, finely chopped
6 tablespoons dry white wine
1 tablespoon chopped flat-leaf parsley

❖Peel the potatoes, wash them and cut them into pieces 2 to 2½ in (5 to 6 cm) long and ½ in (1 cm) wide. Rinse under cold water and dry in a tea towel.
❖Heat the oil in a deep fryer to 350°F (180°C). As soon as it starts to bubble, add the potatoes in a frying basket, in batches if necessary, and fry until a pale straw color. Remove the basket from the oil and set the fries aside; maintain the oil at 350°F (180°C).
❖Pat the steaks dry and season with salt and pepper. Cut the beef marrow into ¼-in (.5-cm) cubes. Drop into a saucepan of simmering water and poach for 3 minutes. Drain in a sieve.
❖Heat the oil in a nonstick 10-in (26-cm) skillet. Add 1 oz (25 g) butter. As soon as it melts, add the steaks and cook for 1½ to 2½ minutes on each side, according to taste. Remove from the pan and keep warm; discard the fat from the pan. Add the shallots and wine and cook over high heat, scraping up browned bits with a wooden spoon, until the liquid is reduced to 1 tablespoon. Remove the pan from the heat and whisk in the remaining butter in small pieces to make a light, foamy sauce. Add the parsley and pour over the steaks. Reheat the marrow in the skillet for 30 seconds and scatter over the meat.
❖Plunge the basket of potatoes back into the hot oil and fry until crisp and golden brown. Drain on paper towels. Sprinkle with salt and turn onto a plate. Serve the steaks immediately, accompanied by the potatoes.

SERVES 4

RIB STEAKS, BERCY-STYLE, WITH FRENCH FRIES
PETER JOHNSON

Provence

DAUBE D'AVIGNON

Avignon Lamb Stew

Although the word daube *refers to a method of cooking in which meat or poultry is simmered for several hours in white or red wine and seasoned with herbs, there are an amazing number of variations of the dish in different towns and villages.*

This is the fragrant, mellow version served in the charming town of Avignon. It is usually accompanied by lightly buttered noodles coated with the juices of the daube *and sprinkled with grated cheese — Emmenthaler or Parmesan, or a mixture of the two.*

3 lb (1.5 kg) lamb from the leg, boned and trimmed of fat
2 onions (3 oz/100 g each) finely chopped
4 cloves garlic, finely chopped
1 sprig thyme, crumbled
1 bay leaf, crumbled
2 tablespoons chopped flat-leaf parsley
2 cloves
6 tablespoons olive oil
1 cup (8 fl oz/250 ml) red wine, such as Côtes du Rhône
2 tablespoons cognac
salt and freshly ground pepper
1 slice pork belly, about 7 oz (200 g)
5 oz (150 g) fresh pork rind
1 strip dried orange rind

❖Cut the meat into 1½-in (4-cm) cubes and place in a large bowl. Add the onion, garlic, thyme, bay leaf, parsley, cloves, oil, wine and cognac. Season with salt and pepper. Stir well, then marinate for 2 hours at room temperature.

❖About 20 minutes before the end of the marinating time, bring a large saucepan of water to boil. Add the pork belly and rind and boil for 5 minutes. Drain, rinse and drain again. Cool to lukewarm, then cut the pork belly into thin strips and the rind into ⅜-in (1-cm) squares. Stir the strips of belly into the marinating mixture.

❖Preheat oven to 350°F (180°C). Scatter the squares of pork rind on the bottom of a 4-qt (4-l) earthenware or enameled casserole. Pour in all the marinating mixture and meat and add the orange rind. Seal the pot airtight by putting waxed paper between casserole and lid, and bake for 5 hours without disturbing the contents.

❖Serve the stew very hot, directly from the casserole.

SERVES 6

Provence

GIGOT FARCI

Stuffed Leg of Lamb

This method of cooking a leg of lamb is found in many parts of France, but the stuffings vary considerably according to the region.

8 oz (250 g) wild mushrooms
1 tablespoon butter
2 oz (50 g) lean smoked bacon, finely chopped
1 heart of fennel, about 3 oz (100 g), chopped
4 tablespoons chopped parsley and fresh chervil, mixed
2 pinches dried thyme

PETER JOHNSON

STUFFED LEG OF LAMB

salt and freshly ground pepper
3 pinches of freshly grated nutmeg
1 oz (25 g) white sandwich bread, crusts trimmed
1 clove garlic
1 leg of lamb, about 3 lb 10 oz (1.8 kg), trimmed and boned
1 teaspoon peanut oil
For the potatoes:
3½ lb (1.7 kg) boiling potatoes
3 oz (80 g) butter
½ teaspoon dried thyme
1 clove garlic

❖Trim the mushroom stems. Wash the mushrooms quickly under cold water and pat dry; chop. Melt 1 table-spoon butter in a nonstick 9-in (22-cm) sauté pan and lightly brown the bacon for 2 minutes, stirring with a wooden spoon. Add the fennel, cover and cook for 2 minutes longer. Add the mushrooms, the parsley mixture, thyme, salt, pepper and nutmeg and cook, half-covered, until the fennel is very tender and all liquid has evaporated.

❖Grind the bread to coarse crumbs in a food processor. Remove the sauté pan from heat. Mix in the crumbs and the crushed garlic.

❖Stuff the leg of lamb with this mixture and sew the opening with kitchen thread. Coat the lamb with oil and season with salt and pepper. Make very shallow crisscross cuts over the surface of the leg. Preheat oven to 450°F (230°C). Peel the potatoes, rinse and pat dry. Slice into very thin rounds. Melt the butter in a 13 x 9-in (32 x 22-cm) baking dish. Add the thyme and the garlic, crushed in a garlic press. Toss the potatoes in this flavored butter to coat well. Spread the slices in the pan and smooth the surface.

❖Place the leg of lamb on the bed of potatoes, rounded side down. Roast for 30 minutes. Turn the lamb and potato slices over and roast 25 minutes longer. Turn off the oven and let the leg of lamb rest in the oven for 10 minutes before serving.

SERVES 8

ROAST LAMB OF PAUILLAC

squeeze out the seeds and finely chop the flesh. Tie together the herbs for the bouquet garni.

❖Heat the oil in a 4-qt (4-l) flameproof casserole, add half the butter and lightly brown the cubes of meat on all sides. Sprinkle with flour and cook, stirring, for 1 minute. Stir in the tomatoes, stock, bouquet garni and garlic. Cover and cook over low heat for 1½ hours.

❖Meanwhile, prepare the vegetables: shell the peas. Peel the carrots and turnips. Peel the onions and cut off the green stalks. Remove the strings from the beans, if necessary. Blanch in a large quantity of boiling water for 5 minutes, then drain.

❖Melt the remaining butter in a nonstick 11-in (28-cm) sauté pan. Add the carrots, turnips and onions and cook over low heat until lightly golden, about 5 minutes, stirring frequently. Add the beans and peas and sprinkle with sugar, salt and pepper. Cook until the vegetables are golden, about 2 minutes longer. Add ¾ cup (6 fl oz/200 ml) of the veal cooking liquid and simmer over low heat for 15 minutes.

❖After the meat has cooked for 1½ hours, add the vegetables and cook over low heat, stirring, for 5 minutes. Remove the meat and vegetables with a slotted spoon, transfer to a shallow dish and keep warm. Boil the cooking liquid until thickened, then remove the garlic and bouquet garni. Stir in the chervil. Pour the sauce over the meat and vegetables and serve.

SERVES 6   *Photograph page 159*

Ile de France

NAVARIN PRINTANIER
Lamb with Spring Vegetables

On October 20, 1827, the French, English and Russian armies together defeated the Egyptian and Turkish fleet at Navarin in Greece in the course of the Greek War of Independence. It is thought that this dish of lamb stewed with vegetables was christened navarin *in honor of the war. Or perhaps the name comes from the* navet *(turnip) which was once the main vegetable used. The mystery remains unsolved.*

3¼ lb (1.6 kg) lamb shoulder, neck and breast, mixed
salt and freshly ground pepper
6 oz (200 g) ripe tomatoes
bouquet garni: 1 bay leaf, 1 sprig thyme, 6 sprigs parsley
1 tablespoon vegetable oil
2 oz (50 g) butter
1 tablespoon all purpose (plain) flour
2 cups (16 fl oz/500 ml) chicken stock (recipe page 34)
2 cloves garlic, halved
1 lb (500 g) fresh peas, in the shell
1 lb (500 g) very small carrots
1 lb (500 g) small turnips
18 small green (spring) onions
6 oz (200 g) slender green beans
1 teaspoon sugar
1 tablespoon chopped fresh chervil

❖Cut the meat into 2-in (5-cm) cubes and season with salt and pepper. Drop the tomatoes into boiling water for 10 seconds. Cool under running water, then peel, halve,

---

Languedoc

AGNEAU RÔTI DE PAUILLAC
Roast Lamb of Pauillac

2½ oz (75 g) stale bread, crusts trimmed
8 cloves garlic
2 oz (50 g) butter
salt and freshly ground pepper
8 tablespoons chopped flat-leaf parsley
1 leg of lamb, about 3½ lb (1.7 kg), trimmed
2 tablespoons peanut (groundnut) oil

❖Preheat oven to 450°F (230°C). Grind the bread to coarse crumbs in a food processor. Finely chop 6 garlic cloves and cut the remaining two into fine slivers. In a bowl, combine the butter, salt, pepper, breadcrumbs, parsley and chopped garlic and mix with a fork to produce a smooth paste.

❖Make slits in the leg of lamb with the point of a knife and insert slivers of garlic in the slits. Season the lamb with salt and pepper and spread the garlic paste over the surface. Coat the lamb with oil and season with salt and pepper.

❖Oil a large baking dish. Place the leg of lamb on a roasting rack in the dish, rounded side down. Roast for 20 minutes, then turn the lamb over and reduce the heat to 425°F (215°C), checking that the juices in the pan are not burning; they should just caramelize. If the juices start to burn, add a few spoonfuls of hot water to the dish from time to time. After 45 minutes of cooking, turn off the oven, turn the leg of lamb over and let it rest for 10 minutes in the oven. Carve in slices, sprinkle over the pan juices and serve.

SERVES 6

PETER JOHNSON

Anjou

CUL DE VEAU À L'ANGEVINE
Veal Pot Roast, Anjou-style

Cul de veau is another name for quasi de veau, the chump end of veal taken from above the thigh of the animal. This Anjou dish is served with sautéed wild mushrooms, glazed carrots or a puree of celeriac.

3 oz (100 g) fresh pork rind, trimmed of all fat
bouquet garni: 1 bay leaf, 1 sprig thyme, 6 sprigs parsley
¾ cup (200 ml) dry white wine
¾ cup (200 ml) chicken stock (recipe page 34)
2 oz (50 g) butter
3½ lb (1.75 kg) veal rump
2 medium carrots, peeled and thinly sliced
2 onions, about 3 oz (100 g) each, thinly sliced
salt and freshly ground pepper

❖Blanch the pork rind in boiling water to cover for 2 minutes; drain. Cut into ¾ x ¼-in (2 x .5-cm) strips. Tie together the herbs for the bouquet garni.
❖Preheat oven to 350°F (180°C). Pour the wine and the stock into a saucepan and boil over high heat until reduced by half. Melt the butter in a pot large enough to hold the piece of veal and lightly brown it on all sides. Remove the meat and set aside. Add the carrots and onions to the pot and cook, stirring, for 5 minutes, then return meat to the pot. Pour in the wine mixture and turn the meat over. Season with salt and pepper; add the pork rind and the bouquet garni. Cover and braise in the oven for 3 hours.
❖Remove the meat from the pot and transfer to a serving plate. Surround with the pork rind, onions and carrots. Boil the cooking liquid until reduced to a syrupy consistency and pour over the meat. Serve immediately.

SERVES 6   *Photograph pages 152 – 153*

Normandie

CÔTES DE VEAU À LA NORMANDE
Veal Chops, Normandy-style

4 Golden Delicious apples, about 7 oz (200 g) each
2½ oz (75 g) butter
4 veal chops (cutlets), about 7 oz (200 g) each
salt and freshly ground pepper
2 tablespoons calvados
¾ cup (6 fl oz/200 ml) heavy (double) cream or crème fraîche

❖Peel, core and quarter the apples; cut each quarter into 3 slices. Melt half the butter in a nonstick 11-in (28-cm) skillet. Add the apple slices and cook over moderate heat for 10 minutes, turning after 5 minutes.
❖Meanwhile, melt the remaining butter in a nonstick 10-in (26-cm) skillet. Sauté the veal over moderate heat for 5 minutes on each side, seasoning with salt and pepper.
❖Arrange the veal and apples on a serving platter and keep warm. Pour the calvados into the pan used for cooking the veal and boil until evaporated, scraping up browned bits

with a wooden spoon. Add the cream and boil until reduced by half, stirring constantly. Pour this sauce over the veal and serve immediately.

SERVES 4

Lyonnais

FOIE DE VEAU À LA LYONNAISE
Calf's Liver, Lyons-style

À la lyonnaise is the term used for any dish cooked with onions that have been chopped and softened in butter with vinegar and chopped parsley added. Among the foods prepared in this way are cardoons and calf's head.

4 slices calf's liver, ⅝ in (1.5 cm) thick and 5 oz (150 g) each
salt and freshly ground pepper
2 oz (50 g) butter
8 oz (250 g) onions, thinly sliced
1 tablespoon red wine vinegar
2 tablespoons chopped flat-leaf parsley

❖Pat the slices of liver dry. Season with salt and pepper. Melt ⅓ of the butter in a nonstick 10-in (26-cm) skillet. Cook the slices of liver over moderate heat for 2 minutes on each side. Remove and keep warm.
❖Melt the remaining butter in the same skillet. Add the onions and cook over low heat, stirring frequently, for 15 minutes or until very soft. Add the vinegar and the juices which have escaped from the liver. Season with salt and pepper and cook, stirring, for 1 minute longer. Divide the onion mixture among four heated plates.
❖Reheat the slices of liver in the skillet for 30 seconds on each side, then arrange them on the plates. Sprinkle with chopped parsley and serve immediately.

SERVES 4

VEAL CHOPS, NORMANDY-STYLE (top)
AND CALF'S LIVER, LYONS-STYLE (bottom)

CREAMED KIDNEYS AND SWEETBREADS

Touraine

BEUCHELLE
Creamed Kidneys and Sweetbreads

The origin of this very old Touraine dish is not known. We only know that it was brought back into fashion by a chef named Edouard Nignon at the Larue restaurant in Paris at the beginning of this century.

2 veal kidneys
salt and freshly ground pepper
2 veal sweetbreads
1 lb (500 g) fresh cèpes (*porcini* mushrooms)
3 oz (100 g) butter
1 cup (8 fl oz/250 ml) heavy (double) cream or crème fraîche
2 oz (50 g) Parmesan cheese, freshly and finely grated

❖Ask the butcher to remove the fat from the kidneys and to cut them into slices ¼ in (.5 cm) thick. Season the kidneys with salt and pepper.
❖Bring a large saucepan of water to boil. Drop in the sweetbreads and blanch for 2 minutes. Drain, then soak for 15 minutes in ice water. Drain, pat dry and cut into slices ¼ in (.5 cm) thick.
❖Trim the stems of the cèpes. Wash quickly under running water, pat dry and cut into slices ¼ in (.5 cm) thick.
❖Melt half the butter in a nonstick 10-in (26-cm) skillet and cook the kidney slices for 2 minutes or until lightly browned, turning with a wooden spoon. Remove from the pan and keep warm. Cook the sweetbread slices in the same way and set aside with the kidneys.
❖Wipe out the skillet, then melt the remaining butter in it. Add the cèpes and cook over high heat until they are golden and do not give out any more liquid. Add the cream and boil, stirring, for 3 minutes or until it thickens and coats the cèpes. Season with salt and pepper.

❖Preheat broiler (griller). Butter a broilerproof dish large enough to hold the meat and cèpes in a 1¼ in (3 cm) layer.
❖Add the sweetbread and kidney slices to the skillet and cook, stirring, for 30 seconds. Pour the mixture into the buttered dish and sprinkle with Parmesan. Broil close to the heat for 2 minutes. Serve immediately from the same dish.

SERVES 6

Ile de France

BLANQUETTE DE VEAU
Veal in White Sauce

3 lb (1.5 kg) veal, on the bone: ⅓ breast, ⅓ shoulder, ⅓ forequarter
1 onion, about 3 oz (100 g)
2 cloves
bouquet garni: 1 bay leaf, 1 sprig thyme, 6 sprigs parsley, 2 celery stalks, white part of 1 leek
1 medium carrot, peeled and cut into 4 chunks
¾ cup (6 fl oz/200 ml) dry white wine
⅔ cup (5 fl oz/150 ml) heavy (double) cream or crème fraîche
2 egg yolks
4 pinches of freshly grated nutmeg
1 tablespoon fresh lemon juice
salt and freshly ground pepper
To garnish:
24 small pickling onions
8 oz (250 g) small (button) mushrooms
2 oz (50 g) butter
6 tablespoons water
1 tablespoon fresh lemon juice

❖Cut the meat into 2-in (5-cm) cubes. Peel the onion and stud with cloves. Tie together the herbs for the bouquet garni. Place the meat in a flameproof casserole and add the carrot, onion and bouquet garni. Pour in the wine and water just to cover. Bring to boil, skimming the surface for the first 10 minutes, then cover and simmer very gently for 2½ hours.
❖About 45 minutes before the meat is ready, prepare the garnish: peel the pickling onions. Trim the mushroom stems; wash the mushrooms and pat dry. Melt half the butter in a nonstick 10-in (26-cm) skillet and cook the onions until golden, about 5 minutes, stirring frequently. Add the water, season with salt and pepper and cook, covered, for 20 minutes or until tender. Melt the remaining butter in a second skillet and add the mushrooms and lemon juice. Season with salt and pepper and cook until mushrooms are golden and no longer give out any liquid. Add to the onions and keep warm.
❖Remove the meat with a slotted spoon and transfer to a heated plate. Surround with the mushrooms and onions.
❖Strain the cooking liquid into a saucepan and boil over high heat until reduced to about 1 cup (250 ml). In a bowl beat the cream and egg yolks; blend in 3 tablespoons of the hot stock. Return to the saucepan and cook, stirring constantly, until slightly thickened; do not boil. Remove from heat and whisk the sauce to a smooth, velvety consistency. Add the nutmeg, lemon juice, salt and pepper and whisk for 30 seconds longer. Pour this sauce over the meat and vegetables; serve immediately.

SERVES 6   *Photograph page 159*

Aquitaine

AILLADE GASCONNE
Veal with Garlic

The large quantity of garlic used in this recipe is responsible for the name of the dish, which is very popular in the southwest.

2 lb (1 kg) veal shoulder, boned and trimmed of all fat
1 oz (25 g) goose fat
10 cloves garlic
⅓ cup (2 oz/50 g) untoasted dried breadcrumbs
1 lb (500 g) ripe tomatoes, quartered
½ teaspoon sugar
salt and freshly ground pepper

❖Cut the meat into 1½-in (4-cm) cubes. Melt the goose fat in a nonstick 10-in (26-cm) sauté pan and lightly brown the veal over moderate heat for about 5 minutes, stirring constantly. Remove with a slotted spoon and set aside. Add the garlic and breadcrumbs to the sauté pan and cook, stirring, until golden brown. Add the tomatoes, sugar, salt and pepper. Return the meat to the sauté pan, stir well and bring to simmer. Cover and cook over low heat for 2 hours, stirring two or three times.

❖Remove the meat with a slotted spoon and transfer to a shallow dish; keep warm. Puree the sauce through the medium holes of a food mill, or use a processor. Pour over the meat and serve immediately.

SERVES 4

Auvergne

FALETTE
Stuffed Breast of Veal

A specialty of Auvergne, this dish is delicious served hot with braised cabbage or sautéed potatoes, or cold with a dandelion and walnut salad. It can also be made from breast of pork, in which case it is called fraude.

1½ lb (750 g) beet greens, Swiss chard or silverbeet
6 tablespoons milk
2 oz (50 g) stale bread, crusts trimmed
5 oz (150 g) fresh pork belly, finely chopped
1 clove garlic, finely chopped
1 tablespoon chopped flat-leaf parsley
1 tablespoon chopped fresh chervil
2 tablespoons cognac
salt and freshly ground pepper
6 pinches of freshly grated nutmeg
2 eggs
3½ lb (1.75 kg) breast of veal, boned and trimmed of all fat
3 oz (100 g) fresh pork rind, trimmed of all fat
bouquet garni: 1 bay leaf, 1 sprig thyme, 10 sprigs parsley
2 tablespoons vegetable oil
1 oz (25 g) butter
1 onion, about 3 oz (100 g), thinly sliced
1 medium carrot, washed and thinly sliced
6 tablespoons dry white wine
¾ cup (6 fl oz/200 ml) chicken stock (recipe page 34)

❖Wash the beet greens and place in a pot with the water clinging to the leaves. Cover and cook over high heat for 4 minutes. Drain the greens and chop finely with a knife.

PETER JOHNSON

VEAL WITH GARLIC (top left), STUFFED BREAST OF VEAL (bottom) AND VEAL ROLLS (top right, recipe page 176)

Bring the milk to boil in a small saucepan. Crumble in the bread. Remove from heat and stir to form a smooth paste. In a bowl, mix the pork belly, garlic, parsley, chervil, cognac, bread paste and beet greens. Season with salt, pepper and nutmeg. Blend in the eggs.

❖Season the veal with salt and pepper. Spread on a work surface and arrange the stuffing lengthwise down the middle. Roll the meat around the stuffing and tie at intervals with kitchen thread.

❖Blanch the pork rind in boiling water to cover for 2 minutes. Drain and cut into ¾-in (2-cm) squares. Tie together the herbs for the bouquet garni.

❖Heat the oil in a heavy pot just large enough to hold the rolled veal. Add the butter and brown the meat on all sides. Remove the meat and discard the cooking fat. Add the onion and carrot to the pot and cook, stirring, for 5 minutes. Return the meat to the pot and pour in the wine and stock. Add the pork rind and bouquet garni; season with salt and pepper. Cover and cook over very low heat for 2 hours.

❖Transfer the meat to a serving plate. Surround it with the pork rind, onion and carrot. Boil the cooking liquid until reduced to a syrupy consistency and pour over the meat. Serve immediately.

SERVES 6–7

Provence
PAUPIETTES
Veal Rolls

The term paupiette *originally referred to a thin slice of veal rolled around some kind of stuffing and tied with string. It was subsequently applied to slices of beef, cabbage leaves or fillets of fish used in the same way.*

12 veal scallops (escalopes), 3 oz (80 g) each
salt and freshly ground pepper
7 oz (200 g) black olives, pitted
7 oz (200 g) cooked ham, finely chopped
2 cloves garlic, finely chopped
2 tablespoons chopped flat-leaf parsley
4 pinches of freshly grated nutmeg
2 tablespoons olive oil
1 oz (25 g) butter
¾ cup (6 fl oz/200 ml) dry white wine

❖Pound the veal scallops until very thin. Season with salt and pepper.
❖Drop the olives into boiling water and blanch for 2 minutes. Refresh them under running water and drain. Finely chop half the olives; halve the remainder.
❖In a bowl mix the ham, chopped olives, garlic, parsley, pepper and nutmeg. Lay one veal scallop on a work surface and spread 1/12 of the mixture to within ⅜ in (1 cm) of the edges. Roll up starting from a narrow end. Tie the roll with kitchen thread. Repeat with the remaining ingredients to produce 12 *paupiettes*.
❖Heat the oil in a heavy 4-qt (4-l) pot. Add the butter and let it melt. Brown the rolls on all sides in two or three batches. Return all the rolls to the pot. Pour in the wine and boil for 1 minute to evaporate the alcohol. Cover and cook over very low heat for 1½ hours, stirring several times.
❖Remove the rolls from the pot and keep warm. Add the remaining olives to the pot and cook for 2 minutes.
❖Remove the strings from the rolls. Reheat the rolls for 5 minutes in the sauce, then arrange on a serving platter. Pour the olive sauce over and serve immediately.

SERVES 6 *Photograph page 175*

Ile de France
VEAU MARENGO
Veal Marengo

On the evening of June 14, 1880, Napoleon defeated the Austrians at Marengo. As the Emperor's cook, Dunand, was organizing the provisions, he improvised a chicken dish, dressing the bird with white wine, garlic, tomatoes and cognac and thus inventing Chicken Marengo. The recipe has since been adapted to shoulder of veal.

2½ lb (1.2 kg) veal shoulder, trimmed of bones and fat
bouquet garni: 1 bay leaf, 1 sprig thyme, 6 sprigs parsley
1 tablespoon vegetable oil
1 oz (30 g) butter
1 medium carrot, peeled and finely chopped
2 onions, about 3 oz (100 g) each, finely chopped
1 tablespoon all purpose (plain) flour
2 cloves garlic, halved
¾ cup (6 fl oz/200 ml) dry white wine

¾ cup (6 fl oz/200 ml) chicken stock (recipe page 34)
¾ cup (6 fl oz/200 ml) tomato puree
salt and freshly ground pepper
1 lemon
1 tablespoon chopped fresh parsley
1 tablespoon chopped fresh tarragon
To garnish:
24 small pickling onions
8 oz (250 g) small (button) mushrooms
1 oz (25 g) butter

❖Cut the meat into 2-in (5-cm) cubes. Tie together the herbs of the bouquet garni.
❖Heat the oil in a nonstick 11-in (28-cm) sauté pan. Add the butter and let melt. Add the meat, carrot and onions and cook over high heat, stirring, for 5 minutes or until lightly browned. Sprinkle with flour and cook, stirring, for 1 minute longer. Add the garlic and bouquet garni, then the white wine. Boil over high heat until reduced by half, then pour in the stock and the tomato puree (the meat should be covered with liquid; if necessary, add a little more stock or water). Season with salt and pepper and bring to boil. Cover and cook over low heat for 1 hour.
❖Meanwhile, prepare the garnish: peel the pickling onions. Trim the mushroom stems, wash the mushrooms and pat dry. Melt the butter in a nonstick 10-in (26-cm) skillet and cook the onions until golden, about 5 minutes, stirring frequently. Remove with a slotted spoon and set aside. Add the mushrooms to the pan and cook until they are golden and give out no more liquid. Set aside with the onions.
❖Wash the lemon and wipe dry. Finely grate half the rind. Halve the lemon and squeeze 1 tablespoon of juice. Stir the onion-mushroom mixture and grated lemon rind into the sauté pan. Cover and cook gently for 45 minutes longer.
❖When the meat is cooked, stir in the lemon juice, parsley and tarragon. Discard the bouquet garni. Remove from heat and turn into a shallow dish. Serve immediately.

SERVES 6 *Photograph pages 152 – 153*

Bourgogne
ROGNONS À LA MOUTARDE
Veal Kidneys in Mustard Sauce

The seeds of a Mediterranean plant are used to make mustard. The vinegar-and-mustard makers guild was formed in Orléans at the end of the sixteenth century, and in Dijon in 1630, to establish rules for its manufacture. Today, verjuice and white wine are added to Dijon mustard; in Meaux, the seeds are coarsely crushed; in Orléans vinegar is added; and in Bordeaux grape must is used.

2 veal kidneys
salt and freshly ground pepper
6 tablespoons heavy (double) cream or crème fraîche
2 tablespoons strong mustard
1 tablespoon vegetable oil
1 oz (25 g) butter
2 French shallots, finely chopped
⅔ cup (5 fl oz/150 ml) dry white wine

❖Ask the butcher to remove the fat from the kidneys. Season them with salt and pepper. Mix the cream and mustard in a bowl.

VEAL KIDNEYS IN MUSTARD SAUCE

❖Heat the oil in a nonstick 10-in (26-cm) sauté pan. Add the butter and let melt. Add the shallots and kidneys and brown the kidneys on all sides, about 5 minutes. Pour in the wine, cover and simmer for 10 minutes, turning the kidneys over after 5 minutes.

❖Remove the kidneys and keep warm. Strain the cooking juices into a saucepan and boil until reduced to 3 table-spoons.

❖Meanwhile, thinly slice the kidneys and divide among 4 heated plates. Pour the juices that escape during slicing into the saucepan. Add the mustard mixture and boil over high heat until the sauce becomes thick and creamy, about 1 minute. Pour over the kidneys and serve immediately.

SERVES 4

Picardie

PORC AUX DEUX POMMES
Pork with Potatoes and Apples

2 lb (1 kg) pork fillet or shoulder, boned and trimmed of fat
salt and freshly ground pepper
1 tablespoon vegetable oil
2 oz (50 g) butter
1 lb (500 g) very small new potatoes, peeled
¾ cup (6 fl oz/200 ml) water
1 lb (500 g) Golden Delicious apples

❖Ask the butcher to tie the meat at intervals. Season with salt and pepper. Heat the oil in an oval pot in which the meat will fit comfortably. Add half the butter and brown the meat on all sides. Remove the meat, add the potatoes to the pot and sauté until golden, about 3 to 4 minutes, turning them over from time to time. Return the meat to the pot, add the water and bring to simmer. Cover and sim-mer for 1½ hours, turning the meat and potatoes several times.

❖About 20 minutes before the end of the cooking time, peel, quarter and core the apples. Cut each quarter into 3 slices. Melt the remaining butter in a nonstick 11-in (28-cm) skillet and cook the apple slices until golden, about 8

minutes, turning them over after 4 minutes. Keep warm.
❖When the meat is cooked, transfer it to a serving platter. Surround with the potatoes and apple slices and serve.

SERVES 4

Bretagne

PORC AU LAIT
Pork Cooked in Milk

1 pork fillet, about 3 lb (1.5 kg), boned and trimmed of fat
salt and freshly ground pepper
4 cloves garlic
1 oz (25 g) butter
1 qt (1 l) whole milk
2 sprigs thyme
1 bay leaf, cut into 4 pieces
4 sprigs parsley, lightly crushed
6 pinches of freshly grated nutmeg

❖Ask the butcher to tie the meat at intervals. Season with salt and pepper. Peel 2 cloves of garlic and cut into fine slivers. Make slits all over the meat and insert the slivers of garlic.

❖Melt the butter in an oval pot just large enough to hold the pork fillet. Brown the meat on all sides. Remove the meat, discard the cooking fat and wipe out the pot. Return the fillet to the pot and cover with milk. Surround it with the thyme, the bay leaf pieces, the parsley and 2 whole garlic cloves, lightly bruised. Season with salt and pepper and add the nutmeg. Bring to the boil over low heat and cook for 2 hours, covered, at a slow simmer, turning the meat over several times.

❖After this time, the meat should be very tender and covered with a golden sauce, reduced and slightly curdled. Transfer to a heated plate. Remove the herbs and garlic from the sauce and puree the sauce in a blender until smooth. Pour into a sauceboat and serve immediately.

SERVES 6

PORK WITH POTATOES AND APPLES (top) AND PORK COOKED IN MILK (bottom)

Lorraine

ÉCHINE À LA BIÈRE
Pork Cooked in Beer

The north and the east, being the two greatest beer-producing areas of France, use beer in their cuisine just as wine is used by the Bordelais. It gives excellent results, producing some very tasty dishes.

2 lb (1 kg) chine of pork or pork shoulder, boned and trimmed of fat
salt and freshly ground pepper
bouquet garni: 1 bay leaf, 1 sprig thyme, 6 sprigs parsley
1 oz (25 g) butter
1½ lb (750 g) onions, thinly sliced
½ teaspoon sugar
½ cup (2 oz/50 g) dried white breadcrumbs
2 cups (16 fl oz/500 ml) beer

❖ Ask the butcher to tie the piece of pork with string to secure it in one piece. Season with salt and pepper. Tie together the herbs for the bouquet garni.

❖ Melt the butter in an oval pot large enough to hold the meat comfortably. Add the meat and brown on all sides, then remove it and set aside. Add the onions to the pot and cook until golden, about 3 to 4 minutes. Stir in the sugar and breadcrumbs and cook, stirring, for 2 minutes longer or until the mixture is golden brown. Place the meat on the bed of onions, pour in the beer and bring to boil. Cover and simmer for 1¾ hours, turning the meat over several times.

❖ Transfer the meat to a serving dish and surround with onions. Boil the cooking juices over high heat until syrupy, then pour over the onions. Serve immediately.

SERVES 4   *Photograph pages 6 – 7*

Languedoc

CASSOULET
Toulouse Casserole

The word cassoulet *comes from* cassole, *the name of the glazed earthenware dish in which the* cassoulet *is gratinéed.*
The main ingredient is haricot beans (originally brought to France from Spain in the sixteenth century), which must be local — either from Cazères or from Pamiers — and must have been picked within the year. To these are added different meats, according to the area.
This version is the simplest, and perhaps the oldest, and originated in Castelnaudary. Carcassonne cooks add leg of lamb, and partridge when it is in season; Toulouse cooks add Toulouse sausage, leg of lamb and confit; *pigs' tails are added in Limoux, chitterlings in Mas d'Azil, and stuffed goose neck and* confit *in Périgord.*

1½ lb (750 g) dried haricot (white) beans
1 lb (500 g) lightly salted pork belly
8 oz (250 g) fresh pork rind, trimmed of all fat
1 lb (500 g) Toulouse (coarse-textured) sausage
1 unsmoked kielbasa (boiling sausage)
8 cloves garlic
1 teaspoon dried thyme
salt and freshly ground pepper

1½ lb (750 g) fresh pork tenderloin (fillet), bones removed and reserved
bouquet garni: 1 bay leaf, 1 sprig thyme, 6 sprigs parsley
13 oz (400 g) ripe tomatoes
8 oz (250 g) onions
2 cloves
2 leeks, white and tender green parts only, washed and thinly sliced
6 oz (200 g) goose fat
3 tablespoons dried white breadcrumbs

❖ Place the beans in a pot and cover with plenty of cold water. Let soak for 4 hours.

❖ Parboil the pork belly and pork rind in water to cover for 5 minutes, then rinse and drain. Cut the pork rind into strips 1¼ in (3 cm) wide. Roll the strips over themselves and secure with kitchen thread. Prick the sausages with a fork to keep them from bursting during cooking.

❖ Peel 2 cloves of garlic and cut each into 6 slivers. Mix the thyme, salt, pepper and garlic slivers. Make 12 slits in the surface of the pork tenderloin and slip a piece of garlic into each. Tie together the herbs for the bouquet garni.

❖ Drop the tomatoes into boiling water for 10 seconds. Cool under running water, peel, halve and squeeze out the seeds; coarsely chop the flesh. Peel 4 cloves of garlic and chop finely. Peel the onions; stud one with cloves and finely chop the remainder.

❖ Drain the beans, discarding the soaking water. Return them to the pot and cover with 3 qt (3 l) of cold water. Add the pork belly, leeks, clove-studded onion, bouquet garni, pork rind and the bone from the pork tenderloin and bring to boil over very low heat. Simmer for 1½ hours.

❖ Meanwhile, melt 3 oz (100 g) goose fat in a heavy pot large enough to hold the tenderloin, and brown it on all sides. Remove and set aside. Add the chopped onions to the pot and cook over low heat until golden, about 5 minutes, stirring with a wooden spoon. Add the chopped garlic and cook, stirring, for 2 minutes. Add the tomatoes and cook for 3 minutes longer. Season with salt and pepper. Return the meat to the pot, cover and cook over low heat for 1 hour.

❖ Remove the meat and add it with the cooking liquid to the beans. Add the sausages and cook for 30 minutes longer.

❖ Preheat oven to 375°F (190°C). Remove the meats from the pot and carve into ¼-in (.5-cm) slices. Remove the thread from the rolls of pork rind and cut them into 1¼ x ¼-in (3 x .5-cm) strips. Discard the onion and bouquet garni.

❖ Halve the remaining 2 cloves of garlic and rub over the inside of a large casserole. Spread a layer of beans on the bottom; cover with a layer of mixed meats. Continue to layer the ingredients, finishing with a layer of beans. Melt the remaining goose fat and pour over the surface. Sprinkle with the breadcrumbs and bake for 1½ hours. Serve directly from the casserole.

SERVES 8 – 10

Alsace

BAECKEOFFE
Baked Meat and Potatoes

The word baeckeoffe *in the dialect of Alsace means baker's oven, and in fact this tasty mixture of meat and vegetables used to be cooked in the baker's oven.*

Once a week, on washing day, the women of Alsace would carry their stewpots to the bakery, and when he had finished making bread for the day the baker would leave their marvelous stews to simmer for many hours in his oven.

1½ lb (750 g) pork shoulder, without bones
1½ lb (750 g) lamb shoulder, without bones
1½ lb (750 g) beef flank, without bones
10 oz (300 g) onions, thinly sliced
8 oz (250 g) carrots, thinly sliced
2 cloves garlic
1 sprig fresh thyme, leaves only
1 bay leaf, broken in half
10 sprigs fresh parsley, bruised
2 cloves
10 peppercorns
salt
2 cups white wine, preferably Riesling or Sylvaner
3 lb (1.5 kg) baking potatoes
⅔ cup (2½ oz/75 g) all purpose (plain) flour

❖Cut the meats into 1½-in (4-cm) cubes and place in a large bowl with the onions and carrots. Peel the garlic cloves and crush with the hand or the side of a cleaver. Add to the bowl with the thyme leaves, bay leaf, parsley, cloves, peppercorns and salt. Pour the wine over and stir. Cover and refrigerate for 12 hours, turning the meats often.
❖Preheat oven to 375°F (190°C). Peel and wash the potatoes; cut into ¼-in (.5-cm) slices. Drain the meat, reserving the vegetable marinade.
❖Arrange a layer of potatoes in a 2-qt (2-l) flameproof earthenware pot with tight-fitting lid. Scatter some of the vegetables from the marinade over the potatoes, then add a layer of meat. Continue alternating layers of meat and potatoes, finishing with potatoes. Pour the marinade over the potatoes.
❖In a small bowl, mix the flour with enough water to produce a smooth, thick paste. Roll into a long, thin sausage shape and lay it around the edge of the pot. Place the lid firmly on the pot, pressing down to ensure a perfect seal. (This operation, called *lutage*, seals the lid so that no evaporation can take place.) Bake for 3 hours.
❖Remove the pot from the oven and break the circle of pastry. Remove the lid and carry the pot straight to the table. Serve hot.

SERVES 8   *Photograph pages 6 – 7*

Alsace

CHOUCROUTE
Sauerkraut with Pork and Sausages

The word comes from the Alsatian dialect term sûrkrût, *which in turn is derived from the German* sauerkraut, *meaning sour herb.*
Choucroute is white cabbage that has been shredded, salted

and fermented and put into wooden barrels or large stone pots. It is served in Alsace and Lorraine, and in some parts of Germany, and is used in stews containing potatoes, salted and smoked pork, and regional charcuterie *products.*

1½ lb (750 g) lightly salted pork shoulder, without bone
2 lb (1 kg) raw sauerkraut
3 cloves garlic
1 bay leaf
3 cloves
1 tablespoon juniper berries
1 teaspoon mixed black and white peppercorns
3 oz (100 g) lard
1 onion, about 3 oz (100 g), finely chopped
2 cups white wine, preferably Riesling or Sylvaner
1 cup (8 fl oz/250 ml) chicken stock (recipe page 34)
1 lb (500 g) smoked bacon
1 lb (500 g) fresh pork belly
1 smoked kielbasa (boiling sausage), about 1 lb (500 g)
6 Strasbourg sausages or frankfurters
1½ lb (750 g) boiling potatoes

❖Parboil the pork shoulder in water to cover for 5 minutes, then cool under running water and drain. Thoroughly wash the sauerkraut under running water and drain. Crush the cloves of garlic with the hand or the side of a cleaver and tie in a square of cheesecloth with the bay leaf, cloves, juniper berries and peppercorns.
❖Melt the lard in a heavy 6-qt (6-l) pot and cook the onion until golden, about 3 minutes, stirring with a wooden spoon. Add the sauerkraut and cook for 5 minutes longer, separating the strands with two forks. Pour in the wine and stock and mix well. Bury the pork shoulder and spice bag in the middle of the sauerkraut. Cover and cook over very low heat for 1½ hours.
❖Add the bacon and pork belly to the sauerkraut, burying them as well, and cook for 1 hour longer.
❖Meanwhile, prick the boiling sausage with a fork to keep it from bursting during cooking. Boil the Strasbourg sausages for 1 minute; let stand in the hot water. Peel and wash the potatoes.
❖Add the boiling sausage to the pot. Place the potatoes on top, cover and cook for 1 hour. About 10 minutes before the end of the cooking time, lay the Strasbourg sausages on top of the potatoes to reheat.
❖Arrange a mound of sauerkraut on a platter and surround with the meat, sausages and potatoes. Serve very hot.

SERVES 6   *Photograph pages 6 – 7*

Périgord

PORC AUX CHÂTAIGNES
Pork with Chestnuts

1 pork fillet, about 2 lb (1 kg), boned and trimmed of fat
salt and freshly ground pepper
1 tablespoon vegetable oil
1 oz (25 g) butter
4 cloves garlic, peeled
3 tablespoons white vermouth
½ teaspoon sugar
6 tablespoons water
1½ lb (750 g) chestnuts

❖Ask the butcher to tie the pork fillet at intervals. Season with salt and pepper.

❖Heat the oil in an oval pot in which the meat will fit comfortably. Add half the butter and the garlic, and brown the meat on all sides.

❖Remove the meat and garlic and discard the cooking fat. Add the vermouth and sugar, and boil over high heat until slightly reduced, scraping up browned bits with a wooden spoon. Return the meat to the pot and turn it over in the liquid. Add the garlic and water and bring to simmer. Cover and cook over low heat for 45 minutes, turning the meat over twice.

❖Meanwhile, make a slash on the flat side of each chestnut. Bring a large saucepan of water to boil. Drop in the chestnuts and boil for 5 minutes. Drain, then shell and remove the brown skin that covers each chestnut.

❖Add the chestnuts to the pot and cook for 45 minutes longer, turning both meat and chestnuts several times.

❖When the meat is cooked, transfer it to a serving plate and surround with chestnuts. Add the remaining butter to the sauce in the pot and stir until it melts. Pour sauce over the chestnuts and serve immediately.

SERVES 4

Périgord/Picardie

PORC AUX PRUNEAUX
Pork with Prunes

1 pork fillet, about 2 lb (1 kg), boned and trimmed of fat
salt
1 bay leaf, crushed

30 prunes
8 walnuts
3 oz (100 g) lean bacon
2 French shallots, finely chopped
4 leaves dried sage
4 tablespoons dry white wine
freshly ground pepper
1 tablespoon vegetable oil

❖Ask the butcher to tie the pork fillet at intervals. Rub the salt and the bay leaf over the pork. Remove the pits from 10 prunes and chop them. Coarsely grate the nuts, using a cylindrical grater with large holes. Remove the rind from the bacon. Finely chop the bacon and cook with the shallots in a nonstick 9-in (22-cm) skillet, stirring often, until lightly browned, about 5 minutes. Remove from heat. Crumble in the sage leaves and add the pepper, grated walnuts, 1 tablespoon wine and the chopped prunes.

❖Pit the remaining 20 prunes, making a single slit in the side. Fill each with a small mound of the stuffing and close the prune over the stuffing. To stuff the roast, make two cuts through the center in the shape of an "X" and make shallow crisscross cuts over the whole surface of the meat. Stuff the meat with the remaining prune mixture, pushing it well in so that the stuffing is not visible from the outside.

❖Lightly oil an oval baking dish just large enough to hold the pork surrounded by the stuffed prunes. Oil the meat and place it in the dish. Place the dish in the oven. Heat the oven to 425°F (215°C) and roast the pork for 30 minutes, then surround the meat with the prunes and pour the remaining wine over them. Reduce the heat to 375°F (190°C) and roast for 1 hour longer. Transfer the roast to a platter, surround with prunes and serve.

SERVES 4

PORK WITH CHESTNUTS (bottom) AND PORK WITH PRUNES (top)

FROM CHARENTES TO THE BASQUE COUNTRY

A joyous accent

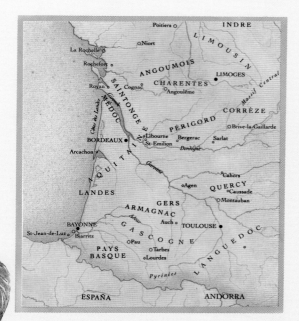

FROM CHARENTES TO THE BASQUE COUNTRY

A joyous accent

This is a country that sings and dances. It is green, undulating, isolated behind its high forests or modest in the shadow of its châteaux. In the southwest there are many reminders of its rich history: separated from the kingdom of France, for three centuries ruled by the Plantagenet dynasty from the time of the marriage of Eleanor of Aquitaine with Henry II, the future king of Great Britain. The provinces of Guyenne, Gascony, Périgord and Saintonge were its vassals; thus were woven enduring ties with England. At Bordeaux, on the wharves of Les Chartrons, oak barrels full of "claret" leave for the port of London. In the Charente, the names of the cognac houses have English connotations. In Périgord, the *bastides* — villages transformed into fortresses — had, by the thirteenth century, become props for the English crown in the Capetian kingdom.

The cuisine amongst all this? It is a solid inheritance, artful, proud of its assets. Almost everywhere, but principally in the Landes of Upper Gascony, in the Périgord and the adjacent Quercy, one is in the kingdom of foie gras, of duck "steaks" (*magrets*), of preserved goose and duck — the birds, fattened on corn, disport themselves in liberty on the fertile soil.

And the whole region is the domain of noble wines and spirits — not only the great vintages of the Gironde, Médoc, Graves, Pomerol and Saint-Emilion, but also *eaux de vie*, distilled in copper alembics by a system of double distillation known as the *double repasse charentaise*. The Saint-Emilion

LEFT: ARTISANS MAKING WINE BARRELS AT THE TONNELLERIE DEMPTOS IN ST-EMILION.

PREVIOUS PAGES: BEYNAC-ET-CAZENAC, A THIRTEENTH-CENTURY CHÂTEAU ON THE DORDOGNE RIVER, COMMANDS A SPECTACULAR VIEW OVER THE TOWN OF LA ROQUE-GAGEAC.
LEO MEIER

THE MAIN SEAPORT OF CHARENTES-MARITIMES, LA ROCHELLE BOASTS ONE OF THE MOST PICTURESQUE HARBORS ON THE ATLANTIC COAST.

them slowly and lovingly in their own fat, then storing them in earthenware pots, is applied to the goose and duck, and also to chicken and even pork. The custom is said to date from the time of the Moorish invasions, but just as important as its historic character is its tenderizing effect, giving the meat a more subtle taste. Potatoes cooked in the style of Sarlat, with garlic, are the standard accompaniment.

Pâté of foie gras is only one of the many forms — a privileged one, to be sure — of the local pâtés, which might equally be based on partridges or chicken livers. The old guard of the Périgord like the traditional way of preparing foie gras, believing that it matures very well in its shiny tins. The truffle is also used in many of the variously shaped terrines. This "black diamond" belongs to a rare variety of fungi, concealed beneath the shady oak trees, which produces a network of white threads — the mycelium —at the soil's surface, so that it can be recognized. People have attributed aphrodisiacal qualities to the truffle, and it must be said that its perfume is one of the most intoxicating imaginable. And this perfume enhances countless dishes in the form of truffle juice, or thin shavings, or more substantial portions. In scrambled eggs or a simple salad, the truffle (supposedly from Périgord, but those found in Provence, and sold at the markets of Tricastin, share the same name) works wonders.

It is difficult to separate the riches of the Périgord from those of its near neighbor, the Quercy. The handsome dwellings of the Périgord seem to confront the more dilapidated houses of Quercy. But the Black Périgord, which follows the course of the Vézère through its snakelike meanderings, encircling belvederes (like that of Domme) alongside the Dordogne, is not to be confused with the Quercy of the *causses*, chalky plateaus of which the best known is that of Gramat.

Here, as there, are high-perched villages of brown stone which take on golden tones from the setting sun; and olive-tinted roofs; and flocks of geese and ducks parading through the fields. The villages of Autoire and Loubressac, of Carennac and Fénélon, in Quercy, are the distant cousins of those others, more splendid, of Beynac-et-Cazenac, la Roque-Gageac and, above all, Sarlat, the proud and high-born city of Périgord.

Périgord, like Quercy, is the realm of the walnut; here ancient mills produce a velvety, pure and aromatic oil. In both regions, the queen of the pâtisserie is the *pastis*, made from a paper-thin pastry and flavored with apples and Armagnac. It has a strong similarity to the Moroccan *bstilla* — demonstrating, in the same way as does the *confit*, the influence of the passage through the region by the Moors. The method is simple: a noodle dough, made with flour, vanilla sugar, salt, eggs and water, is kneaded the night before, then very gently stretched out over long tables to produce the thinnest pastry possible.

grape is used in the Charentes, the Colombard at Cognac, the Folle blanche or the Ugni blanc in Armagnac. These "waters of life," aged in oak barrels encircled by bands of iron, have a soft, silky texture and the wonderful fragrance of mature plums.

Of all the regions of the Southwest, the Périgord is undoubtedly the one which has best preserved its traditions. One sees history itself in the golden stone of the villages of the region known as the Black Périgord, centered on Sarlat; the chalky white stone of Nontron, at Bourdeilles; the rustic charm of the "green" Périgord, from the waters of the Dronne which laps Bourdeilles, the ancient town of Saint-Jean-de-Cole; the markets of Bergerac and Thiviers; the noble mansions of Trémolat, Saint-Léon-sur-Vézère; the countless caves of Les Eyzies-de-Tayac, world capital of prehistory; the châteaux of Beynac, Castelnaud, and Puyguilhem; the abbeys of Saint-Cyprien, Cadouin and Brantôme.

The older people here wear berets, and walk with canes; they sit in their armchairs beside the fire and shell chestnuts and walnuts. Traditional ingredients abound, and end up in dishes that bring the aroma of the whole country to the tastebuds: stuffed goose neck, preserved goose and duck *confits*, foie gras and truffles. The time-honored practice of preserving meats by cooking

LEO MEIER

PLAYING *BOULES*, WHERE THE AIM IS TO TOSS A HEAVY METAL BALL AS CLOSE AS POSSIBLE TO THE SMALL CENTRAL BALL. FAVORED BY FRENCHMEN OF ALL AGES, INCLUDING THIS GROUP IN BERGERAC, *BOULES* IS WITHOUT A DOUBT FRANCE'S MOST POPULAR GAME.

Soule, in the middle of the Pyrenees, past the green hills of Labourdine, with their white cottages with green and red painted wood panels and high-pitched roofs.

The air of the region is also the salty air of the old fishing port of Saint-Jean-de-Luz, where the boats unload their cargoes of tuna, baby eels, shad, hake and *louvines*, the local species of bass; of the waterfalls near the fresh waters of the Nive; and of the alleys of Saint-Jean-Pied-de-Port, capital of the interior.

Adding to the Basque country's allure is Bayonne ham, raw, salted, dried and rubbed with red peppers; *tourons*, tiny treats of delicately tinted and decorated almond paste; macaroons; chocolate caramels known as *kanouga*; pure chocolate originally imported by the Spanish Jews; the local *gâteau basque*, made with eggs, sugar and flour, flavored with rum and enriched with fruits such as black cherries or dried apricots.

The flavor of the region? It comes from the pimento, or red pepper. Grown in the charming village of Espelette, this sweet red pepper turns up in every dish: the black pudding called *tripoxa*, peppers stuffed with cod, the *pipérade*, which is nothing other than eggs scrambled with cooked peppers and tomatoes. And also in the sauces that accompany shrimp and fish from the gulf of Saint-Jean-de-Luz, and in the fish soup, the slow-cooked *ttorro* of the fishermen.

And more again: bull beef, very red and very tough, which is eaten in Bayonne on the evenings of the *corridas*; the *palombes*, or ring-doves, that are hunted in autumn in the valley of the Aldudes, in a totally preserved landscape, green and mountainous, dotted with little cabins called *palombières*; Pyrenees lamb, naturally raised, its flesh aromatic and juicy; the salmon which returns to the river of the Adour, and which is simply grilled and accompanied by a bearnaise sauce; the *piballes*, the baby eels that are caught in bad weather and cooked with garlic and peppers, *à la basquaise*; the strong wine of Irouléguy; the fruit spirits made from plums and pears from the orchards around Saint-Etienne-de-Baïgorry; the robust green Izarra or the softer, yellow version, resulting from the maceration of mountain herbs; ewe's milk cheese, with a grassy, hazelnut flavor.

Perhaps you've had enough — but now you will believe anyone who tells you how exciting it is, this Basque country, the most southerly of the small regions of the great southwest.

VEGETABLES

A garden of Eden

LEO MEIER

NO OTHER VEGETABLE IS USED SO OFTEN IN FRENCH REGIONAL CUISINE AS THE POTATO, AND IT
APPEARS MOST OFTEN IN NORTHERN AND CENTRAL FRENCH COOKING.

VEGETABLES

A garden of Eden

France is one large garden, lavishly planted from north to south. Large-scale farming, glasshouse culture, market gardens: these are the sources of some splendid ingredients.

There is nothing more agreeable than to choose one's vegetables at the Marché d'Intérêt National, situated at Rungis. To the great regret of those who enjoy strolling around the capital, Rungis has replaced the old and venerated market of Les Halles, with its decorative ironwork designed by the architect Baltard. In this world of concrete and galvanized iron, the professional — restaurateur or wholesaler of fruit and vegetables — comes in search of the best of the best. Purple artichokes from Provence, cabbages from Alsace and the Auvergne, endives from Flanders, beans from Poitou, broad beans from Aquitaine, peas from Vendée, potatoes from Ile-de-France: all are here, according to season, and they do not even begin to exhaust the enormous richness of the French vegetable garden.

Each vegetable speaks for a region. The zucchini, pepper and olive evoke the markets of Provence and the Côte d'Azur. The market of Forville, at Cannes, bears witness to the prodigality of this land of sunshine. Brittany has elected as king and queen the artichoke and the potato. The sweet

pepper is the glory of the Basque village of Espelette. And if beets belong to the north, cardoons — fine-flavored but stringy cousins of the artichoke that are eaten as a gratin and with beef marrow — are part of the territory of Lyons.

The noble asparagus is found as readily in Sologne, at Vineuil, as it is in the Lubéron at Pertuis, in Alsace at Village-Neuf or Hoerdt, in the Val de Loire near Chinon. Anyone willing to trade it for the "common" leek would be delighted to discover that the latter is, in fact, just as rich in possibilities as its better-born neighbor.

Behind one vegetable is often hidden another. Cabbage, Savoy cabbage, white cabbage, red cabbage, green cabbage, Brussels sprouts, sauerkraut cabbage: a vegetable with a thousand uses. Artichokes — stewed *à la barigoule*; in vinaigrette, first the leaves savored and finally the heart; the bases, or *fonds*, garnishing a pâté de foie gras. Or a combination of vegetables — a bouquet of peas, baby carrots, onions, turnips and green beans epitomizing spring, ratatouille and exquisitely stuffed vegetables symbolizing Provence. Vegetables to be eaten as fritters, pan-fried, flavored with onion, garlic, fresh herbs, butter or oil; vegetables to be fried, roasted, simmered, braised — in a bain-marie, in a cast-iron casserole, in the oven.

PREVIOUS PAGES: BRAISED ARTICHOKES (left, recipe page 204),
RATATOUILLE (center, recipe page 195), AND TOMATOES, PROVENÇAL-STYLE
(right, recipe page 195), PHOTOGRAPHED IN PROVENCE.
PIERRE HUSSENOT/AGENCE TOP

LEO MEIER

SHOPPING FOR FRESH VEGETABLES AND FRUIT IN FRANCE IS NOT A SOLITARY STROLL
DOWN A SUPERMARKET AISLE, IT IS A RITUAL OF DAILY LIFE.

THE IDEAL WAY TO PREPARE *LACTAIRES DÉLICIEUSES*, THE MOST COMMON MUSHROOM IN PROVENCE, IS TO SAUTÉ THEM *À LA PROVENÇAL* — IN OLIVE OIL WITH CHOPPED GARLIC, PARSLEY AND A SQUEEZE OF LEMON.

A CAREFULLY TENDED GARDEN LIKE THIS ONE IN THE LOIRE VALLEY WILL YIELD THE MOST BEAUTIFUL FLOWERS AND SUCCULENT VEGETABLES.

What fine and wholesome vegetables they are! Alone, they might constitute a whole meal: witness the *aligot* of the Aubrac, a creamy-smooth potato puree flavored with garlic and blended with the fresh local cheese, which is turned over and over, drawn out with the spoon, and is enough in itself; the *truffade* of Auvergne; a dish of lentils enriched with cubes of salt pork; cabbage filled with a succulent stuffing. In countless traditional dishes, vegetables are the central element; they give the dish its flavor, its unity, its *raison d'être*. In the Middle Ages they were somewhat neglected, and the nineteenth century practically stifled them under a heap of over-refined sauces. Nouvelle cuisine has restored vegetables to a position of honor, recommending cooks to make the most of their healthful variety.

Some chefs abused the craze for baby vegetables and for mousses more appropriate to infants. Other chefs have been able to extract new accents from beets, snow and sugar-snap peas, celery, turnips (exquisite when served as *confits*, coated with a sweet glaze), endive with its hint of sweetness, even the simple potato, which give an unexpected lift to the most classical preparations of meat and fish. Indeed, if today we had to do without these fine fresh vegetables, we would be wondering what was happening to the *grande cuisine française*.

Provence

TOMATES À LA PROVENÇALE
Tomatoes, Provençal-style

6 large, firm-ripe tomatoes, about 7 oz (200 g) each
2 cloves garlic, finely chopped
2 tablespoons chopped flat-leaf parsley
5 tablespoons olive oil
salt and freshly ground pepper
1 tablespoon sugar

❖Preheat oven to 425°F (215°C). Wash the tomatoes and halve horizontally. Remove the seeds with a small spoon. Combine the garlic and parsley.
❖Lightly oil a baking dish large enough to hold the tomato halves in a single layer. Arrange the tomatoes in the dish, cut side up. Drizzle with the remaining oil and sprinkle with the garlic mixture, salt, pepper and sugar.
❖Bake the tomatoes for 1 hour. Serve hot.

SERVES 4   *Photograph pages 190 – 191*

Provence

RATATOUILLE
Ratatouille

Although it is often called ratatouille niçoise, *this is a summer favorite not only in the Nice area but all along the Mediterranean coast.*

2 red peppers (capsicums), about 7 oz (200 g) each
10 oz (300 g) small eggplants (aubergines)
2 lb (1 kg) small zucchini (courgettes)
2 lb (1 kg) ripe tomatoes
12 tablespoons peanut (groundnut) oil
1 lb (500 g) onions
4 tablespoons olive oil
1 bay leaf
2 sprigs fresh thyme
4 cloves garlic
salt and freshly ground pepper
1 teaspoon sugar
6 sprigs fresh basil

❖Broil the peppers until the skins are blackened, about 25 minutes, turning frequently. Place in a dish, cover and let cool.
❖Cut the eggplants and zucchini into ¾-in (2-cm) cubes. Drop the tomatoes into boiling water for 10 seconds, then cool under running water. Peel, halve and squeeze out the seeds; coarsely chop the flesh.
❖Peel the skins from the broiled peppers. Halve them and remove the seeds and veins. Cut the flesh into ¾ x 1½-in (2 x 4-cm) rectangles.
❖Heat 2 tablespoons peanut oil in a nonstick 10-in (26-cm) skillet. Add the peppers and cook for 2 minutes. Transfer to a colander and discard the cooking oil.
❖Add 4 tablespoons peanut oil to the skillet and lightly brown the onions. Drain and add to the peppers.
❖Add another 3 tablespoons peanut oil to the skillet and lightly brown the zucchini. Drain and add to the other vegetables in the colander.

❖Pour the last 3 tablespoons peanut oil into the frying pan and lightly brown the eggplant cubes. Drain and add to the other vegetables in the colander.
❖In a nonstick 11-in (28-cm) sauté pan combine the tomatoes, olive oil, bay leaf, thyme and the garlic crushed in a garlic press. Bring to boil and add salt, pepper and sugar. Transfer the other vegetables to the sauté pan and return to boil. Cover and cook over moderate heat for about 30 minutes or until very tender, turning the ingredients from time to time.
❖Meanwhile, strip the basil leaves from the stems and chop coarsely. Remove the thyme and bay leaf from the ratatouille. Stir in the chopped basil. Serve hot, lukewarm or cold.

SERVES 4   *Photograph pages 190 – 191*

Bourgogne

PETS DE NONNE
Cheese Beignets

1 scant cup (3 oz/100 g) all purpose (plain) flour
¾ cup (6 fl oz/200 ml) water
½ teaspoon salt
2½ oz (80 g) butter
3 oz (100 g) Comté cheese, freshly and finely grated
5 eggs
1 qt (1 l) peanut oil

❖Prepare a choux pastry according to the recipe on page 247, omitting the sugar and adding the cheese just before the eggs.
❖Heat the oil in a small deep-fryer to 325°F (160°C). Drop in small spoonfuls of the mixture, pushing them off with a second lightly oiled teaspoon so that they drop into the oil in the shape of little balls. They will puff up as soon as they are in the oil and will rotate so that all sides are cooked. Fry until golden brown, about 5 minutes, then remove with a slotted spoon. Drain on paper towels and serve immediately as a side dish.

SERVES 6

CHEESE BEIGNETS

PETER JOHNSON

PETER JOHNSON

GNOCCHI

Corse

POLENTA DE CHÂTAIGNES
Chestnut-flour Polenta

salt
2 cups (8 oz/250 g) chestnut flour
For serving:
fresh *broccio* cheese, ricotta or lightly salted feta cheese
olive oil
freshly ground pepper

❖Pour 1 qt (1 l) water into a saucepan and bring to boil. Season with salt. Pour in the chestnut flour and cook, stirring with a wooden spoon, until the mixture thickens into a solid mass that comes away from the sides of the saucepan, about 15 minutes.
❖Pour the polenta out onto a moistened tea towel. Cut into portions using a knife dipped in cold water. Serve immediately, accompanying with the cheese. Drizzle each slice with olive oil and season to taste with pepper.
❖Any leftover polenta may be browned in olive oil and eaten with a seasonal salad.

SERVES 6

Corse

COURGETTES AU BROCCIO
Corsican-style Stuffed Zucchini

10 small round zucchini (courgettes), about 2½ lb (1.2 kg)
2 tablespoons olive oil
1 clove garlic, finely chopped
1 tablespoon chopped fresh basil
salt and freshly ground pepper
1 slice white bread, crusts trimmed
8 oz (250 g) fresh Corsican *broccio* cheese or ricotta
½ oz (15 g) finely grated Parmesan cheese
1 tablespoon dried currants
1 tablespoon pine nuts

❖Scrub the zucchini under running water and trim the ends. Halve lengthwise and steam for 15 minutes. Using a small teaspoon, hollow out the flesh, leaving a shell ⅜ in (1 cm) thick. Coarsely chop the pulp removed. Let the shells cool.
❖Heat 1 tablespoon oil in a nonstick 10-in (26-cm) skillet and cook the chopped zucchini for 3 minutes, stirring constantly with a wooden spoon. Add the garlic and basil and cook, stirring, for 2 minutes longer. Remove from heat and season with salt and pepper.
❖In a blender or food processor, grind the bread to crumbs. Crush the cheese with a fork and mix in the breadcrumbs, Parmesan, currants and pine nuts. Add the contents of the skillet and stir well.
❖Preheat oven to 425°F (215°C). Pat the insides of the zucchini shells dry with paper towels. Fill with the cheese mixture, piling it into a dome shape. With the remaining tablespoon of oil, grease a shallow baking dish large enough to hold the zucchini in a single layer. Arrange them in the dish. Bake for 45 minutes or until the stuffing is puffed and browned. Serve hot or warm.

SERVES 5

Provence

GNOCCHI
Gnocchi

2 lb (1 kg) baking potatoes
1 egg
2 tablespoons olive oil
about 2 cups (8 oz/250 g) all purpose (plain) flour, sifted
salt and freshly ground pepper
For serving:
tomato sauce, or the sauce from a beef *daube* combined with cream and butter to taste
freshly and finely grated Parmesan cheese

❖Scrub the potatoes under running water and place in a saucepan. Cover with plenty of cold salted water. Bring to boil and cook for about 25 minutes or until the potatoes are very tender and easily pierced with a knife.
❖Drain the potatoes and refresh under running water. Peel them and puree through the finest holes of a food mill. Add the egg, oil, flour, salt and pepper and stir with a wooden spoon until well blended, then work the mixture with your hands to produce a smooth dough that comes away from the fingers. (Depending on the type of flour used, you may need more or less than 2 cups.)
❖Roll the dough into sausage shapes ⅜ in (1 cm) diameter, then cut into ¾-in (1.5-cm) chunks. Dip a fork in flour. Place the rounded side of the fork on a work surface and roll each chunk of dough over the fork, from the tips of the tines towards the handle, using a floured finger. Place each formed gnocchi on a tea towel.
❖Bring a large pot of salted water to boil. Drop in the gnocchi. As soon as they float to the surface, in about 2 to 3 minutes, remove with a slotted spoon and transfer to a serving dish. Mix in the desired sauce and serve with grated Parmesan.

SERVES 8

CHESTNUT-FLOUR POLENTA AND CORSICAN-STYLE
STUFFED ZUCCHINI
PIERRE HUSSENOT/AGENCE TOP

PETER JOHNSON

STEWED BROAD BEANS

Aquitaine

FÈVES EN RAGOÛT
Stewed Broad Beans

4 lb (2 kg) fresh broad beans
2 oz (50 g) goose fat
6 small carrots, peeled and thinly sliced
8 green onions (scallions or spring onions), trimmed
3 oz (100 g) streaky bacon, finely chopped
1 sprig fresh thyme, leaves only
⅔ cup (5 fl oz/150 ml) chicken stock (recipe page 34)
salt and freshly ground pepper

❖Shell the beans and peel off the green skin covering each bean. Melt the goose fat in a nonstick 10-in (26-cm) sauté pan. Add the carrots, onions, bacon and thyme and cook over low heat, stirring often, for 5 minutes or until the vegetables are golden. Add the beans and stock, season lightly with salt and pepper, cover and cook for 10 minutes or until the beans are tender.
❖Turn the beans into a shallow dish and serve immediately.

SERVES 4

Ile de France

POMMES ANNA
Potatoes Anna

This dish was invented by Adolphe Dugléré in honor of Anna Deslions, a "lioness" of the Second Empire. In restaurants it is cooked in a special little copper dish with a tight-fitting lid to ensure that the potatoes cook perfectly.

5 oz (150 g) butter
1½ lb (750 g) boiling potatoes
salt

❖Preheat oven to 400°F (200°C). To clarify the butter, melt it in a saucepan and let cool to lukewarm. Skim off the froth from the surface, then carefully pour the clear liquid into a bowl, discarding the white milk solids at the bottom of the saucepan.
❖Peel and wash the potatoes and pat dry. Cut into ⅛-in (3-mm) slices.
❖Butter a 9-in (22-cm) round pan and layer the potato slices in it, seasoning each layer with salt and adding some of the clarified butter to each layer. Cover with aluminum or waxed paper and bake for 1 hour. Let rest at room temperature for 5 minutes before unmolding onto a plate. Serve immediately.

SERVES 4

Dauphiné

GRATIN DAUPHINOIS
Dauphiné-style Potato Gratin

1 clove garlic
¾ cup (6 fl oz/200 ml) milk
6 tablespoons heavy (double) cream
1 lb (500 g) boiling potatoes
salt and freshly ground pepper
2 pinches of cinnamon
4 pinches of freshly grated nutmeg

❖Preheat oven to 375°F (190°C). Peel the garlic and crush in a garlic press into a large saucepan. Add the milk and cream and bring to boil over low heat.
❖Meanwhile, peel the potatoes, wash and pat dry. Using the shredder attachment of a food processor, slice them very thinly. Add to the saucepan with salt, pepper, cinnamon and nutmeg. Cook for 5 minutes, turning the potatoes carefully.
❖Butter a 10x7-in (26x18-cm) baking dish. Add the potatoes and smooth the surface with a wooden spoon. Bake until golden brown, about 50 minutes. Serve hot from the baking dish.

SERVES 4

Bretagne

POMMES DE TERRE À LA BRETONNE
Potato Casserole

2 lb (1 kg) boiling potatoes
13 oz (400 g) ripe tomatoes
2 oz (50 g) butter
7 oz (200 g) onions, thinly sliced
3 cloves garlic, finely chopped
1 sprig thyme
1 bay leaf
salt and freshly ground pepper
2 cups (16 fl oz/500 ml) chicken stock (recipe page 34)

PETER JOHNSON

POTATOES ANNA (left), DAUPHINÉ-STYLE POTATO GRATIN (bottom right)
AND POTATO CASSEROLE (top right)

❖Preheat oven to 375°F (190°C). Peel the potatoes, wash and pat dry. Cut into ¾-in (1.5-cm) cubes. Drop the tomatoes into boiling water for 10 seconds. Cool under running water, peel, halve and squeeze out the seeds; coarsely chop the flesh.

❖Use half the butter to grease an 8 x 12-in (20 x 30-cm) baking dish. Add the potatoes, onions, garlic, herbs, tomatoes, salt and pepper and stir gently to mix. Pour in the stock and dot the surface with the remaining butter.

❖Bake for about 1 hour or until the potatoes are tender and golden brown and the stock has been absorbed. Serve hot, directly from the dish.

SERVES 4

Provence

FLEURS DE COURGETTE FARCIES
Stuffed Zucchini Flowers

18 large zucchini (courgette) flowers
8 oz (250 g) fresh sheep's milk cheese
grated rind of 1 lemon

⅓ cup (1½ oz/40 g) dried breadcrumbs
2 oz (50 g) freshly and finely grated Parmesan cheese
2 tablespoons chopped flat-leaf parsley
salt and freshly ground pepper
2 egg whites
1½ oz (40 g) butter

❖Preheat oven to 425°F (215°C). Butter a 13 x 9-in (32 x 22-cm) baking dish. Remove the stamens from the zucchini flowers without destroying their shape or separating the petals. Wipe the flowers with a dampened cloth and set aside. Using a fork, mash the fresh cheese in a bowl. Add the lemon rind, breadcrumbs, half the Parmesan and the parsley. Season liberally with salt and pepper and mix well.

❖Beat the egg whites to stiff peaks and fold into the breadcrumb mixture. Fill each flower with a portion of this mixture and roll up tightly to seal.

❖Arrange the stuffed flowers in the baking dish. Melt the butter in a small saucepan and pour over the flowers. Sprinkle with the remaining Parmesan. Bake for 15 minutes or until the flowers have puffed up and become golden. Serve immediately.

SERVES 6   *Photograph pages 8 – 9*

199

EMBEURRÉE DE CHOU
Buttered Cabbage

1 white cabbage, about 2 lb (1 kg)
3 oz (100 g) butter
salt and freshly ground pepper

❖Remove the large outside leaves of the cabbage, then cook the cabbage in a large pot of boiling water for 10 minutes. Drain, cut into quarters and remove the hard core. Cut each quarter into very fine strips, cutting away the hard ribs.
❖Melt half the butter in a nonstick 11-in (28-cm) sauté pan. Add the cabbage, season with salt and pepper and cook for about 20 minutes or until the cabbage is very soft. Remove from heat, add the remaining butter and stir well, mashing the cabbage slightly.
❖Turn the buttered cabbage into a shallow plate and serve immediately.

SERVES 4

HARICOTS VERTS À L'AIL
Green Beans with Garlic

1½ lb (750 g) young, very slender green beans
2 tablespoons extra virgin olive oil
6 cloves garlic, minced
2 tablespoons dried white breadcrumbs
2 tablespoons chopped flat-leaf parsley
salt and freshly ground pepper
1 oz (25 g) butter

❖Drop the beans into a large pot of boiling salted water and cook uncovered over high heat for about 6 to 8 minutes or until slightly crisp. Drain the beans in a colander, then drop them immediately into a large quantity of very cold water so that they retain their bright green color. Drain.
❖Heat the oil in a nonstick 10-in (26-cm) sauté pan over low heat. Add the garlic, breadcrumbs, parsley and salt and pepper and cook, stirring, for 1 minute. Add the butter and, when it has melted, add the beans and stir to reheat. Serve immediately.

SERVES 4

Flandres

ENDIVES À LA FLAMANDE
Endives, Flemish-style

The endive is a vegetable from Belgium which first appeared in France in 1879. It also goes under the names "Brussels chicory" and chicon.

2 lb (1 kg) medium-size Belgian endives (witloof or chicory)
2 oz (50 g) butter
1 tablespoon sugar
salt and freshly ground pepper
¼ cup (2 fl oz/60 ml) fresh lemon juice

❖Pull off the outside leaves of the endives and the bitter part of the heart. Rinse the endives and pat dry.
❖Preheat oven to 400°F (200°C). Using a small amount of the butter, grease a baking dish large enough to hold the endives in a single layer. Arrange them in the dish, season with sugar, salt and pepper, and sprinkle with lemon juice. Dot with the remaining butter.
❖Bake for 45 minutes or until soft and caramelized, turning the endives over halfway through cooking. Arrange on a platter and serve immediately.

SERVES 4

BEIGNETS DE LEGUMES
Vegetable Fritters

For the batter:
1¼ cups (5 oz/150 g) all purpose (plain) flour
salt
⅔ cup (5 fl oz/150 ml) milk
1 tablespoon olive oil
2 eggs, separated
For the vegetables:
1 eggplant (aubergine), about 5 oz (150 g)
1 zucchini (courgette), about 5 oz (150 g)
6 zucchini (courgette) flowers
2 artichokes, about 4 oz (125 g) each
½ lemon
For cooking:
3 cups (24 fl oz/750 ml) peanut (groundnut) oil

❖Prepare the fritter batter: sift the flour into a bowl. Whisk in the salt, milk and oil, then the egg yolks, whisking until the batter is smooth and homogeneous. Cover and let rest for 2 hours.
❖After this time, prepare the vegetables: cut the eggplant and zucchini diagonally into ¼-in (.5-cm) slices. Remove the stamens from the zucchini flowers and cut each flower into 2 or 3 pieces, according to size. Break off the stalk of the artichokes level with the heart. Remove the tough outside leaves and cut off the tips of the tender leaves to within ½ in (1 cm) of the heart. Remove the chokes and rub the hearts with the lemon half to keep them from discoloring. Slice each artichoke vertically and sprinkle with lemon juice.
❖Beat the egg whites to stiff peaks and fold into the batter. Heat the oil in a small deep fryer or saucepan to 375°F (190°C). Dip the artichoke, eggplant and zucchini slices and the zucchini flowers into the batter, then drop into the hot oil a few at a time and fry for 1 to 2 minutes or until golden brown.
❖Remove the fritters with a slotted spoon and drain on paper towels. Arrange on a plate and serve immediately.

SERVES 4   *Photograph pages 8 – 9*

BUTTERED CABBAGE (top right), GREEN BEANS WITH GARLIC (top left)
AND ENDIVES, FLEMISH-STYLE (bottom)
PETER JOHNSON

Périgord

CÈPES FARCIS
Stuffed Mushrooms

12 large fresh cèpes (*porcini* mushrooms)
3 tablespoons olive oil
3½ oz (100 g) prosciutto or other raw ham, finely chopped
3½ oz (100 g) *ventrèche, pancetta* or rindless bacon, chopped
2 cloves garlic, finely chopped
2 French shallots, finely chopped
2 tablespoons chopped flat-leaf parsley
salt and freshly ground pepper
2 eggs, beaten

❖Remove the stems of the mushrooms and trim off the base. Quickly wash the caps and stems under cold running water and pat dry. Finely chop the stems.
❖Heat 1 tablespoon oil in a nonstick 10-in (26-cm) skillet and cook the ham and *ventrèche* for 2 minutes, stirring. Add the garlic and shallots and cook for 2 more minutes, stirring. Add the chopped mushroom stems and parsley and cook until golden. Remove from heat. Season lightly with salt and pepper. Add the eggs and mix well.
❖Preheat oven to 400°F (200°C). Lightly oil a baking dish large enough to hold the mushroom caps in one layer. Arrange the caps upside down in the dish and fill with the stuffing. Sprinkle with the remaining oil. Bake for 25 minutes or until the mushrooms are tender and the stuffing is golden brown. Arrange on a platter and serve immediately.

SERVES 4   *Photograph page 207*

Languedoc

MILLAS
Cornmeal Mush

This corn galette is sometimes served as a dessert, sprinkled with sugar.

1 qt (1 l) water
2½ oz (75 g) lard
salt and freshly ground pepper
1½ cups (8 oz/250 g) cornmeal

❖Pour the water into a large saucepan. Add the lard, salt and pepper and bring to boil. Pour in the cornmeal and cook, stirring with a wooden spoon, for 15 minutes or until the mixture forms a solid mass which comes away from the sides of the saucepan.
❖Turn the mixture onto a dampened linen towel; it will spread out of its own accord. Cut it with a knife dipped in cold water and serve hot. When cold, it may be cut into slices and fried.
❖*Millas* is served hot as an accompaniment to beef stews (*daubes*) and similar dishes. When cold, it is fried in lard, then served warm with a garlic-seasoned salad. It can also be sprinkled with cheese and baked until crusty.

SERVES 6

CORNMEAL MUSH (top), HARICOT BEANS, PÉRIGORD-STYLE (bottom)
AND HARICOT BEANS IN CREAM SAUCE (right)
PETER JOHNSON

Périgord

HARICOTS À LA PÉRIGOURDINE
Haricot Beans, Périgord-style

7 oz (200 g) fresh pork rind, trimmed of fat
1 lb (500 g) ripe tomatoes
4 lb (2 kg) fresh haricot beans (or flageolet beans), shelled
1 onion, about 3 oz (100 g), finely chopped
20 sprigs parsley
4 cloves garlic, finely chopped
7 oz (200 g) fresh pork belly, finely chopped
salt and freshly ground pepper

❖Boil the pork rind in water to cover for 5 minutes, then cool under running water and cut into ⅜-in (1-cm) squares. Drop the tomatoes into boiling water for 10 seconds. Cool under running water, peel, halve and squeeze out the seeds; coarsely chop the flesh.
❖Place the beans in a large saucepan and cover with plenty of water. Add the pork rind, onion and tomatoes and bring to boil. Cook for 1 hour over low heat, stirring from time to time.
❖Meanwhile, wash and dry the parsley. Remove the stalks and finely chop the leaves. Combine with the garlic and pork belly.
❖Add the parsley mixture to the beans and cook for 30 minutes longer, stirring from time to time and adding a little water if necessary. Season with salt and pepper, turn the beans into a shallow dish and serve immediately.

SERVES 6

Poitou

HARICOTS BLANCS À LA CRÈME
Haricot Beans in Cream Sauce

1 medium onion
2 cloves
bouquet garni: 1 bay leaf, 1 sprig thyme, 6 sprigs parsley,
    2 celery stalks
4 lb (2 kg) fresh haricot beans (or flageolet beans), shelled
1 medium carrot, peeled and cut into 6 pieces
2 cloves garlic, halved
1 cup (8 fl oz/250 ml) heavy (double) cream or
    crème fraîche
1 oz (25 g) butter
salt and freshly ground pepper
4 pinches of freshly grated nutmeg

❖Peel the onion and stud with the cloves. Tie together the herbs for the bouquet garni.
❖Place the beans in a pot and cover with plenty of cold water. Add the carrot, onion, garlic and bouquet garni and bring to boil. Cook over low heat for 1½ hours, stirring from time to time and adding a little extra water if necessary.
❖When the beans are cooked, pour the cream into a large saucepan. Add the butter, salt, pepper and nutmeg and place over low heat. Drain the beans and discard the carrot, onion, garlic and bouquet garni. Add the beans to the cream and stir to coat well. Turn into a shallow dish and serve immediately.

SERVES 6

HERB RISOTTO FROM LES BAUX

Provence

RISOTTO DES BAUX

Herb Risotto from Les Baux

1 clove garlic, finely chopped
2 French shallots, finely chopped
1 sprig thyme
1 sprig rosemary
1 bay leaf
2 sage leaves
3 oz (80 g) butter, softened
1 tablespoon olive oil
2 cups (10 oz/300 g) long-grain or Camargue rice
salt and freshly ground pepper
6 tablespoons dry white wine
3¼ cups (26 fl oz/800 ml) water
12 sprigs basil, leaves only

❖In a 4-qt (4-l) enameled pot combine the garlic, shallots, thyme, rosemary, bay leaf and sage. Add half the butter and oil and cook for 2 minutes over low heat, stirring constantly with a wooden spoon. Add the rice, season with salt and pepper and cook over low heat, stirring, for 3 minutes.
❖Sprinkle the wine over the rice and let it evaporate. Add 1¾ cups (14 fl oz/400 ml) water, cover and cook for 10 minutes. Add ¾ cup (6 fl oz/200 ml) more water, cover and cook for 5 minutes. Again add ¾ cup water and cook until the rice has absorbed all the liquid, about 25 minutes total; do not stir the rice during cooking.
❖Coarsely chop the basil. When the rice is cooked, remove the thyme, rosemary, bay leaf and sage. Add the remaining butter and the basil and season with pepper. Stir well and serve immediately from the pot.

SERVES 6

Aquitaine

CÈPES À LA BORDELAISE

Cèpes, Bordelaise-style

1½ lb (750 g) small fresh cèpes (*porcini* mushrooms)
¼ cup (2 fl oz/60 ml) olive oil
2 cloves garlic, finely chopped
3 tablespoons chopped flat-leaf parsley
salt and freshly ground pepper

❖Cut off the stalks of the cèpes at the level of the cap. Quickly wash the caps under running water and pat dry.
❖Heat the oil in a nonstick 10-in (26-cm) sauté pan over high heat. Add the cèpes; they will immediately give out a lot of liquid. Cook over very high heat, stirring constantly, until all liquid evaporates. Remove the cèpes. Add the garlic and parsley to the pan and cook, stirring, for 2 minutes, then turn out of the pan onto a plate.
❖Return the cèpes to the pan, rounded surface up. Sprinkle with the garlic and parsley and season with salt and pepper. Cover and cook over low heat for 30 minutes.
❖Arrange the cèpes on a serving plate. Boil the pan juices until reduced to a syrupy consistency. Pour over the cèpes and serve immediately.

SERVES 4

Provence

ARTICHAUTS À LA BARIGOULE

Braised Artichokes

Artichokes came to France with Catherine de'Medici. At first they were served simply grilled, like mushrooms. Barigoulo, the name of a mushroom in the Provençal dialect, is a recipe that has evolved into this fragrant sauté which still goes by the original name.

12 young artichokes, about 4 oz (125 g) each
1 lemon, halved
¼ cup (2 fl oz/60 ml) olive oil
4 large onions, finely chopped
3 small carrots, peeled and thinly sliced
3 cloves garlic, cut into fine slivers
1 sprig thyme, crumbled
1 bay leaf
6 tablespoons dry white wine
6 tablespoons water
salt and freshly ground pepper

❖Trim the artichoke stalks ¾ in (2 cm) from the heart and strip off the tough leaves. Cut off the tips of the tender leaves to within ¾ in (2 cm) of the heart. Pare the heart and stalks and rub with lemon.
❖Heat the oil in an enameled pot just large enough to hold the artichokes. Add the onions and carrots and cook for 5 minutes without allowing them to color. Add the garlic and cook, stirring, for 1 minute longer. Rinse the artichokes and pat dry. Add to the pot with the thyme and bay leaf and cook, stirring, for 2 minutes. Add the wine and water and season with salt and pepper. Cover and cook over very low heat for about 1 hour or until the artichokes are easily pierced with a knife and are coated with a reduced sauce. Serve warm.

SERVES 4

CÈPES, BORDELAISE-STYLE (top) AND BRAISED ARTICHOKES (bottom)
PETER JOHNSON

Auvergne

CHOU FARCI
Stuffed Cabbage

1 Savoy cabbage, about 3 lb (1.5 kg)
1 tablespoon vegetable oil
2 cloves garlic, finely chopped
2 French shallots, finely chopped
6 tablespoons milk
2 oz (50 g) soft bread, crusts trimmed
12 oz (400 g) beef round steak (top round) or porterhouse
12 oz (400 g) fresh pork shoulder, boned and trimmed of fat
6 oz (200 g) fresh pork belly, boned
1 egg
2 tablespoons finely chopped mixed fresh parsley and
    chives
½ teaspoon dried thyme
½ teaspoon *quatre-épices* (see glossary)
salt and freshly ground pepper
1 sheet pork caul fat (*crépine*)
bouquet garni: 1 bay leaf, 1 sprig thyme, 10 sprigs parsley
1 oz (25 g) butter
6 oz (200 g) onions, thinly sliced
6 oz (200 g) carrots, peeled and thinly sliced
1 cup (8 fl oz/250 ml) chicken stock (recipe page 34)

❖Remove the tough outer leaves from the cabbage and parboil the cabbage for 10 minutes in water to cover. Drain and let cool.

❖Heat the oil in a nonstick 8-in (20-cm) skillet and cook the garlic and shallots until golden. Pour the milk into a small saucepan and bring to boil. Crumble in the bread, remove from heat and stir to form a smooth paste. Let cool.

❖Grind (mince) the three meats in a grinder or food processor. Add the garlic and bread mixtures, egg, herbs, *quatre-épices*, salt and pepper and mix well.

❖To stuff the cabbage, stand it on its base and delicately spread the outside leaves, taking care not to tear them; as each leaf is spread out, cut away the thick white stalk from the base with a small knife. Continue in this way to the heart of the cabbage. Place half the stuffing in the heart. Fold the leaves back over the heart, adding a few spoonfuls of stuffing between the leaves. Use the last layer of leaves to cover the whole cabbage. Rinse the caul fat under cold water, drain and use it to wrap the cabbage.

❖Preheat oven to 425°F (215°C). Tie together the herbs of the bouquet garni. Melt the butter in a heavy pot just large enough to hold the cabbage. Cook the onions and carrots until golden, stirring with a wooden spoon, about 5 minutes. Add the bouquet garni, salt, pepper and stock. Place the cabbage on top and cover. Bake for 1½ hours undisturbed.

❖Transfer the cabbage to a serving platter. Strain the cooking liquid into a sauceboat. Quarter the cabbage, pour the sauce over and serve.

SERVES 8

STUFFED CABBAGE (top right), STUFFED MUSHROOMS (center right, recipe page 203), POTATO CREAM PIE (bottom right, recipe page 212), AND AUVERGNE-STYLE LENTILS (left, recipe page 214), PHOTOGRAPHED IN PÉRIGORD.

PIERRE HUSSENOT/AGENCE TOP

PETER JOHNSON

TOMATO AND EGGPLANT CASSEROLE

BOHÉMIENNE
Tomato and Eggplant Casserole

This dish is served throughout the summer in the town of Avignon.

4 tablespoons olive oil
6 tablespoons water
2 lb (1 kg) eggplants (aubergines), peeled and cut into ¾-in (2-cm) cubes
1½ lb (750 g) ripe tomatoes
6 cloves garlic
1 teaspoon sugar
salt and freshly ground pepper
1 bay leaf
¼ cup (2 fl oz/60 ml) milk
6 anchovy fillets in oil
2 oz (50 g) freshly and finely grated Parmesan cheese

❖Heat 2 tablespoons oil in a nonstick 10-in (26-cm) sauté pan. Add the water and eggplant cubes, cover and cook over low heat, stirring frequently, for 1 hour or until the eggplant is very tender.
❖Drop the tomatoes into boiling water for 10 seconds. Cool under running water; peel, halve and squeeze out the seeds. Chop the flesh into small pieces.
❖Heat the remaining oil in a nonstick 10-in (26-cm) skillet. Add the garlic, forced through a garlic press. Stir in the tomatoes, sugar, salt, pepper and bay leaf and cook over high heat for 20 minutes or until all liquid has evaporated. Add the milk and the anchovies and cook, stirring, for 5 minutes or until the anchovies dissolve.
❖Preheat oven to 400 °F (200 °C). Discard the bay leaf. Add the tomato sauce to the eggplant and mix well. Pour into a 10-in (26-cm) oval baking dish. Sprinkle with Parmesan and bake for 20 minutes. Serve hot from the baking dish.

SERVES 4

EPINARDS AUX PIGNONS
Spinach with Pine Nuts

2½ oz (75 g) dried currants
3 lb (1.5 kg) fresh spinach
3 tablespoons olive oil
salt and freshly ground pepper
2½ oz (75 g) pine nuts
6 drops orangeflower water

❖Cover the currants with warm water in a small bowl. Trim the stalks from the spinach; wash the leaves and dry in a salad spinner.
❖Heat 2 tablespoons oil in a nonstick 11-in (28-cm) sauté pan and cook the spinach in batches over high heat, turning constantly, for 5 minutes. Season with salt and pepper and keep hot.
❖Heat the remaining oil in a nonstick 8-in (20-cm) skillet. Add the drained currants and pine nuts and cook, stirring, for 2 minutes or until the pine nuts are golden. Add the pine nuts, currants and orangeflower water to the sauté pan with the spinach and stir for 30 seconds, then remove from heat. Arrange the spinach on a serving plate and serve immediately.

SERVES 4

PALETS DE MARRONS
Chestnut Patties

2 lb (1 kg) fresh chestnuts
2 tender celery stalks, with leaves, chopped
3 oz (100 g) butter
6 tablespoons water
salt and freshly ground pepper
3 egg yolks, beaten

❖Make a small incision on the flat face of each chestnut. Bring a large saucepan of water to boil and drop in the chestnuts. Boil for 5 minutes, then drain and remove both the outside shells and the inner skins.
❖Combine the chestnuts, celery and 2 oz (60 g) butter in a nonstick 10-in (26-cm) sauté pan over low heat. Add the water and cook, stirring often, for about 1 hour or until the chestnuts are very soft. Season with salt and pepper during cooking.
❖Puree the chestnuts through the finest holes of a food mill into a bowl. Add the egg yolks and refrigerate for 2 hours.
❖Shape the mixture into rounds 2 in (5 cm) in diameter and ⅜ in (1 cm) thick. Melt the remaining butter in a nonstick 11-in (28-cm) skillet and fry the patties for 2 minutes on each side. Arrange on a platter and serve immediately.

SERVES 6

SPINACH WITH PINE NUTS (top) AND CHESTNUT PATTIES (bottom)
PETER JOHNSON

Languedoc

POMMES SARLADAISES
Potatoes, Sarlat-style

1½ lb (750 g) boiling potatoes
2 oz (50 g) goose fat
4 cloves garlic, finely chopped
2 tablespoons chopped flat-leaf parsley
salt and freshly ground pepper

❖Peel the potatoes, wash and slice into ⅛-in (3-mm) rounds.
❖Melt the goose fat in a nonstick 10-in (26-cm) skillet. Add the potatoes and turn them over in the hot fat for 10 minutes. Add the garlic and parsley, season with salt and pepper and stir again. Cover and cook over low heat for 20 minutes or until the potatoes are tender, turning them several times.
❖Transfer the potatoes to a shallow dish and serve hot.

SERVES 4

Savoie

GRATIN SAVOYARD
Potato Gratin, Savoy-style

1¼ cups (10 fl oz/300 ml) chicken stock
salt and freshly ground pepper
6 pinches of freshly grated nutmeg
1¼ lb (625 g) boiling potatoes
1½ oz (40 g) butter
4 oz (125 g) Beaufort or Emmenthaler cheese, freshly and finely grated

❖Preheat oven to 375°F (190°C). Bring the chicken stock to boil over low heat. Add salt, pepper and nutmeg and remove from heat.
❖Peel the potatoes, wash them and pat dry. Using the shredder attachment of a food processor, slice the potatoes very thinly.
❖Using a small amount of the butter, grease a 10x7-in (26x18-cm) baking dish. Spread a layer of potatoes over the bottom, then a layer of cheese. Continue layering the remaining potatoes and cheese, ending with cheese. Pour the hot stock over and dot with the remaining butter.
❖Bake until golden brown, about 50 minutes. Serve hot from the baking dish.

SERVES 4

Provence

BARBOUIADO DE FÈVES ET D'ARTICHAUTS
Braised Broad Beans and Artichokes

3 lb (1.5 kg) fresh broad beans
3 oz (100 g) streaky bacon
5 small artichokes, about 4 oz (125 g) each

½ lemon
2 tablespoons olive oil
1 green onion (scallion or spring onion), finely chopped
1 sprig thyme
1 sprig savory
3 tablespoons water
salt and freshly ground pepper

❖Shell the broad beans and peel off the soft green skin from each bean. Remove the rind from the bacon and cut the meat into thin matchsticks.
❖Trim each artichoke stalk at the base of the heart. Remove the tough outside leaves. Cut off the tips of the tender leaves to within ¼ in (½ cm) of the heart. Trim the hearts and rub with the cut surface of the lemon. Cut each heart into quarters and remove the choke. Cut each quarter into 3 slices.
❖Heat the oil in a 4-qt (4-l) pot. Add the onion, bacon, thyme and savory and cook gently for 2 minutes, stirring with a wooden spoon. Add the artichokes and cook over moderate heat, stirring constantly, until light golden and almost tender, about 7 to 8 minutes.
❖Add the water and beans and season with salt and pepper. Mix well. Cover and cook for 5 minutes longer. Remove from heat and discard the thyme and savory. Turn into a shallow dish and serve immediately.

SERVES 4

POTATOES, SARLAT-STYLE (bottom), POTATO GRATIN, SAVOY-STYLE (top left)
AND BRAISED BROAD BEANS AND ARTICHOKES (right)

Franche-Comté

MORILLES À LA CRÈME

Morels in Cream Sauce

1 lb (500 g) fresh morels
1 tablespoon fresh lemon juice
6 tablespoons heavy (double) cream or crème fraîche
2 oz (50 g) butter
2 French shallots, finely chopped
salt and freshly ground pepper

❖Trim the ends of the morel stalks. Wash and dry the morels. Place in a saucepan with the lemon juice and cook over low heat for 15 minutes.
❖Remove the morels with a slotted spoon, add the cream to the saucepan and mix well.
❖Melt the butter in a nonstick 10-in (26-cm) skillet and cook the shallots until golden, about 3 minutes, stirring with a wooden spoon. Add the morels, season with salt and pepper, then add the cream sauce from the saucepan. Increase heat and cook until the mixture reduces to form a thick, creamy sauce to coat the morels, about 2 to 3 minutes.
❖Turn them into a shallow dish and serve immediately.

SERVES 4

Provence

TIAN DE COURGETTES

Baked Zucchini with Tomatoes and Onions

Tian is the name of the square or rectangular glazed earthenware dish in which vegetable, meat or fish dishes are baked. Because of this, all Provençal gratins have taken the name of tians.

1 lb (500 g) green (spring) onions
1 lb 10 oz (800 g) medium zucchini (courgettes)
1½ lb (750 g) firm-ripe tomatoes
6 tablespoons olive oil
2 cloves garlic, finely chopped
salt and freshly ground pepper
1 sprig fresh thyme, leaves only
1 sprig fresh savory, leaves only (optional)

❖Cut the onions into ¼-in (.5-cm) slices, including the green stalk. Cut the zucchini diagonally into ¼-in (.5-cm) slices; cut the tomatoes into similar-size slices.
❖Preheat oven to 400°F (200°C). Heat 4 tablespoons oil in a nonstick 10-in (26-cm) skillet and cook the onions over low heat, stirring frequently, until soft and transparent, about 8 minutes. Add the garlic, salt and pepper and cook, stirring, for 2 minutes longer.
❖Transfer the mixture to a 10 x 7-in (26 x 18-cm) baking dish and smooth the surface. Arrange 4 lengthwise rows of tomato and zucchini slices on top of the onions. Sprinkle with thyme and savory. Pour the remaining oil over and season with salt and pepper.
❖Bake until the vegetables are very soft and slightly browned, about 1 hour. Serve directly from the baking dish, hot or lukewarm.

SERVES 4 – 5   *Photograph pages 8 – 9*

PETER JOHNSON

211

TRUFFAT
Potato Cream Pie

2½ cups (10 oz/300 g) all purpose (plain) flour
5 oz (150 g) butter
¼ cup (2 fl oz/60 ml) water
salt
5 oz (150 g) smoked bacon
1 tablespoon peanut (groundnut) oil
1 onion, about 4 oz (125 g), finely chopped
1 lb 10 oz (800 g) boiling potatoes
freshly ground pepper
6 pinches freshly grated nutmeg
1 egg yolk
1 tablespoon milk
⅔ cup (5 oz/150 ml) heavy (double) cream or crème fraîche

❖Sift the flour onto a work surface and make a well in the center. Add the butter, water and 3 pinches of salt. Combine the ingredients with the fingertips to produce a smooth dough. Roll it into a ball and refrigerate for 1 hour.
❖Meanwhile, remove the rind from the bacon and chop the meat finely with a knife. Heat the oil in a nonstick 9-in (22-cm) skillet and cook the onion and bacon over low heat until golden, stirring with a wooden spoon. Remove from heat.
❖Wash the potatoes and slice thinly. Turn into a bowl and add salt, pepper, nutmeg, and the mixture from the skillet. Combine carefully so that the potato slices do not break.
❖Preheat oven to 425°F (215°C). Cut the pastry into two portions, one slightly larger than the other. Roll out the larger portion to a 12-in (30-cm) circle. Butter a 10-in (26-cm) cake pan and line with pastry. Turn the potato mixture into the pastry case and smooth the surface. Roll out the second portion of pastry into a 10-in (26-cm) circle for the lid. Place on top of the filling and press the edges together firmly to seal.
❖Beat together the egg yolk and milk and brush the surface of the pastry with this mixture. Bake for 1¼ hours or until the pastry is light golden. Cut a ¾-in (2-cm) circle of pastry from the center of the lid and pour the cream through this opening. Replace the circle of pastry and return the *truffat* to the oven for 10 minutes longer. Serve hot.

SERVES 6 *Photograph page 207*

PAPETON D'AUBERGINES
Eggplant Charlotte

This is a specialty of Avignon, once the city of the Popes. In the old days it was baked in a mold shaped like a papal tiara. It is sometimes called "aubergines of the Popes."

3 lb (1.5 kg) eggplant (aubergine), the long oval variety
4 tablespoons olive oil
6 tablespoons water
2 sprigs fresh thyme, leaves only
1 clove garlic, finely chopped
salt and freshly ground pepper
5 eggs

2½ oz (75 g) freshly and finely grated Parmesan
For serving:
fresh tomato sauce flavored with basil

❖Wash the eggplant and wipe dry. Cut into 2-in (5-cm) cubes. Heat 3 tablespoons oil in a nonstick 11-in (28-cm) sauté pan. Add the water, thyme and garlic and cook for 1 minute, then add the eggplant. Season with salt and pepper. Cover and cook over low heat, stirring from time to time, until the eggplant is tender, about 30 minutes.
❖Preheat oven to 400°F (200°C). Puree the cooked eggplant through the medium holes of a food mill. Beat the eggs with a fork. Add the eggs and cheese to the eggplant puree and mix well. Oil a charlotte mold 7 in (18 cm) in diameter. Turn the eggplant mixture into the mold and smooth the surface. Bake for 40 minutes or until the surface is golden brown.
❖Let the *papeton* rest for 10 minutes at room temperature, then unmold. Serve hot or lukewarm with tomato sauce.

SERVES 6

COUSINAT
Cousinat

This dish is a specialty of the town of Bayonne.

1 lb (500 g) fresh broad beans
1 red bell pepper (capsicum), about 7 oz (200 g)
7 oz (200 g) ripe tomatoes
4 small artichokes, about 4 oz (125 g) each
1 oz (25 g) goose fat
2 slices prosciutto or other raw ham, ½ in (1 cm) thick, diced
12 green onions (scallions or spring onions), trimmed
7 oz (200 g) small carrots, peeled and thinly sliced
4 oz (125 g) slender green beans
6 tablespoons dry white wine
salt and freshly ground pepper

❖Shell the broad beans and peel off the soft green skin from each bean. Quarter the pepper, remove the seeds and veins and cut into thin strips.
❖Drop the tomatoes into boiling water for 10 seconds. Cool under running water, peel, halve and squeeze out the seeds; coarsely chop the flesh. Cut off the stalk of each artichoke at the base of the heart. Remove the tough outside leaves. Cut off the tips of the tender leaves to within ¾ in (2 cm) of the heart; trim the heart.
❖Melt the goose fat in a 4-qt (4-l) pot and lightly brown the cubes of ham for 3 minutes, stirring with a wooden spoon. Add the onions, pepper, artichokes and carrots and cook, stirring, for 2 minutes. Add the tomatoes and beans and cook for 10 minutes, stirring often. Pour in the wine and boil for 5 minutes. Season with salt and pepper, cover and cook over very low heat for 1 hour, stirring from time to time; the vegetables should be tender and coated with a syrupy glaze. Turn into a shallow dish and serve.

SERVES 4

EGGPLANT CHARLOTTE (top) AND COUSINAT (bottom)
PETER JOHNSON

GREEN PEAS, VENDÉE-STYLE

Vendée

PETITS POIS À LA VENDÉENNE
Green Peas, Vendée-style

1 sprig thyme
1 sprig hyssop
1 sprig savory
1 sprig flat-leaf parsley
2 oz (50 g) butter
16 fresh green onions (scallions or spring onions)
3 lb (1.5 kg) green peas, shelled
2 lettuce hearts, quartered
salt and freshly ground pepper
1 teaspoon sugar

❖Strip the leaves from the thyme, hyssop, savory and parsley.
❖Melt the butter in a nonstick 10-in (26-cm) sauté pan. Add the onions and herbs and cook over low heat, stirring, for 3 minutes or until the onions are golden. Add the peas and cook, stirring, for 2 minutes longer. Add the lettuce hearts, season with salt, pepper and sugar and add cold water just to cover.
❖Cover the pan and cook for 1 hour, stirring from time to time. Turn the peas into a shallow dish and serve immediately.

SERVES 4

Auvergne

LENTILLES À L'AUVERGNATE
Auvergne-style Lentils

10 oz (300 g) carrots
10 oz (300 g) onions
2 cloves

bouquet garni: 1 bay leaf, 1 sprig thyme, 6 sprigs parsley
2 cloves garlic
1 lb (500 g) lentils
7 oz (200 g) smoked bacon, in one piece
1 oz (25 g) lard
1 tablespoon chopped flat-leaf parsley
1 tablespoon chopped fresh chives
salt and freshly ground pepper

❖Cut the carrots into ¼-in (.5-cm) slices. Peel the onions; stud one onion with cloves and finely chop the remainder. Tie together the herbs of the bouquet garni. Crush the cloves of garlic with your hand or the side of a cleaver.
❖Rinse the lentils, then place them in a large pot. Add the bacon, whole onion, garlic, carrots and bouquet garni. Cover with plenty of cold water and bring to boil over low heat. Cook for 45 minutes.
❖Lift out the bacon, remove the rind and fat and break the lean meat into small pieces. Melt the lard in a nonstick 10-in (26-cm) skillet and cook the chopped onions until golden, about 3 minutes, stirring with a wooden spoon. Add the bacon and cook, stirring, for 2 more minutes. Drain the lentils and discard the whole onion, garlic and bouquet garni. Stir in the contents of the skillet with the parsley and chives. Season with salt and pepper. Turn the lentils into a shallow dish and serve immediately.

SERVES 6   *Photograph page 207*

Ile de France

POMMES SOUFFLÉES
Puffed Potatoes

The date of the inauguration of the railway line between Paris and St Germain-en-Laye, August 26, 1837, apparently marked the entirely accidental creation of this dish.

When someone told the chef at the celebration banquet that the guests were arriving, he plunged the prepared potatoes into the frying oil; but alas, the guests had been held up. The same thing happened a second time: another frying, and still no guests. At the third attempt, the chef was astonished to see his potatoes puffing up in the hot oil. When they were drained, they remained light and golden, and were praised by all who tasted them.

So a new recipe was born, and for a long time it bore the title pommes soufflées de Saint-Germain-en-Laye.

1½ lb (750 g) boiling potatoes
2 qt (2 l) peanut (groundnut) oil
salt

❖Peel the potatoes and trim them to a roughly rectangular shape. Rinse, pat dry and slice each potato into ⅛-in (3-mm) slices. Pour 1 qt (1 l) oil into each of two deep fryers or large saucepans. Heat one to 212°F (100°C) and the second to 425°F (220°C).
❖Place the potatoes in a frying basket and plunge into the fryer with the 212°F oil. Cook until they are just beginning to color, then lift out the basket and immediately plunge it into the second fryer; the potatoes will puff up. Drain immediately on paper towels and transfer to a serving plate. Season with salt and serve at once.

SERVES 4

OURBONNAIS, ROUERGUE

Cheeses, mountains and plateaus

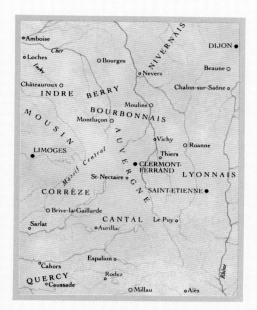

AUVERGNE, BOURBONNAIS, ROUERGUE

Cheeses, mountains and plateaus

"The Auvergne," wrote Alexandre Vialatte, "produces government ministers, cheeses and volcanoes." As far as cheeses go, he is absolutely right. Together with those of Savoy, they are the kings of the French mountains. Their taste of natural pastures, their undeniable wholesomeness, their genuine flavor — in sum, their authenticity and the vigor of their aroma, all the result of good-quality cow's milk, give them pride of place in the cheese-lover's heart: the grassy Saint-Nectaire, with its handsome grey or purplish crust, which seems to come directly from the pasturages where it was born — not to be confused with the Murol, similarly shaped but with a hole in the center, a commercial cheese, of plastic appearance and neutral flavor; the solid and powerful Cantal, whose reputation is not eclipsed by that of its near cousins from Laguiole-en-Aubrac and Salers, with their distinctive flavor of pressed curds and dried hazelnuts; the Fourme d'Ambert, with its light veining and slightly bitter aftertaste, a cheese as fine as English Stilton and which goes well with a good port. But also the *bleu d'Auvergne*, the *Tomme de Brach*, the *Brique de Livradois*, the *Galette de la Chaise-Dieu* — all local cheeses which amply justify the local saying that the Auvergne is one immense cheese platter.

With its southern appendage of the Rouergue, which produces Roquefort, the Auvergne is the very symbol of the tourist's eternal France, peaceful and cheese-producing. Roquefort is the star of

LEFT: A SHEPHERD FROM ST-BERAIN NEAR LE PUY STARTS HIS DAY.

PREVIOUS PAGES: LE PUY'S BEAUTIFUL ROMANESQUE CATHÉDRALE NÔTRE-DAME IS STILL AN IMPORTANT PILGRIMAGE SITE, AND IT TOWERS OVER THE RED-TILED ROOFS AND NARROW COBBLESTONE STREETS OF THE TOWN.

the Rouergue Midi. Made from the milk of sheep of the Lacaune breed, the cheese is handsomely veined, soft-textured and moist-crusted, containing a minimum of 52% fat. It comes from the village of Roquefort-sur-Soulzon in the *département* of Aveyron, in the south of the Auvergne, wrapped in foil that is stamped with the name of the producer. Somewhat acidic, Roquefort marries admirably with sweet white wines like those of Sauternes or Montbazillac. The *Bleu des Causses*, made from cow's milk, is its first cousin. These are the cheeses of this splendid country, the Auvergne.

But the volcanoes? They are a source of pure air and sparkling water (the many brands of mineral water bottled in the region are renowned for their purifying properties) and of open pastures. To crisscross from the Bourbonnais to Clermont-Ferrand, which dominates the landscape of Puy de Dôme, then to turn towards the charming village of Salers, with its old houses of black lava, its Renaissance-style former bailey and its Templars' House, is to experience a rich and self-contained land, closed around its treasures — which are, first of all, a group of extinct volcanoes unique in France.

Puy de Sancy, Puy Mary, Puy de Montchal, the deservedly famous Puy de Dôme, which offers a spectacular view over the nearby craters and a green and grassy landscape that looks more like the moon. On this rich, lush, ancient earth the flocks graze without risk. The cattle give a juicy, flavorful, marbled beef — Charolais in the north, Salers in the south, the long-horned Aubrac on the plateau of the same name. Cattle with a smooth, orange-red coat, which have never eaten anything but tender grass.

In the Auvergne, the cuisine is generous, rustic, country- rather than city-style. The traditional dish is *aligot*: a potato puree mixed with fresh *tomme* cheese and a hint of garlic. In the Aubrac mountains in summer it is prepared in the open air in front of the *burons*, small shepherds' huts made of stone. It will be accompanied by some good sausages, dried or grilled, or by pig's trotters or *andouillette*. The star of local vegetables is the green lentil from Le Puy, jokingly called the "caviar of the poor," since in appearance it recalls those small, luxurious black pearls. The *gigot brayaude* is a leg of lamb cooked in a closed pot, very gently, for seven hours, with salt pork, garlic cloves, onions and carrots. It is a true peasant dish, appetizingly aromatic, the meat so soft and tender that it can be eaten with a spoon. *Mourtayrol* is the plentiful pot-au-feu of feast days. *Falette* is a boned breast of veal, stuffed with ham, bacon, veal, onions and garlic, which is slowly cooked over gentle heat and served with braised cabbage. The *potée auvergnat* calls for cabbage and salted pork, in particular the head and knuckle. Mountain trout are cooked *au bleu*, in a court bouillon, and enhanced with melted butter. The *omble-chevalier*, a highly esteemed, pink-fleshed trout which is the glory of the Savoy lakes, is equally the pride of

IN THE HEART OF FRANCE, AUVERGNE'S CHARACTERISTIC MOUNTAINS ARE EXTINCT VOLCANOES, AND THE ONCE-FIERY CRATERS ARE NOW INVITING BLUE LAKES LIKE LAC CHAMBON, SOUTH OF CLERMONT-FERRAND.

ROSINE MAZIN/AGENCE TOP

Lake Pavin. Mushrooms come in infinite variety — *chanterelles, girolles, lactaires, morilles, gyromitres*. In Velay, and also in Combrailles and Aubrac, they make for a real treasure hunt.

The *truffade* or *truffado* makes use of the "truffle" of the Auvergne, otherwise known as a potato, which is cut into thick slices and fried with cubes of salt pork and slivers of cheese — certainly solid fare, but what flavor! But then, the whole of Auvergne is a land of substantial flavors, of powerful aromas. Its liqueurs come from the plants of its mountains: the verveine, which is the glory of the Velay, and which also serves to make soothing infusions, and the deep-rooted gentian, yellow-flowered, herbaceous, bitter and sweet at the same time, from which results one of the best of the bitter aperitifs, Suze. The red wines, from Gamay grapes, are light: Chanturgue and Châteaugay around Clermont-Ferrand, Côtes du Forez and Roannaise between Roanne and Saint-Etienne. In the Bourbonnais, the light, fresh Saint-Pourçain wine, made from Gamay, Pinot noir, Sauvignon and Chardonnay grapes, comes in white, red and rosé styles.

The Bourbonnais in the northeast is another region that could very well stand on its own. On the edge of the Auvergne, renowned for such spa resorts as Vichy and Bourbon-l'Archambault, it borders with the Nivernais, the Berry and the

IN THE TINY TOWN OF ESPALION IN THE AVEYRON REGION OF AUVERGNE, AN ANCIENT BRIDGE SPANS THE RIVER LOT.

Loire. As in Auvergne, this is still the territory of the cabbage, which goes into the *potée* — the pot-au-feu of the region — and the celebrated *soupe aux choux*, aromatic and restorative. But at the same time it enriches this heritage with its own original dishes: *pâté de tartouffes*, a potato pie with cubes of salt pork, onions and cream, and a crust of short pastry; *pompes au graıtons*, with yeast-raised dough and pieces of salt pork; duck *à la Du Chambet*, served with cinnamon-scented apples and a sauce enriched with cubes of foie gras. All are succulent, earthy dishes which have contributed to the fame of the Hôtel de Paris at Moulins.

Rouergue could be split in two. The southern part, towards Millau, resembles the Midi and the Languedoc; the north, from Rodez to Conques, from the countryside of Marcillac with its red brick houses, vivid and rustic, as far as the highlands of the Aubrac, is a foretaste of the Auvergne. Shaded green forests, luxuriant foliage: in the lost valley of Conques, one of the most magnificent villages of the Auvergne, the traveler will re-experience the rich splendor of the region, first encountered at Murols and Saint-Nectaire.

This is still a region of hearty meals and rib-sticking dishes, where offal is in no way disdained. Many of the dishes that are said to be *auvergnat* in Paris actually belong to the Rouergue: the *florès* of Rodez, made from veal tripe; the dried hams of

Naucelle; the *tripoux*, which are little, tied-up parcels of mutton tripe, braised in a tomato sauce over gentle heat; *estofinado*, made from dried cod cooked with potatoes; *fouace*, a cake flavored with orangeflower water. But the real wealth of the country, apart from the aforementioned *aligot*, which belongs equally to the Rouergue and the Auvergne, is the Roquefort.

The people of the Auvergne, solid and honest gourmands, are first and foremost hard workers. Many proprietors of cafes and lively brasseries in Paris today are former waiters and owners of *bois-charbons*, where they sold not only the means of heating but also the young red wine. Most of them came from the famous triangle Espalion-Estaing-Saint-Chély-d'Apcher. It is a harsh region, this Upper Rouergue, touching the nearby Auvergne on the vast plateau of Aubrac, crossed by *drailles*, paths made of dry stone. Many of its countrymen migrated, working day and night to earn their daily bread and, eventually, buy their own bistros. One such is Marcellin Cazes, who was a water carrier before he became the force behind the Brasserie Lipp on the Boulevard Saint-Germain. These citizens have been the most valiant ambassadors of their region. And of its wonderful dishes — *truffade, falette, tripoux* and *aligot* — which you eat with the horn-handled knife of Laguiole, and which sing with joy of the great land of the Auvergne.

221

DESSERTS

How sweet they are!

LEO MEIER

A SELECTION OF DECORATIVE *CONFISERIES* — "THISTLE" PRALINES
AND SWEET FRUIT AND ALMOND PASTES.

DESSERTS

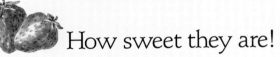

How sweet they are!

NOT ONLY DO THE FRENCH GROW GRAPES FOR WINE-MAKING, BUT THEY
ALSO USE *RAISINS* IN ALL KINDS OF REGIONAL DISHES INCLUDING THE TASTY
ALSACE DESSERT *KUGELHOPF*.

Let's start with the cheeses. Brillat-Savarin deemed them the *premier des desserts*, the most important. But in France, cheeses in all their diversity ("a country with four hundred different cheeses will never die," promised Churchill during the debacle of 1940), remain a prelude to dessert.

The land of good things to eat, France does not ignore the appeal of sugar. The markets of eastern France feel the influence of central Europe, with Vienna at its hub, where cafes are meeting places. The town of Metz, for example, has one of the best chocolatiers in the whole country — Pierre Koenig, who exports his chocolate truffles, pralines and semisweet chocolate creams around the world — as well as a dozen or so top-quality *pâtisseries-salons de thé*. Strasbourg is obviously one of the most deliciously sweet towns in the world. Its specialties are many, starting with *kugelhopf*, *büeraweka* (a fruit loaf), fruity *Bettelmann* cake, and *schnecke*, known throughout the rest of France as *pain aux raisins*. Besides, many of the pâtisserie specialties of eastern France have spread to other parts of the country: the *meringue chantilly*, meringue with whipped cream, that is also found in Ile-de-France, for example; the *nid d'abeilles*, or bee's nest (a brioche dough sprinkled with sugar and filled with a custard cream), which finds its counterparts in the *tarte au sucre* of Artois and Picardy and the *tarte tropézienne* of the Var.

LEO MEIER

PREVIOUS PAGES: SNOW EGGS (top left, recipe page 232), MERINGUES
CHANTILLY (center left, recipe page 231), PRALINE BUTTER CREAM CAKE
(top right, recipe page 246) AND ORANGE LIQUEUR CRÊPES (bottom right,
recipe page 250), PHOTOGRAPHED IN THE ILE DE FRANCE.
PIERRE HUSSENOT/AGENCE TOP

224

Certain other regions have their own specialties, which rely on local resources: for example, in Brittany, *kouigh amann au miel*, prune-studded *far*, the rich butter cake known as *quatre-quarts*, and *galettes*, pastries made with salted butter. The *clafoutis* is now found everywhere, although it originated in the Limousin. The baba — is it a native of Lorraine? — becomes *savarin* when served in Paris, garnished with whipped cream.

Ice cream, introduced to the French court by Catherine de' Medici, who married the future Henri II, did not properly arrive in Paris until the following century, when Francesco Procopio opened the first cafe in Paris. This frozen treat — which became based on cream and eggs only around 1775 — and sorbets, made from all kinds of fruit, were an immediate hit. In the eighteenth century, Paris had 250 *limonadiers* selling ice creams during summer.

Since that time, the elaborately decorated and molded confections known as *bombes glacées* and similar preparations have vulgarized the use of iced desserts. Modern dietetics has endorsed the serving of sorbets — an ancient Chinese practice, passed on to the Persians and Arabs — which use neither eggs nor fats. Based on fruit pulp, preferably fresh, sorbets calmly follow the rhythm of the changing seasons.

Tarts, too, wed the fruits of all regions, all seasons. *Crêpes* are not necessarily Breton, as evi-

THE FRENCH ARE VERY PARTICULAR ABOUT USING THE FRESHEST INGREDIENTS. THEY ARE DISCERNING CUSTOMERS AND TAKE TIME TO SELECT THE BEST PRODUCE.

MILLE-FEUILLES, TARTE AUX MIRABELLES (TARTS WITH YELLOW PLUMS), *CHOUX A LA CHANTILLY* (CREAM PUFFS) AND *MOUSSE FRAISE* (STRAWBERRY MOUSSE), AS WELL AS *RELIGIEUSES* (LITTLE NUN CAKES) AND *ÉCLAIRES*, ARE SOME OF THE DELICIOUS PASTRIES YOU WILL FIND IN ANY FRENCH *PÂTISSERIE*.

denced by the very Parisian *crêpes Suzette*, delicately flavored with orange zest and dramatically flamed at the table. The dessert that finishes the meal should also be a feast for the eyes — hence the importance given to presentation. The great chefs have never been indifferent to this. Urbain Dubois, who was the chef of the Rocher de Cancale, then of the Café Anglais before exercising his talents in the service of Prince Orloff in Russia and William I in Germany, set down his rules of aesthetics in a work which has since become a classic, *La Cuisine Artistique*, dating from 1870 and predating by thirteen years his *Grand Livre des Pâtissiers et des Cuisiniers*.

A century later, Gaston Lenôtre, a pâtissier at Pont-Audemer, became the most famous caterer in the world; he understood, as did his predecessor Urbain Dubois, that if the dinner does not climax in dessert, even the finest cuisine will be a disappointment, and that the dessert will never be complete unless it is properly presented. His parades of elaborately constructed *pièces montées* borne by an army of white-hatted kitchen boys, a splendid array of ice creams and light and fruity sorbets, remain in the memory like living paintings worthy of Watteau. At the end of the twentieth century, French festivities — like those of the whole world — are indebted to Gaston Lenôtre for something of their sweet sparkle and a great deal of their magic.

CATERING FOR EVERYONE'S TASTES, THIS SHOP IN DINAN, BRETAGNE IS A *BOULANGERIE, PÂTISSERIE* AND DELICATESSEN.

FRUIT TARTS AND *GÂTEAUX*, BAKED DAILY, DECORATE THIS *PÂTISSERIE* WINDOW IN QUIMPER. REFLECTED IN THE GLASS IS THE STREET SCENE — THE OLD QUARTER OF TOWN WITH ATTRACTIVELY RESTORED HOUSES AND COBBLESTONE STREETS.

Aquitaine

LE NÈGRE
Flourless Chocolate Cake

Made with dark chocolate, butter and sugar this cake is served all along the Aquitaine coast from Bayonne to Bordeaux. Different families have different ways of preparing it, but the important thing is not to use flour, so that a very soft-textured cake rather like a baked mousse is achieved, served warm or cold, with custard cream.

7 oz (200 g) semisweet or bittersweet (plain) chocolate
7 oz (200 g) soft butter
1 cup (7 oz/200 g) sugar
4 eggs, separated

❖Preheat oven to 375°F (190°C). Butter an 8-in (22-cm) round cake pan. Break the chocolate up into small pieces and melt over hot water. Add the butter and stir with a spatula until smooth.
❖Add half the sugar to the egg yolks and whisk until the mixture is pale in color. Beat in the chocolate mixture. Beat the egg whites to soft peaks. Gradually add the remaining sugar, beating until the mixture is smooth and shiny. Fold gently into the chocolate mixture with a rubber spatula.
❖Pour the batter into the prepared pan and bake for 40 minutes or until a tester inserted in the center comes out clean.
❖Let the cake rest at room temperature for 10 minutes before turning it out of the pan. Serve warm, at room temperature or chilled.

SERVES 6

FLOURLESS CHOCOLATE CAKE

APRICOT PASTRY

Maine

JALOUSIES
Apricot Pastry

1 scant cup (7 oz/200 g) apricot jam
1¼ lb (600 g) puff pastry (recipe page 44)
To glaze:
1 egg yolk
1 tablespoon milk

❖Preheat oven to 425°F (215°C). Heat the jam in a small saucepan, then put it through a fine sieve to remove the skin of the fruit. Let cool. Roll out the puff pastry into two 8 x 3-in (20 x 8-cm) strips.
❖Lightly moisten a baking sheet and place one pastry strip on it. Spread with the jam to within ⅜ in (1 cm) of the edges. Place the second pastry strip on top, smooth side up (i.e., the side that was in contact with the work surface). Press down all around the edges so they will stick together. Make small knife cuts at ⅜-in (1-cm) intervals around the edges.
❖Beat the egg yolk and milk together and brush the surface of the pastry with the mixture; do not let the glaze run over the edges as this would keep the pastry from rising. With the point of a knife, make deep slanting cuts in the pastry ⅜ in (1 cm) apart and ¼ in (.5 cm) from the edges. Bake the pastry for 30 minutes or until golden brown. Transfer to a plate and serve warm.

SERVES 6

PUFF PASTRY WITH ALMOND FILLING

PITHIVIERS

Puff Pastry with Almond Filling

1¼ lb (600 g) puff pastry (recipe page 44)
For the filling:
5 oz (150 g) ground blanched almonds
1 cup (5 oz/150 g) powdered (icing) sugar
5 oz (150 g) soft butter
2 eggs
2 tablespoons dark rum
For the glaze:
1 egg yolk
1 tablespoon milk
2 tablespoons powdered (icing) sugar

❖Prepare the filling: mix the ground almonds and sugar in a small bowl. Cream the butter in a large bowl. Blend in the almond mixture, eggs and rum.

❖Preheat oven to 425°F (215°C). Cut the puff pastry into 2 equal parts and roll out into two 12-in (30-cm) circles, using a large plate or cake pan as a guide. Hold the knife very straight so that the pastry is not crushed, which would prevent it from rising evenly during baking.

❖Lightly moisten a baking sheet and lay one of the pastry circles on it. Spread with almond mixture to within ⅜ in (1 cm) of the edge. Place the second pastry disc on top of this, smooth side up (i.e. the side that was in contact with the work surface). Press firmly all around the edge of the pastry so that the two circles will stick together. Make small cuts in the edge of the *pithiviers* ⅜ in (1 cm) apart.

❖Prepare the glaze: beat the egg yolk and milk together and brush the mixture over the surface of the pastry; do not let it run over the edge, as this would prevent the pastry from rising as it bakes. Using the point of a knife, make very shallow curved cuts on the surface of the pastry, from the outside edge into the center.

❖Bake for 30 minutes. Sprinkle with powdered sugar and bake for 5 more minutes or until the surface is shiny and slightly caramelized. Transfer the pastry to a serving plate and serve warm.

SERVES 6

FAR

Warm Prune Tart

This is one of the most popular of Bretagne's desserts. It is served in different ways according to the region — plain in Saint Pol de Léon, filled with prunes at Quiberon, and with raisins at Brest.

11 oz (350 g) prunes
2 cups (16 fl oz/500 ml) milk
3 eggs
½ cup (4 oz/125 g) sugar
⅔ cup (2½ oz/75 g) all purpose (plain) flour

❖Soak the prunes in warm water to cover for 2 hours. Preheat oven to 400°F (200°C). Heat the milk in a small saucepan over gentle heat. Combine the eggs and sugar in a bowl and whisk until the mixture is pale in color. Whisk in the flour, then the milk.

❖Butter a 10-in (26-cm) deep-sided flameproof china tart plate. Drain the prunes and arrange in the plate. Cover with the batter and bake for about 45 minutes or until browned. Let the tart cool slightly. Serve warm from the baking dish.

SERVES 6

KOUIGH AMANN

Buttered Pastry

The Douarnenez region is the home of this cake, whose name means bread and butter.

7 oz (220 g) low-salt butter
10 oz (300 g) bread dough (page 41)
1 cup (7 oz/220 g) plus 2 tablespoons superfine (caster) sugar

❖Place the butter in a deep plate and work it with a fork until it is soft and the same consistency as the dough. Roll out the dough on a work surface into a square ⅜ in (1 cm) thick. Spread with butter to within ¾ in (2 cm) of the edges; sprinkle with 1 cup sugar. Fold the dough in thirds one way, then in thirds the opposite way. Roll it out as thinly as possible, being careful not to let any of the butter or sugar escape. Fold the pastry again, as before.

❖Butter a 10-in (26-cm) cake pan. Lay the dough in it and push down gently with your fingers, taking care not to break it. Start from the center and work outwards until the whole pan is covered with an even thickness of dough. Let rise for 30 minutes, preheating the oven to 425°F (200°C) after 10 minutes of rising. Bake the tart for 35 minutes, basting with the butter that rises to the surface during the last 15 minutes of baking.

❖Sprinkle the tart with the remaining 2 tablespoons sugar. Let cool slightly, then turn it out and serve.

SERVES 6

WARM PRUNE TART (left) AND BUTTERED PASTRY (right),
PHOTOGRAPHED IN BRETAGNE
PIERRE HUSSENOT/AGENCE TOP

BAKED CHERRY CUSTARD

Lorraine

BABA
Rum Baba

Finding the kugelhopf too dry for his taste, Stanislas Leszczynski had the idea of moistening it with Malaga wine. He christened the new dish "Ali Baba" in honor of his favorite book, the Thousand and One Nights. *Subsequently it became known simply as a* baba, *and the Malaga wine was replaced by rum.*

3 teaspoons sugar
¼ cup (2 fl oz/60 ml) warm water
1 envelope (½ oz/15 g) dry yeast
3 tablespoons milk
2 oz (60 g) butter
1 cup (4 oz/125 g) all purpose (plain) flour
2 eggs
3 pinches of salt
For the syrup:
¾ cup (6½ oz/200 g) sugar
1½ cups (12 fl oz/400 ml) water
6 tablespoons dark rum

❖Place 1 teaspoon sugar in a 1-cup (8-fl-oz/250-ml) measure. Add the warm water and stir until the sugar dissolves. Sprinkle the yeast over the surface and let stand in a warm place for about 10 minutes or until the mixture has risen almost to the top of the cup.
❖Meanwhile, heat the milk to lukewarm in a small saucepan. Work the butter with a wooden spoon until creamy. Sift the flour into a mixing bowl and make a well in the

Limousin

CLAFOUTIS
Baked Cherry Custard

The origin of the clafoutis *is not known, but both the Limousin and the Auvergne — where the very similar* millard *is made — claim this honor.*

1½ lb (750 g) ripe black cherries, not pitted
2 eggs
1 egg yolk
½ cup (4 oz/125 g) sugar
2½ oz (75 g) butter, melted
⅔ cup (2½ oz/75 g) all purpose (plain) flour
1 cup (8 fl oz/250 ml) milk
vanilla sugar

❖Preheat oven to 400°F (200°C). Wash, dry and stem the cherries.
❖Butter an ovenproof china or glazed earthenware mold large enough to hold the cherries in a single layer. Place the cherries in it. Combine the eggs and yolk in a bowl, add the sugar and whisk until the mixture is pale in color. Whisk in the butter. Sift in the flour and mix well, then mix in the milk. Continue beating until the batter is smooth, then pour over the cherries.
❖Bake for 40 minutes or until browned. Remove the *clafoutis* from the oven and sprinkle with vanilla sugar. Serve lukewarm, from the baking dish.

SERVES 6

center. Add the eggs, salt, the remaining sugar, the milk and the yeast mixture to the well and mix. Add the butter and mix again. Knead the dough until smooth and elastic, lifting it as high as possible and letting it fall to force in as much air as possible.

❖Butter a 9-in (24-cm) baba mold and place the dough in it. Cover with a cloth and let rise until level with the edge of the mold, about 1 hour.

❖Preheat oven to 400°F (200°C). Bake the baba for 25 minutes.

❖Meanwhile, prepare the syrup: combine the sugar and water in a saucepan and bring to boil. Remove from heat and stir in the rum.

❖When the baba is baked, turn it out onto a serving plate. Prick it all over and spoon the syrup over, scooping up the syrup that runs down onto the plate and spooning it back over the cake until it is soaked all over. Refrigerate for at least 4 hours before serving.

SERVES 6

Ile de France

MERINGUES À LA CHANTILLY
Meringues Chantilly

In 1720, during his exile in Alsace, the former king of Poland Stanislas Leszczynski, a great gourmet, had the pastrycook Gasparini brought over from Switzerland. He created a cake which was called "meringue" after the Swiss village of Mehringen where he was born. As for the chantilly, it had been created earlier, in 1714, by a chef named Vatel who officiated in the château at Chantilly.

For the meringues:
4 egg whites
⅔ cup (5 oz/150 g) superfine (caster) sugar
⅔ cup (3½ oz/100 g) powdered (icing) sugar
For the chantilly:
2 cups (16 fl oz/500 ml) very cold heavy (double) cream
2 tablespoons superfine (caster) sugar

❖Make the meringues: preheat the oven to 225°F (110°C). Butter and flour a baking sheet. Beat the egg whites to soft peaks in a large mixing bowl. Gradually add ¼ cup (2 oz/60 g) superfine sugar and continue to beat until the mixture is smooth and shiny. Add the remaining superfine sugar and beat for another 2 minutes at low speed. Fold in the powdered sugar with a rubber spatula.

❖Transfer the meringue to a pastry bag fitted with a ¾-in (2-cm) fluted tip and pipe onto the prepared baking sheet in small domes or swirls as desired.

❖Bake the meringues for about 1 hour, without letting them brown. They should be ivory-colored; if they begin to brown, lower the heat. Remove the baked meringues with a metal spatula and let cool on a rack.

❖Prepare the chantilly: shortly before serving, whip the cream with an electric mixer until firm. Add the sugar and beat until the cream forms soft peaks.

❖Place the cream in a pastry bag fitted with a small smooth or fluted tip. Pipe it onto the flat side of one meringue and sandwich with a second meringue. Continue with the remaining meringues and cream. Serve at once.

MAKES APPROXIMATELY 16   *Photograph pages 222 – 223*

PRUNES COOKED IN WINE (top) AND ANGEVINE PEARS (bottom, recipe page 232)

Val de Loire

PRUNEAUX AU VIN
Prunes Cooked in Wine

2 lemons
1 vanilla bean (pod)
2 lb (1 kg) prunes
3 cups (24 fl oz/750 ml) red wine, such as Vouvray
1 cinnamon stick, 4 in (10 cm) long
⅓ cup (2½ oz/75 g) sugar

❖Wash the lemons and wipe dry. Remove the zest of each in a long strip; reserve the pulp for another use. Split the vanilla bean in two lengthwise.

❖Place the prunes in a large bowl and cover with the wine. Add the lemon zest, vanilla bean and cinnamon stick. Cover and let the prunes soak for 4 hours.

❖Drain the prunes and pour the wine into a large nonaluminum saucepan with the lemon zest, vanilla bean, cinnamon stick and sugar. Bring to boil over high heat, stirring until the sugar has dissolved. Add the prunes and poach gently for 10 minutes. Drain and set them aside. Boil the cooking liquid over high heat until reduced to about 1 cup (8 fl oz/250 ml) of syrupy, fragrant liquid. Pour this over the prunes and discard the lemon zest, cinnamon stick and vanilla bean. Let cool, then cover and refrigerate for 12 hours before serving.

SERVES 6

POIRES BELLES-ANGEVINE

Angevine Pears

1 lemon
3 cups (24 fl oz/750 ml) red wine
1 cinnamon stick, 4 in (10 cm) long
½ cup (4 oz/125 g) sugar
4 large perfumed pears, about 7 oz (220 g) each

❖Wash the lemon and wipe dry. Remove the zest in a long strip; reserve the pulp for another use. Pour the wine into a large nonaluminum saucepan. Stir in the lemon zest, cinnamon stick and sugar. Bring to boil over high heat, stirring until the sugar dissolves.
❖Peel the pears, leaving them whole; do not remove the stems. Arrange on their sides in a flameproof deep-sided dish big enough to hold them without overlapping. Pour the wine mixture over them and poach for 20 minutes over gentle heat, turning often.
❖Drain the pears and set aside in a bowl. Boil the cooking liquid over high heat until reduced to about 1 cup (8 fl oz/250 ml) of fragrant syrup. Remove the lemon zest and cinnamon stick. Coat the pears with the wine syrup and let cool. Refrigerate for at least 2 hours before serving.

SERVES 4 *Photograph page 231*

Alsace

SOUFFLÉ AU KIRSCH

Kirsch Soufflé

5 tablespoons sugar
1 tablespoon cornstarch (cornflour) or potato flour
5 tablespoons milk
4 teaspoons butter
3 tablespoons kirsch
2 egg yolks
3 egg whites
pinch of salt

❖Preheat oven to 390°F (200°C). Butter the bottom and sides of a soufflé dish 6 in (16 cm) in diameter and 4 in (10 cm) deep. Sprinkle with 1 tablespoon sugar and turn the dish in your hands so that the sugar coats the entire inside surface.
❖Combine 2 tablespoons sugar, the cornstarch and the milk in a saucepan and beat briskly with a whisk. Place over moderate heat and bring just to boil, whisking constantly. As soon as the first bubbles appear, remove from heat and whisk in first the butter, then the kirsch and finally the egg yolks.
❖Combine the egg whites and salt in a bowl and beat until stiff. Add the remaining sugar and beat until smooth and shiny. Whisk a large tablespoonful of the whites into the soufflé base in the saucepan, then pour the contents of the saucepan over the remaining whites and fold together with a rubber spatula. Turn the mixture into the soufflé dish and bake for 25 minutes or until puffed and golden. Serve immediately.

SERVES 2

KIRSCH SOUFFLÉ

Ile de France

OEUFS À LA NEIGE

Snow Eggs

1 vanilla bean (pod)
1 qt (1 l) whole milk
8 eggs, separated
⅔ cup (5 oz/150 g) superfine (caster) sugar
For the caramel:
⅓ cup (3 oz/90 g) superfine (caster) sugar
3 tablespoons water

❖Split the vanilla bean lengthwise using a small knife. Place in a saucepan and add the milk. Bring to boil, then remove from heat, cover and let stand to infuse. Place the egg whites in a large bowl and the yolks in a large saucepan.
❖Sprinkle ⅔ of the sugar over the yolks, beating with a whisk or hand beater until the mixture is very pale in color. Beat in the hot milk. Place over low heat and cook, stirring constantly, until the custard coats the spoon. Remove from heat. Strain the mixture into a bowl and let cool, stirring from time to time.
❖Beat the egg whites until very stiff, then beat in the remaining sugar; continue beating until the mixture is the consistency of meringue. Bring several inches of water to boil in an 11-in (28-cm) sauté pan, then reduce the heat so that it barely simmers.
❖Dip a large, long-handled spoon into cold water, then scoop spoonfuls of the egg white from the bowl and place one by one into the simmering water; plunge the spoon into cold water beforehand so that the egg white will slide off easily. Turn each spoonful after 30 seconds and cook for 30 seconds on the other side. When the whites are cooked, use a skimmer to remove them from the water. Set on a wire rack that is covered with a cloth, not touching one another.

❖To serve, pour the custard into a bowl and pile the cooked egg whites on it in a dome shape. To prepare the caramel, cook the sugar and water in a saucepan over gentle heat to form an amber-colored syrup. Pour over the eggs in a thin stream and serve at once.

SERVES 6   *Photograph pages 222 – 223*

Bretagne

SORBET AUX FRAISES
Strawberry Water Ice

From May to July the whole of France enjoys the wonderfully sweet and fragrant fruit known as the strawberry. The most sought-after is the variety from Plougastel (Bretagne's "strawberry capital"), with its incomparable taste and flavor.

⅔ cup (5 oz/160 g) sugar
6 tablespoons water
13 oz (400 g) strawberries
1 tablespoon fresh lemon juice
To serve:
red fruits, such as strawberries, raspberries and/or red
   currants

❖Place the sugar in a saucepan, add the water and bring to boil. Remove from heat. Cool the syrup by plunging the bottom of the pan into cold water

❖Wash and drain the strawberries; remove the hulls. Put through the fine holes of a food mill (if you do not want the seeds in your sorbet) or puree in a blender or processor. Transfer the puree to a bowl and mix in the lemon juice and syrup.

❖Freeze the sorbet in an ice cream maker, following manufacturer's instructions. Serve in scoops in ice cream dishes, accompanied by fruits.

SERVES 4

Anjou

POIRIER D'ANJOU
Pear Cake

1 cup (8 oz/250 g) sugar
2 cups (16 fl oz/500 ml) water
1 vanilla bean (pod), halved lengthwise
2 lb (1 kg) large perfumed pears
3 oz (90 g) butter
¾ cup (6 fl oz/200 ml) milk
1⅔ cups (6½ oz/200 g) all purpose (plain) flour
2 teaspoons baking powder
2 eggs
2 tablespoons red currant jelly
3 tablespoons cointreau

❖Place ⅓ cup (90 g) sugar in a large saucepan. Add the water and vanilla bean and bring to boil over low heat. Halve, peel and core the pears. Place the pear halves in the boiling syrup and cook for 30 minutes or until just tender. Drain, reserving the syrup.

❖Preheat oven to 425°F (215°C). Melt the butter in a small saucepan and let cool slightly. Butter a 9-in (24-cm) cake pan. Combine the flour and baking powder in a food processor. Add the eggs, the remaining sugar, the butter and milk and blend to form a smooth batter. Pour into the cake pan. Cut each pear half vertically into slices ⅜ in (1 cm) thick and arrange on top of the batter in a rose pattern, starting from the center. Bake for 40 minutes or until a tester inserted in the center comes out clean.

❖Meanwhile, boil the syrup in which the pears were cooked over high heat until very thick and syrupy. Add the red currant jelly and boil for 1 minute more. Add the cointreau and remove from heat.

❖Coat the cake with this syrup and bake for another 5 minutes. Unmold onto a serving plate. Serve warm or cold.

SERVES 6

STRAWBERRY WATER ICE

PETER JOHNSON

PEAR CAKE

PETER JOHNSON

CHESTNUT MERINGUE

Savoie

MONT BLANC

Chestnut Meringue

A mound of chestnut puree with whipped cream piled on top —
homage to Mont Blanc.

4 lb (2 kg) chestnuts
1 qt (1 l) whole milk
1 vanilla bean (pod), halved lengthwise
¾ cup (6½ oz/200 g) sugar
1 cup (8 fl oz/250 ml) chilled heavy (double) cream
1 envelope vanilla sugar or 3 drops vanilla extract (essence)

❖Make a slash in the flat side of each chestnut. Bring a large saucepan of water to boil. Drop in the chestnuts and boil for 5 minutes. Drain and remove the outer shell and the brown inner skin. Pour the milk into a large saucepan, add the vanilla bean and bring to boil. Add the chestnuts. Cover and cook for 30 minutes, stirring from time to time.

❖Stir in the sugar and cook, stirring frequently, for about 30 minutes more or until the mixture forms a thick puree that comes away from the sides of the saucepan.

❖Put the puree through the fine holes of a food mill, held over a serving plate. Try not to break the vermicelli-like threads of chestnut if possible. Refrigerate for at least 2 hours.

❖At serving time, whip the cream with the vanilla sugar. Transfer it to a piping bag fitted with a small smooth or fluted tip and decorate the top and sides of the Mont Blanc. Serve immediately.

SERVES 6

Languedoc

GIMBLETTES D'ALBI

Albi Rings

Ring cookies used to form part of the decorations hung on olive branches on Palm Sunday. Nowadays they have become an everyday cookie.

2 tablespoons sugar
3 tablespoons warm water
1 envelope (½ oz/15 g) dry yeast
3 tablespoons milk
2 oz (60 g) butter
3¼ cups (13 oz/400 g) all purpose (plain) flour
3 eggs
grated rind of 1 lemon
2 oz (60 g) candied citron peel, diced
1 teaspoon orangeflower water
For the glaze:
1 egg yolk
1 tablespoon milk

❖Combine 1 teaspoon sugar and the warm water in a 6-oz (200-ml) glass and stir until the sugar dissolves. Sprinkle the yeast on top and mix it in. Let stand in a warm place for 10 minutes.

❖Heat the milk in a small saucepan. Add the butter and stir until it melts, then let cool slightly.

❖Sift the flour into a mixing bowl and mix in the remaining sugar. Make a well in the center and add the milk mixture, eggs, lemon rind, citron peel, orangeflower water and yeast mixture. Blend with a spatula, starting from the center and working out, until the dough becomes too thick to work with the spatula. Then knead with your hands for 10 minutes, lifting and letting the dough drop to the work surface frequently to incorporate as much air as possible. Roll the dough into a ball and return to the mixing bowl. Cover the bowl with a cloth and let the dough rise in a warm place for about 1½ hours or until it has doubled in volume.

❖Knead the dough for 2 minutes, then divide it into 1½-oz (40-g) pieces. Roll into small balls and push a hole into the center of each with your index finger dipped in flour. Rotate each ball on your finger to make a ring shape. Bring a large saucepan of water to a slow boil. Drop in the rings of dough and cook for about 30 seconds or until they puff up and rise to the surface. Lift out with a skimmer and arrange on a cloth.

❖Preheat oven to 400°F (200°C). Butter a baking sheet and arrange the rings on it. Beat the egg yolk and milk with a fork and brush each ring with the mixture. Bake the cookies for 20 minutes or until browned. Cool on racks before serving.

MAKES ABOUT 20 COOKIES

ALBI RINGS (right) AND SWEET BREAD (left)

PASTIS LANDAIS
Sweet Bread

5 tablespoons superfine (caster) sugar
3 tablespoons warm water
1 envelope (½ oz/15 g) dry yeast
2 oz (60 g) butter
2½ cups (10 oz/300 g) all purpose (plain) flour
3 pinches of salt
2 tablespoons anise liqueur
1 tablespoon orangeflower water
grated rind of 1 lemon
½ teaspoon vanilla extract (essence)
2 eggs, separated

❖Combine 1 teaspoon sugar and the warm water in a 6 oz (200 ml) glass and stir until the sugar dissolves. Sprinkle the yeast on top and mix it in. Let stand in a warm place for 10 minutes.

❖Melt the butter in a small saucepan and let cool.

❖Sift the flour into a mixing bowl and mix in the remaining sugar and the salt. Make a well in the center and add the liqueur, orangeflower water, lemon rind, vanilla, melted butter, egg yolks and yeast mixture to the well. Blend with a spatula, starting from the center and working out, until the dough becomes too thick to work with the spatula. Knead it with your hands for 10 minutes, lifting and letting the dough drop to the work surface frequently to incorporate as much air as possible. Return the dough to the bowl.

❖Beat the egg whites to soft peaks. Beat ⅓ into the dough to loosen it, then fold in the remaining whites in two portions. Cover the bowl with a cloth and let rise in a warm place for about 1½ hours or until doubled in volume.

❖Butter a 7-in (18-cm) charlotte mold. Place the dough in the mold and let rise for 45 minutes or until it reaches the top of the mold.

❖Preheat oven to 400°F (200°C). Bake the *pastis* for 45 minutes or until risen and browned.

❖Let cool for 10 minutes, then turn out onto a rack to cool.

SERVES 6

GÂTEAU DE NANCY
Nancy Cake

5 oz (150 g) semisweet or bittersweet (plain) chocolate
4 oz (125 g) butter
½ cup (4 oz/125 g) superfine (caster) sugar
4 eggs, separated
1 cup (3½ oz/100 g) ground almonds
1 level tablespoon potato starch (potato flour)
For serving:
2 tablespoons powdered (icing) sugar

❖Preheat oven to 375°F (190°C). Butter an 8-in (22-cm) cake pan. Melt the chocolate over hot water, add the butter and stir with a spatula until smooth. Let cool slightly.

❖Combine the sugar and egg yolks and whisk until pale in color. Beat in the chocolate mixture. Combine the

NANCY CAKE (bottom) AND ORANGE TARTLETS (top)

ground almonds and potato starch and stir in. Beat the egg whites to soft peaks and fold into the batter.

❖Pour the batter into the prepared pan and bake for 35 minutes or until a tester inserted in the center comes out clean.

❖Let the cake rest at room temperature for 10 minutes before turning it out onto a plate. Let cool completely. Sift the powdered sugar over it before serving.

SERVES 6

BARQUETTES D'ORANGES
Orange Tartlets

1½ cups (7 oz/200 g) blanched almonds
1 cup (7 oz/200 g) superfine (caster) sugar
9 tablespoons potato starch (potato flour)
3 tablespoons curaçao
2 oranges
4 egg whites
3 tablespoons granulated sugar

❖Preheat oven to 375°F (190°C). Butter 24 3-in (8-cm) oval tartlet molds (*barquettes*).

❖In a food processor, grind the almonds and ⅔ cup (5 oz/150 g) superfine sugar to a fine powder. Transfer to a mixing bowl. Sift in the potato starch and add the curaçao. Wash and dry the oranges and remove the rind with a lemon zester. Add the strips of rind to the bowl.

❖Beat the egg whites to soft peaks. Gradually add the remaining superfine sugar and continue beating to stiff peaks. Fold in the almond mixture.

❖Divide the dough among the prepared molds and flatten lightly with the back of a spoon to level the surface. Sprinkle granulated sugar over each tartlet.

❖Arrange the molds on a baking sheet and bake for 25 minutes or until browned. Let cool in the tins for 10 minutes before turning them out onto a wire rack to cool completely.

SERVES 6

VANILLA CUSTARD WITH CARAMEL SAUCE

Ile de France

CRÈME CARAMEL
Vanilla Custard with Caramel Sauce

This family dessert is sometimes made without the caramel, in which case it goes by the name of oeufs au lait *(eggs with milk).*

1 vanilla bean (pod)
1 qt (1 l) whole milk
¾ cup (6½ oz/200 g) sugar
½ teaspoon fresh lemon juice
2 tablespoons water
8 eggs

❖Preheat oven to 340°F (170°C). Split the vanilla bean in two lengthwise and place in a saucepan with the milk. Bring to simmer, then remove from heat. Cover and let stand to infuse.
❖Place half the sugar in a small saucepan. Add the lemon juice and water and bring to boil. Cook until an amber-colored caramel forms. Remove from heat and pour the caramel into a 2-qt (2-l) metal charlotte mold, soufflé dish or cake tin; it may also be divided among individual soufflé dishes. Quickly turn the mold in your hands so the caramel coats the bottom and sides.
❖Break the eggs into a large bowl and add the remaining sugar. Whisk until well blended, then whisk in the hot milk. Put the mixture into the mold through a fine sieve.
❖Place the mold in a bain-marie and bake for 1 hour (45 minutes for individual molds), or until the custard ıs set and a knife inserted in the center comes out clean.
❖Remove the *crème caramel* from the water bath and let cool. Unmold onto a plate and serve at room temperature or cold. If it is to be served cold, keep refrigerated until serving time, then plunge the bottom of the mold into hot water for 30 seconds before unmolding the custard.

SERVES 6 – 8

Bretagne

TARTE AUX FRAISES
Strawberry Tart

10 oz (300 g) sweet pastry (recipe page 246)
½ cup (6½ oz/200 g) raspberry jam
2 tablespoons water
2 lb (1 kg) strawberries

❖Preheat oven to 425°F (215°C). Butter a 10-in (26-cm) tart plate (flan tin). Roll out the pastry into a 12-in (30-cm) circle and line the plate with it. Line with parchment paper and fill with dried beans or pie weights. Bake the pastry for 15 minutes, then remove the beans and paper and bake until the bottom is golden, about 20 minutes. Cool the tart shell on a wire rack. (The shell may be prepared several hours in advance.)
❖An hour before serving time, combine the raspberry jam and water in a small saucepan and cook over low heat until the jam melts. Remove from heat and let cool. Wash, drain and hull the strawberries. Dry with paper towels and refrigerate.
❖Fifteen minutes before serving, arrange the strawberries in the pastry shell, pointed ends up. Coat with the cooled jam and serve.

SERVES 8

Alsace

TARTE AUX POMMES À L'ALSACIENNE
Alsatian Apple Tart

10 oz (300 g) sweet pastry (recipe page 246)
1 lb (500 g) Golden Delicious or pippin apples
4 egg yolks
⅓ cup (3 oz/90 g) sugar
1 envelope vanilla sugar or 3 drops vanilla extract (essence)
4 pinches of cinnamon
¾ cup (6 fl oz/200 ml) heavy (double) cream

❖Preheat oven to 425°F (215°C). Butter a 10-in (26-cm) deep tart plate (flan tin). Roll out the pastry dough into a 12-in (30-cm) circle and line the plate with it.
❖Peel, quarter and core the apples. Cut each quarter into 4 slices. Arrange evenly over the pastry in the form of a rose, starting from the outside and overlapping the slices slightly. Bake for 15 minutes.
❖Meanwhile, combine the egg yolks, sugar, vanilla sugar and cinnamon and beat well. Beat in the cream. Coat the apples with this mixture and bake for another 35 minutes or until the apples are tender. Serve warm.

SERVES 6

STRAWBERRY TART (top) AND
ALSATIAN APPLE TART (bottom)
PETER JOHNSON

Provence

TARTE AU CITRON
Lemon Tart

8 oz (250 g) sweet pastry (recipe page 246)
3 lemons
4 eggs
4 oz (125 g) butter
1 cup (7 oz/220 g) superfine (caster) sugar

❖Preheat oven to 425°F (215°C). Butter a 9-in (24-cm) tart plate (flan tin). Roll out the dough to an 11-in (28-cm) circle and line the tart plate with it. Line with parchment paper and fill with dried beans or pie weights. Bake for 15 minutes.

❖Meanwhile, prepare the filling: wash and dry lemons. Grate the rinds into a bowl. Halve the lemons and squeeze out the juice; pour ¾ cup (6 fl oz/200 ml) of the juice into the bowl. Separate 3 of the eggs. Combine the yolks and whole egg and beat with a fork. Place the whites in a larger bowl.

❖Melt the butter in a saucepan, add ¾ cup (6 oz/185 g) of the sugar and mix well. Add the egg yolk and lemon mixtures and cook over low heat, beating constantly, for 5 minutes or until the mixture thickens. Strain into a large bowl and let cool.

❖Remove the beans and paper from the tart shell and bake until browned, about 10 more minutes. Pour in the lemon filling. Beat the egg whites until very stiff, then beat in the remaining sugar to form a meringue. Spread the meringue evenly over the surface of the tart, using either a large spoon or a piping bag with plain tip. Return the tart to the oven for 10 to 15 minutes or until the meringue is golden. Let cool completely before serving.

SERVES 6   *Photograph page 4*

Provence

TOURTE AUX BLETTES
Swiss Chard Pie

13 oz (400 g) sweet pastry (recipe page 246)
1½ lb (800 g) Swiss chard greens (silverbeet)
2 eggs
½ cup (3½ oz/100 g) firmly packed brown sugar
2 oz (60 g) Edam, Gouda or Emmenthaler cheese, freshly and finely grated
⅔ cup (3 oz/90 g) currants
2½ oz (75 g) pine nuts
1 teaspoon grated lemon rind
freshly ground pepper
1 egg yolk
1 tablespoon milk

❖Preheat oven to 400°F (200°C). Butter an 8-in (22-cm) deep-sided ovenproof china pie plate. Divide the dough in two, one piece a little larger than the other. Roll out the larger piece into a 10-in (25-cm) circle and line the pie plate with it.

❖Wash the chard and place in a very large pot with the water still clinging to the leaves. Cover and cook over high heat for 5 minutes. Drain in a colander and let cool. Squeeze the chard between your hands to get rid of as much moisture as possible, then chop it coarsely.

❖Break the eggs into a mixing bowl and beat in the sugar with a fork. Add the cheese, chard, currants, pine nuts, lemon rind and pepper and mix well. Pour this filling into the pastry shell. Using a pastry brush, moisten the edge of the pastry, then lay the remaining pastry over the top of the filling and crimp the edges of the pastry to seal.

❖Beat the egg yolk and milk and brush the entire surface of the pie with this mixture. Bake for 45 minutes or until the crust is golden. Let the pie cool for 10 minutes before turning it out onto a wire rack. Serve at room temperature.

Provence

FOUGASSE
Provençal Fruit Loaf

Originally this "hearth-cake" was one of the thirteen Provençal Christmas desserts. In some areas it is called fouace, *in others* pompe *or* pogne.

Today you can buy it in any bakery all year round, either savory, filled with anchovies or bacon, or sweet and filled with candied fruit or sprinkled with coarsely crushed loaf sugar.

1 tablespoon superfine (caster) sugar
¼ cup (2 fl oz/60 ml) warm water
1 envelope (½ oz/15 g) dry yeast
7 tablespoons milk
4 cups (1 lb/500 g) all purpose (plain) flour
3 pinches of salt
3 tablespoons olive oil
1 tablespoon orangeflower water
6½ oz (200 g) mixed candied fruit and peel
1 egg yolk
1 tablespoon milk

❖Place the sugar in a 1-cup (250-ml) measure. Add the warm water and stir until the sugar dissolves. Sprinkle the yeast over the surface, stir in and let stand in a warm place for about 10 minutes or until the mixture has risen almost to the top of the cup. Meanwhile, heat 6 tablespoons milk to lukewarm in a small saucepan.

❖Sift the flour into a mixing bowl and make a well in the center. Add the salt, oil, orangeflower water, milk and yeast mixture to the well and mix. Knead the dough until it is smooth and comes away from your fingers. Cover with a cloth and let rise until doubled in volume, about 2 hours.

❖Preheat oven to 425°F (215°C). Chop the candied fruit and peel into ¼-in (.5-cm) cubes. Punch the dough down and knead in half the fruit. Form into a large figure 8.

❖Oil a baking sheet and place the dough on it. Arrange the remaining candied fruit and peel on top, pushing the pieces lightly into the dough. Let rise for 20 minutes.

❖Beat the egg yolk and 1 tablespoon milk and brush the dough with this mixture. Bake for about 30 minutes or until the *fougasse* has risen and browned. Let cool on a wire rack before serving.

SERVES 6

Bretagne

GALETTE BRETONNE
Rum and Butter Cake

2 oz (60 g) candied angelica, finely diced
3 tablespoons rum
5 oz (150 g) soft unsalted butter
⅔ cup (5 oz/150 g) superfine (caster) sugar
pinch of salt
2 cups (8 oz/250 g) all purpose (plain) flour
2 eggs
To glaze:
1 egg yolk
1 tablespoon milk

❖Preheat oven to 400°F (200°C). Butter a deep 9-in (24-cm) ovenproof china tart plate or quiche dish. Place the angelica in a small bowl, sprinkle with the rum and stir.
❖Cream the butter, sugar and salt until pale in color. Using a rubber spatula, stir in half the flour and the eggs, then the remaining flour and the rum-soaked angelica. Add any unabsorbed rum. Press the dough into the center of the tart plate and out to the edge, keeping the surface as smooth as possible.
❖Beat the egg yolk and milk together with a fork and brush over the surface of the *galette*. With the point of a knife, mark the surface with a grid pattern. Bake until browned, about 30 minutes. Turn out onto a rack to cool before serving.

SERVES 6

PROVENÇAL FRUIT LOAF (top) AND RUM AND
BUTTER CAKE (bottom)

PETER JOHNSON

CREAM MOLDS WITH FRUIT

PETER JOHNSON

Anjou

CREMETS
Cream Molds with Fruit

1½ cups (12 fl oz/400 ml) heavy (double) cream
2 egg whites
To serve:
superfine (caster) sugar
chilled heavy (double) cream
red fruits, such as strawberries, raspberries and/or
    red currants

❖Whip the cream until it forms soft peaks. Whisk the egg whites until stiff but not dry. Gently whisk together the two ingredients.
❖Line 4 small round or heart-shaped perforated molds with cheesecloth (muslin). Each should be large enough to hold a quarter of the mixture. Divide the mixture among them and fold the corners of the cheesecloth over the top. Set the molds on a plate and refrigerate for 3 hours.
❖Fold back the corners of the cheesecloth. Unmold each *cremet* onto a dessert plate and remove the cloth. Serve with sugar to taste, cream, and fruits of your choice.

SERVES 4

PETER JOHNSON

NORMANDY COOKIES (top) AND CRISP HONEY COOKIES (bottom)

Normandie

SABLÉS NORMANDS

Normandy Cookies

These little shortbread cookies are also found in Bretagne, where they are made with low-salt butter and given an egg glaze.

1¼ cups (5 oz/150 g) all purpose (plain) flour
5 tablespoons superfine (caster) sugar
3 oz (90 g) soft butter
2 egg yolks

❖Sift the flour onto a work surface and mix in the sugar. Make a well in the center. Add the butter and egg yolks to the well and mix rapidly with your fingertips until all the ingredients are amalgamated. Roll the dough into a ball and let rest in a cool place for 1 hour.
❖Preheat oven to 375°F (190°C). Butter one large or two small baking sheets. Roll the dough out to a thickness of ¼ in (.5 cm) and cut into 1¼-in to 1½-in (3- to 4-cm) circles using a smooth or fluted round cutter.
❖Arrange the *sablés* on the baking sheet(s) and bake until just turning golden, about 10 minutes. Cool on a rack before serving. *Sablés* will keep for several weeks in an airtight tin.

MAKES APPROXIMATELY 20 COOKIES

Auvergne

CROQUANTS

Crisp Honey Cookies

These particularly crunchy little cakes are a specialty of Mauriac, a pretty little town in Cantal.

2 cups (8 oz/250 g) all purpose (plain) flour
6 tablespoons superfine (caster) sugar

3 tablespoons honey
8 oz (250 g) soft butter
2 eggs
To glaze:
1 egg yolk
1 tablespoon honey

❖Sift the flour onto a work surface and make a well in the center. Add the sugar, honey, butter and eggs and mix quickly with the tips of your fingers to form a smooth, stiff dough. Roll it into a ball and let rest in a cool place for 1 hour.
❖Preheat oven to 375°F (190°C). Butter one large or two small baking sheets. Roll the dough out on a lightly floured surface to a thickness of ¼ in (.5 cm). Cut into different shapes (leaves, hearts, wreaths, etc.) with cookie cutters. Arrange the cookies on the baking sheet(s). Beat the egg yolk and honey together and brush over the cookies. Bake until lightly browned, 15 minutes. Cool on a rack before serving.

MAKES APPROXIMATELY 15 – 25 COOKIES

Artois

TARTE AU SUCRE

Sugar Tart

⅓ cup (2½ oz/75 g) sugar
¼ cup (2 fl oz/60 ml) warm water
1 envelope (½ oz/15 g) dry yeast
6 tablespoons milk
2 cups (8 oz/250 g) all purpose (plain) flour
2½ oz (75 g) soft butter
2 egg yolks
6 pinches of salt
For the topping:
¾ cup (4 oz/125 g) firmly packed brown sugar
2 oz (60 g) butter

❖Place a teaspoonful of sugar into a 1-cup (250-ml) measure. Add the warm water and stir until the sugar is dissolved. Sprinkle the yeast onto the surface, stir to mix and let stand in a warm place for about 10 minutes or until the mixture has risen almost to the top of the cup.
❖Meanwhile, heat the milk to lukewarm in a small saucepan. Sift the flour into a mixing bowl and make a well in the center. Cream the butter in another bowl. Add the remaining sugar and beat until pale in color. Add the egg yolks, milk, yeast mixture and salt and mix well. Pour into the center of the flour and mix to form a smooth dough.
❖Place the dough on a work surface and knead for 10 minutes or until it is smooth and comes away from your fingers. Place it in a mixing bowl, cover with a cloth and let rise in a warm place for 2 hours or until doubled in volume.
❖Preheat oven to 425°F (215°C). Butter an 8-in (22-cm) cake pan. Punch the dough down and knead again for 5 minutes. Roll out into an 8-in (22-cm) circle and lay it in the cake pan. Sprinkle with the brown sugar and dot with the butter. Let rise to the top of the pan, about 20 minutes. Bake for about 30 minutes or until puffed and golden. Serve warm or at room temperature.

SERVES 6

Lorraine

TARTE AU FROMAGE BLANC
Cheese Tart

8 oz (250 g) sweet pastry (recipe page 246)
1 lemon
½ cup (4 oz/125 g) sugar
3 whole eggs
1 egg yolk
1 teaspoon all purpose (plain) flour
6 tablespoons heavy (double) cream or crème fraîche
1 lb (500 g) ricotta cheese, drained

❖Preheat oven to 400°F (200°C). Butter a 9-in (24-cm) deep-sided ovenproof china tart plate. Roll out the pastry into an 11-in (28-cm) circle and line the tart plate with it.
❖Wash and dry the lemon and grate the rind into a bowl. Add the sugar, the whole eggs, the yolk and the flour, and beat with a hand beater until the mixture turns pale in color. Add the cream and the drained cheese and continue beating until smooth.
❖Pour the filling into the pastry shell and smooth the surface with a spatula. Bake for 50 minutes or until the filling is puffed and golden. Let the tart cool before serving.

SERVES 6

Lorraine

GÂTEAU DE METZ
Metz Cake

4 eggs
1 cup (7 oz/200 g) superfine (caster) sugar
1 cup (4 oz/125 g) all purpose (plain) flour
1 scant cup (7 oz/200 g) heavy (double) cream or crème fraîche
4 oz (125 g) semisweet or bittersweet (plain) chocolate, grated

❖Preheat oven to 375°F (190°C). Butter an 8-in (22-cm) round cake pan.
❖Beat the eggs and sugar until the mixture is pale in color. Sift the flour and blend in. Add the cream and chocolate and mix well.
❖Pour the batter into the prepared pan and bake for 45 minutes or until a tester inserted in the center comes out clean.
❖Turn the cake out onto a rack and cool completely before serving.

SERVES 6

SUGAR TART (bottom left), CHEESE TART (bottom right) AND METZ CAKE (top)

PETER JOHNSON

241

CREAM HORNS (top) AND MADELEINES (bottom)

Lorraine

MADELEINES DE COMMERCY
Madeleines

Stanislas Leszczynski, Marie Leszcynska's cook, Talleyrand's cook Avice, and Mme Perrotin de Barmond's cook, Madeleine Paulmier — have all been credited with the invention of the madeleine. This "little shell of cake, so generously sensual beneath the piety of its stern pleating," as Marcel Proust described it, remains, however, the uncontested specialty of the small town of Commercy.

3 eggs
¼ cup (2 oz/60 g) superfine (caster) sugar
½ teaspoon orangeflower water
2 oz (60 g) soft butter
½ cup (2 oz/60 g) all purpose (plain) flour

❖Preheat oven to 375°F (190°C). Butter 20 to 24 madeleine tins, depending on size.
❖Combine the eggs and sugar and beat until the mixture is pale in color. Stir in the orangeflower water and butter. Sift in the flour and fold in gently.
❖Divide the batter among the molds, filling them ¾ full. Bake for 15 minutes or until the madeleines have risen and are lightly browned. Turn out and cool on a rack before serving.

MAKES APPROXIMATELY 24 MADELEINES

Auvergne

CORNETS DE MURAT
Cream Horns

2 oz (60 g) butter
2 egg whites
6 tablespoons superfine (caster) sugar
½ cup (2 oz/60 g) all purpose (plain) flour
1 tablespoon dark rum
For the filling:
2½ cups (20 fl oz/600 ml) very cold heavy (double) cream
1 envelope vanilla sugar or ¼ teaspoon vanilla extract (essence)

❖Preheat oven to 375°F (190°C). Butter one large or two small baking sheets. Melt the butter in a small saucepan, then remove from heat and let cool.
❖Beat the egg whites with a fork until frothy. Mix in the sugar. Sift in the flour and stir, then beat in the butter and rum. Drop the batter by tablespoonfuls onto the baking sheet(s); it will spread out slightly to form small circles.
❖Bake for 8 to 10 minutes or until the pastry circles are just golden. Quickly form the hot wafers into cone shapes, inserting the point of the pastry into the neck of a bottle and it will hold its shape until it cools. Let cool completely.
❖At serving time, whip the cream and vanilla sugar to soft peaks. Spoon into a pastry bag filled with a small fluted tip and pipe into the cones.
❖The cream horns may be prepared several hours in advance, but should be served as soon as they are filled.

SERVES 6

Lorraine

MACARONS DE NANCY
Nancy Macaroons

At the time of the French Revolution, when the monastic orders were dispersed in 1792, some nuns found refuge at the home of a middle-class family in rue de la Hache, Nancy. To pay for their lodging they baked these little delicacies, and so great was their success that the nuns who began selling them became known as the "macaroon sisters."

⅔ cup (5 oz/150 g) superfine (caster) sugar
1⅓ cups (5 oz/150 g) ground almonds
2 egg whites
1 tablespoon powdered (icing) sugar

❖Mix the sugar and ground almonds in a mixing bowl. Add the egg whites and beat rapidly with a wooden spoon until well mixed. Cover the bowl and refrigerate for at least 2 and not more than 8 hours.
❖Preheat oven to 350°F (180°C). Lightly oil a baking sheet and line with waxed paper; oil the paper. Divide the dough into 16 balls, shaping them with wet hands. Arrange on the waxed paper and flatten into discs ¼ in (.5 cm) thick. Sift the powdered sugar over them.
❖Bake the macaroons for 15 minutes or until barely colored.
❖Place the waxed paper on a wet tea towel and let the macaroons cool completely. They will come away from the paper very easily.

MAKES APPROXIMATELY 12 MACAROONS

NANCY MACAROONS (center right), BEE'S NEST CAKE (bottom, recipe page 244) AND ALMOND AND RAISIN CAKE (top, recipe page 244), PHOTOGRAPHED IN ALSACE
PIERRE HUSSENOT/AGENCE TOP

Alsace

NID D'ABEILLES

Bee's Nest Cake

For the bread dough:
2 cups (8 oz/250 g) all purpose (plain) flour
3 oz (90 g) soft butter
1 egg
6 tablespoons warm milk
1 envelope (½ oz/15 g) dry yeast
2 tablespoons sugar
3 pinches of salt
For the glaze:
2 oz (60 g) butter
1 tablespoon honey
⅓ cup (3 oz/90 g) superfine (caster) sugar
3 oz (90 g) slivered (flaked) almonds
For the custard:
2 cups (16 fl oz/500 ml) milk
3 egg yolks
⅓ cup (3 oz/90 g) sugar
⅓ cup (1½ oz/50 g) all purpose (plain) flour
1 tablespoon kirsch

❖Prepare the bread dough according to the recipe on page 41, adding the butter and egg with the milk. Let rise until doubled in volume, about 2 hours.
❖Butter a deep-sided 10-in (26-cm) ovenproof china tart plate. Pat down the dough to its original volume and spread in the tart plate.
❖Prepare the glaze: heat the butter and honey in a saucepan over gentle heat, stirring until melted. Mix in the sugar and almonds and remove from heat. Distribute this mixture evenly in teaspoonfuls over the dough. Let rise in a warm place until doubled in volume, about 30 minutes.
❖Preheat oven to 400°F (200°C). Bake the cake for 25 minutes; if it seems to be browning too much, lower the heat to 375°F (190°C).
❖Meanwhile, prepare the custard: bring the milk to boil in a small saucepan. In a large saucepan, whisk the egg yolks and sugar until pale in color. Add the flour and mix well. Whisk in the boiling milk. Place over medium heat and beat until the custard thickens; let it boil for another minute. Remove from heat and add the kirsch. Let cool, stirring from time to time.
❖Let the cake cool for 5 minutes, then cover it with a sheet of foil and invert it onto a plate. Turn it back again onto a wire rack to cool completely. Cut horizontally into two halves, fill with the custard and serve.

SERVES 8 *Photograph page 243*

Alsace

KUGELHOPF

Almond and Raisin Cake

Legend has it that a certain Kügel, a potter by trade, offered hospitality to the Three Wise Men on their way home from Bethlehem. By way of thanks, they are supposed to have made a special mold, the kugelhopf, *and baked a cake in it.*

The real story of this cake is not known, but it appears that Marie Antoinette brought it to France from Austria, and it has since become one of the glories of the Alsace cuisine.

6 tablespoons raisins
2 tablespoons kirsch
¼ cup (2 oz/60 g) superfine (caster) sugar
¼ cup (2 fl oz/60 ml) warm water
1 envelope (½ oz/15 g) dry yeast
6 tablespoons milk
4 oz (125 g) soft butter
2 cups (8 oz/250 g) all purpose (plain) flour
2 eggs
4 pinches of salt
For the mold:
1 tablespoon butter
2 tablespoons all purpose (plain) flour
2 tablespoons slivered (flaked) almonds
To serve:
1 tablespoon powdered (icing) sugar

❖Wash the raisins under warm water, drain and place in a bowl. Sprinkle with kirsch.
❖Place ⅓ of the sugar in a 6-oz (200-ml) glass. Add the warm water and stir until the sugar dissolves. Sprinkle the yeast over the surface and mix in. Let stand in a warm place for about 10 minutes or until the mixture is level with the rim of the glass.
❖Meanwhile, warm the milk in a small saucepan. Work the butter with a spatula until creamy.
❖Sift the flour into a mixing bowl. Make a well in the center and add the eggs, salt, remaining sugar, milk and yeast mixture and blend well. Add the butter and mix again. Turn the dough out onto a work surface and knead by hand, adding the raisins; lift the dough as high as possible and let it fall again to achieve maximum aeration.
❖Butter and flour a 9-in (22-cm) kugelhopf mold. Turn it in your hands and shake it to remove excess flour; press the slivered almonds into the grooves of the fluting. Place the dough mixture into the mold. Cover with a clean towel and let rise for about 1 hour or until it is level with the rim of the mold.
❖Preheat oven to 375°F (190°C). Bake the kugelhopf for 40 minutes or until golden brown. Turn it out onto a wire rack to cool, then transfer to a serving plate. Sprinkle with powdered sugar and serve.

SERVES 6 *Photograph page 243*

Languedoc

CASTANHET

Chestnut Cake

This cake was traditionally eaten with a glass of the local liqueur after chestnut-gathering in the Cévennes and the Ardèche.

2 lb (1 kg) chestnuts
2 oz (50 g) butter
2 eggs
⅔ cup (5 oz/150 g) superfine (caster) sugar
1 envelope vanilla sugar or 3 drops vanilla extract (essence)

❖Make a slash on the flat side of each chestnut. Bring a large saucepan of water to boil. Drop in the chestnuts and boil for 30 minutes; drain. While still hot, remove the outer shell and the brown inner skin.
❖Preheat oven to 400°F (200°C). Butter a 9-in (24-cm) cake pan. Put the chestnuts through the fine holes of a food mill.

Blend in the butter, using a wooden spoon. Whisk the eggs and sugar in a bowl until the mixture is pale in color. Blend in the chestnut puree. Pour into the prepared pan and bake for 30 minutes. Turn the cake out onto a serving plate. Dust the top with vanilla sugar. Let cool before serving.

SERVES 6

Limoges/Auvergne

GÂTEAU AU POTIRON
Pumpkin Cake

2 lb (1 kg) peeled and seeded pumpkin
3 eggs, separated
½ cup (4 oz/125 g) sugar
2 tablespoons dark rum
⅓ cup (1½ oz/50 g) cornstarch (cornflour)
¼ cup (1 oz/25 g) all purpose (plain) flour

❖ Cut the pumpkin into ¾-in (2-cm) cubes and steam for 20 minutes or until very soft. Drain in a colander, then put it through the fine holes of a food mill or blend to a smooth puree in a food processor.

❖ Preheat oven to 400°F (200°C). Butter a 9-in (24-cm) cake pan or mold. Combine the egg yolks and sugar and whisk until the mixture is pale in color. Stir in the rum and pumpkin puree, then the cornstarch and flour. Beat the egg whites until stiff and fold them gently into the mixture.

❖ Pour the batter into the prepared pan and bake for 40 minutes.

❖ Let the cake cool for 10 minutes in the pan, then turn out on a rack and cool completely before serving.

SERVES 6

PETER JOHNSON   PUMPKIN CAKE (top) AND CHESTNUT CAKE (bottom)

PETER JOHNSON

ICE CREAM PLOMBIÈRES

Lorraine

GLACE PLOMBIÈRES
Ice Cream Plombières

In 1858 Napoleon III met Cavour at Plombières-les-Bains. In honor of the visit, the keeper of a local eating-house invented this dessert, christened plombières, *or* glace plombières. *Today the name is also given to an ice cream made with candied fruits soaked in kirsch, which are added to an almond custard base.*

6 cups (48 fl oz/1.5 l) heavy (double) cream
1⅓ cups (7 oz/220 g) blanched almonds
1 cup (8 fl oz/250 ml) milk
10 egg yolks
1 cup (7 oz/220 g) sugar
½ teaspoon almond extract (essence)
¾ cup (8 oz/250 g) apricot jam

❖ Bring 4 cups (32 fl oz/1 l) cream to boil in a saucepan. Remove from heat. Combine the almonds and milk in a food processor. Blend until the almonds are ground, then pour the mixture through a strainer into the cream in the saucepan.

❖ Combine the egg yolks and sugar in a second saucepan and whisk until the mixture is very pale in color. Add the almond milk and cook over gentle heat, stirring constantly, until the custard coats the spoon. Remove from heat and add the almond extract. Let cool, stirring from time to time.

❖ When the custard is completely cooled, whip the remaining cream until it forms soft peaks. Fold into the almond mixture. Pour into a large round or square mold and freeze until firm.

❖ Meanwhile, heat the jam in a small saucepan. Force through a fine strainer and let cool.

❖ Plunge the mold into hot water for 20 seconds; then unmold the ice cream onto a plate. Coat with the jam and serve immediately.

SERVES 8

UPSIDE DOWN APPLE TART

Orléanais

TARTE TATIN
Upside Down Apple Tart

The Tatin sisters ran a restaurant at Lamotte-Beuvron in Sologne at the beginning of this century. They created this tart, with its crusty golden pastry beneath a filling of soft caramelized apples. Being cooked upside down, it also goes by the name of tarte renversée *or* tarte à l'envers.

3 oz (90 g) soft butter
⅓ cup (3 oz/90 g) sugar
3 lb (1.5 kg) Golden Delicious or pippin apples
8 oz (250 g) sweet pastry (recipe below)

❖Preheat oven to 425°F (215°C). Grease a 9-in (24-cm) cake pan with ⅔ of the butter, then sprinkle over ⅔ of the sugar. Cut the apples in two, peel and core them, and arrange the halves upright, tightly packed in the cake pan. Sprinkle with the remaining sugar and the butter which has been cut into small pieces. Place the pan over medium heat and cook for 20 minutes or until a light caramel forms on the bottom.
❖Transfer the pan to the oven and bake for 5 minutes to cook the top surface. Remove from the oven.
❖Roll out the dough to a 10-in (26-cm) circle. Place over the cake pan and pass the rolling pin around the edge to remove the overhanging pastry. The dough will sink down the sides of the tin onto the top of the apples.
❖Return the pan to the oven and bake for 20 minutes or until the pastry is well browned. Invert the tart onto a serving plate and serve at once.

SERVES 6

PÂTE SUCRÉE
Sweet Short (Shortcrust) Pastry

For approximately 1 lb (500 g) pastry: *
4 oz (125 g) soft butter
⅓ cup (3 oz/90 g) superfine (caster) sugar
1 egg
2 cups (8 oz/250 g) all purpose (plain) flour
2 pinches of salt

❖Cream the butter and sugar until pale and fluffy. Add the egg and mix for 30 seconds. Add the flour and salt and mix until a smooth dough forms.
❖Place the pastry on a work surface and knead, pushing it out with the palm of the hand then reforming it into a ball, until the dough is smooth and elastic; this should take about 5 minutes. Wrap the ball of dough in plastic and refrigerate for at least 2 hours, preferably longer. Remove from the refrigerator 1 hour before using. Any leftover pastry can be stored in the refrigerator for 4 days or frozen.
❖The egg will prevent this pastry from becoming soggy, even when cooked directly with the filling. It may also be baked blind, in large or small pans, by covering the pastry with waxed or parchment paper and filling it with rice, dried beans or pie weights.

* *Makes enough to line two 9- to 10-inch (24- to 26-cm) pans.*

Ile de France

PARIS–BREST
Praline Butter Cream Cake

A Paris pastrycook was watching the Paris-to-Brest cycling race passing in front of his shop in 1891 when he had the idea of creating this cake, which is ring-shaped like a bicycle wheel.

13 oz (400 g) choux pastry (recipe page 247)
1 egg white
2 oz (60 g) slivered (flaked) almonds
For the filling:
1⅓ cups (11 oz/350 ml) milk
3 egg yolks
⅓ cup (3 oz/90 g) superfine (caster) sugar
½ vanilla bean (pod)
¾ cup (3 oz/90 g) all purpose (plain) flour
100 g powdered praline (see below)
3 oz (90 g) soft butter
2 tablespoons powdered (icing) sugar
For the praline:
2 oz (60 g) almonds, coarsely chopped
¼ cup (2 oz/60 g) sugar
3 drops lemon juice

❖Preheat oven to 425°F (215°C). Lightly oil a nonstick baking sheet. Place an 8-in (20-cm) plate in the center of it. Place the choux pastry dough into a pastry bag fitted with a plain ¾-in (1.5-cm) tip and pipe a circle of pastry around the edge of the plate. Remove the plate and pipe another circle of pastry inside the first one, then pipe a third circle overlapping the first two. Lightly beat the egg white with a fork until frothy and brush over the pastry. Scatter the slivered almonds over. Bake for 15 minutes, then lower the heat to 375°F (190°C) and bake for 15 minutes longer.
❖Meanwhile, prepare the filling: bring the milk to boil in a small saucepan. Combine the egg yolks, sugar and vanilla bean in a large saucepan and whisk until the mixture turns pale in color. Add the flour and mix again. Whisk in the boiling milk. Place over moderate heat and cook the custard, beating constantly, until it thickens. Let it boil for 1 minute, then remove from heat and let cool, stirring occasionally. When cool, add the praline and then the butter, beating by hand for 2 minutes. Refrigerate.
❖To make the praline: in a dry pan over medium heat,

lightly brown the almonds for 5 minutes. In a separate pan melt the sugar with the lemon juice to make a light caramel. Add the almonds and mix for 2 minutes until the caramel darkens. Pour onto a marble slab and let cool completely. Break the caramel and pound or grind to a fine powder.

❖Let pastry stand in the turned-off oven for 10 minutes with the oven door slightly ajar. Remove from the oven and let cool. Cut the pastry in two horizontally, a third of the way from the top; the bottom part, which is to be filled, must be higher.

❖Place the cooled filling in a pastry bag fitted with a fluted ¾-in (2-cm) tip. Fill the bottom of the pastry with the custard, letting it overlap the edges slightly. Replace the top third of the pastry. Sprinkle with powdered sugar and keep in a cool place until serving time.

SERVES 6	*Photograph pages 222 – 223*

PÂTE À CHOUX
Choux Pastry

For approximately 1 lb 10 oz (800 g) pastry:
1¼ cups (150 g) all purpose (plain) flour
1 cup (8 fl oz/250 ml) water
2 teaspoons sugar
1 teaspoon salt
3 oz (90 g) butter
5 eggs

❖Sift the flour into a large bowl. Combine the water, sugar, salt and butter in a saucepan over low heat and bring just to boil. Remove from heat. Pour in all the flour, stirring quickly with a wooden spoon.

❖Return the saucepan to the stove and stir over low heat for 1 minute longer to dry out the mixture. Remove from heat and beat in the eggs one at a time, completely incorporating each before the next is added. Once the last egg has been mixed in, stop stirring; this helps produce smooth, uniform puffs.

❖The finished pastry may be used immediately or wrapped in plastic and refrigerated for several days.

Provence

OREILLETTES
Pastry Puffs

Oreillettes *in Provence,* bottereaux *in Vendée,* bugnes *in Lyon,* frivolles *in Champagne,* merveilles *in Charentes,* guenilles *in Auvergne,* carquelin *in Savoie — all these are names for the fritters that are made all over France for Mardi Gras, Mid-Lent, Christmas, and at times of family celebration.*

2½ cups (10 oz/300 g) all purpose (plain) flour
3 eggs
1 oz (30 g) soft butter
grated rind of 1 orange and 1 lemon
1 teaspoon orangeflower water
3 pinches of salt
2 qt (2 l) peanut (groundnut) oil
To serve:
superfine (caster) sugar

❖Sift the flour onto a work surface and make a well in the center. Add the eggs, butter, grated rinds, orangeflower water and salt and mix with your fingertips, beginning from the center and working out. Then work the dough by pushing it away from you repeatedly with the flat of your hand until it is smooth and soft and comes away from your fingers.

❖Roll the dough into a ball, wrap in plastic and refrigerate for 4 hours.

❖Roll the dough out on a floured surface as thinly as possible. Cut into 3 x 1½-in (8 x 4-cm) rectangles. Heat the oil in a deep fryer to 375°F (190°C). Drop in the dough pieces in batches and fry until puffed and brown. Turn with a skimmer, remove and then drain on paper towels.

❖When all the pastries are cooked, pile them on a plate, sprinkling sugar over each layer. They should be served the day they are made.

MAKES APPROXIMATELY 20 – 30	*Photograph page 4*

Normandie

TERRINÉE
Caramel Rice Pudding

Also known as beurgoule *or* teurgoule, *the* terrinée *is a traditional dessert of Normandie. In the old days it was left to cook all night in the baker's oven.*

It is often served with a slice of fallue *— a kind of brioche — or with the Normandie version of* sablés.

2 qt (2 l) whole milk
⅔ cup (4 oz/125 g) short-grain rice
½ cup (4 oz/125 g) superfine (caster) sugar
4 pinches of cinnamon

❖Preheat oven to 175°F (80°C). Pour the milk into a saucepan and bring to boil. Let cool.

❖Mix the rice, sugar and cinnamon in a 4-qt (4-l) baking dish. Stir in the cooled milk. Bake uncovered for 6 hours without disturbing. When the *terrinée* is cooked, the rice will be covered with a thick, shiny brown skin which has a delicious caramel taste. Serve the pudding warm or hot.

SERVES 6

CARAMEL RICE PUDDING

PETER JOHNSON

PETER JOHNSON

GINGERBREAD

Bourgogne

PAIN D'ÉPICES
Gingerbread

References to pain d'épices — a mixture of flours, honey and spices — are found throughout history. In France the most famous version today is that of Dijon, which has taken over from the success of the Rheims pain d'épices.

Its origins certainly go back to 1452, when Philippe Le Bon tasted a galette with honey and spices in Flandres and at once took into his service the man who had prepared it. So began a time of glory for Dijon, with the three feathers in its cap: mustard, cassis and pain d'épices.

½ cup (4 fl oz/125 ml) water
½ cup (4 oz/125 g) sugar
⅓ cup (4 oz/125 g) honey
2 cups (8 oz/250 g) all purpose (plain) flour
½ cup (2 oz/60 g) rye flour
2 teaspoons baking powder
grated rind of 1 orange
1 tablespoon cinnamon
1 teaspoon ground aniseed
½ teaspoon ground ginger
pinch of salt

❖Preheat oven to 375°F (190°C). Butter a 9-in (24-cm) square cake pan. Combine the water and sugar in a saucepan and bring to boil. Cook for 5 minutes over low heat. Remove from heat and stir in the honey.
❖Sift the two flours and the baking powder into a large mixing bowl. Mix in the orange rind, spices and salt. Make a well in the center, pour in the contents of the saucepan and stir for 5 minutes. Turn the batter into the prepared pan.

❖Bake for 40 minutes or until a tester inserted in the center comes out clean. Let cool for 15 minutes in the pan, then turn out onto a rack to finish cooling.
❖The gingerbread will keep for several weeks in an airtight tin.

SERVES 6

Pays Basque

GÂTEAU BASQUE
Basque Cake

In Itxassou and Sarre gâteau Basque is filled with black cherries in syrup and cherry jam rather than crème pâtissière.

4½ oz (140 g) butter
2 eggs
11 tablespoons superfine (caster) sugar
1 teaspoon vanilla extract (essence)
1 tablespoon dark rum
2¼ cups (9 oz/280 g) all purpose (plain) flour
1 teaspoon baking powder
2 pinches of salt
For the filling:
1 cup (8 fl oz/250 ml) milk
3 egg yolks
⅓ cup (3 oz/90 g) superfine (caster) sugar
¼ cup (1 oz/30 g) all purpose (plain) flour
1 tablespoon dark rum
1 teaspoon vanilla extract (essence)
For the glaze:
1 egg yolk
1 tablespoon milk

❖Melt the butter in a small saucepan over low heat, then let cool. Combine the eggs, sugar and vanilla and mix well. Blend in the butter and rum. Sift in the flour, baking powder and salt and stir until a soft dough forms. Refrigerate for 1 hour.
❖Meanwhile, prepare the filling: bring the milk to simmer in a small saucepan. Combine the egg yolks and sugar in a large saucepan and whisk until pale in color. Mix in the flour. Beat in the hot milk. Place the saucepan over moderate heat and cook the custard until it thickens, beating constantly. Let boil for 1 minute, then remove from heat and add the rum and vanilla. Let cool, stirring occasionally.
❖Preheat oven to 400°F (200°C). Butter a 10-in (26-cm) round cake pan. Divide the dough into two pieces, one a little larger than the other. Roll out the larger portion into a 9-in (24-cm) circle ⅜ in (1 cm) thick. Carefully line the cake pan with the dough, flattening it against the sides. Spread the custard on top and turn the edge of the dough circle back over the custard, but do not press down. Moisten the edge of the dough with a pastry brush dipped in cold water. Roll out the remaining dough into a 9-in (24-cm) circle and lower it into the pan to cover the custard.
❖For the glaze, beat the egg yolk and milk and brush over the top of the cake. Bake the cake for 40 minutes or until golden brown. Let cool before turning out of the pan. Let the cake rest at room temperature for a few hours before serving.

SERVES 8

BASQUE CAKE
PIERRE HUSSENOT/AGENCE TOP

Ile de France

CRÊPES SUZETTE

Orange Liqueur Crêpes

Were these famous pancakes invented in 1896 at the Café de Paris when the Prince of Wales visited in the company of a lady named Suzette, or in 1898 at the Maire restaurant? The mystery remains. As for their filling, some people maintain that mandarin oranges are indispensable; others prefer oranges.

For the batter:
1 cup (4 oz/125 g) all purpose (plain) flour
2 cups (16 fl oz/500 ml) milk
2 eggs
1 tablespoon sugar
1 envelope vanilla sugar or 3 drops vanilla extract (essence)
1 tablespoon peanut (groundnut) oil
4 pinches of salt
For the garnish:
4 oz (125 g) soft butter
2 mandarin oranges
⅓ cup (3 oz/90 g) sugar
3 tablespoons cognac
6 tablespoons curaçao

❖Make the batter: place the flour in a food processor. Add the milk, eggs, sugar and vanilla sugar, oil and salt and process until you have a smooth, liquid batter. Pour through a strainer into a bowl and let rest for 1 hour.
❖Melt 1 oz (20 g) butter in a nonstick 8-in (22-cm) skillet, then pour it into a bowl. Using a small ladle, pour some batter into the skillet and tilt it so that the mixture spreads to cover the bottom. When it is golden on the bottom, about 40 seconds, turn the crêpe over with a spatula and cook for about 30 seconds longer.
❖Ten minutes before serving, wash the mandarin oranges and wipe dry. Grate the rind finely into the skillet in which the crêpes were cooked. Halve the oranges and squeeze the juice into the skillet. Add the remaining butter, the sugar, 1 tablespoon cognac and 3 tablespoons curaçao and boil until a thick syrup forms, about 1 minute. Dip the crêpes into the syrup one by one, fold each in quarters and arrange on a large plate; keep warm. Drizzle with the syrup remaining in the skillet.
❖Heat the remaining cognac and curaçao in a small saucepan. Bring the crêpes to the table. Pour the boiling alcohol mixture over them and ignite. Serve as soon as the flames subside.

SERVES 6   *Photograph pages 222 – 223*

Savoie

BISCUIT DE SAVOIE

Savoy Sponge

1 cup (8 oz/250 g) superfine (caster) sugar
7 eggs, separated
2 teaspoons vanilla extract (essence) or the grated rind of 1 lemon
1 scant cup (3½ oz/100 g) all purpose (plain) flour
¾ cup (3½ oz/100 g) potato starch (potato flour)
For serving:

1 tablespoon powdered (icing) sugar

❖Preheat oven to 280°F (140°C). Butter and flour a 9-in (24-cm) round cake pan.
❖Combine the sugar, egg yolks and vanilla and beat with an electric mixer at high speed until the mixture is pale in color and tripled in volume. Sift the flour and potato starch and fold in. Beat the egg whites to stiff peaks and fold quickly into the batter.
❖Spread the batter in the prepared pan and bake for 50 minutes or until the cake is golden brown and a tester inserted in the center comes out clean.
❖Turn off the oven and let the cake rest for 10 minutes in the oven with the door open, then turn out of the pan onto a wire rack to cool completely. Sprinkle with powdered sugar before serving.
❖The sponge may be eaten as is or filled with chocolate cream, jam, pastry cream or custard. It can also be used as a base for any kind of charlotte.

SERVES 6

Savoie-Dauphiné

GRENOBLOIS

Grenoble Caramel Walnut Cake

10 oz (300 g) butter
8 oz (250 g) walnuts
6 eggs, separated
1 cup (7 oz/200 g) superfine (caster) sugar
3 tablespoons dark rum
1 teaspoon coffee extract (or 1 teaspoon instant coffee dissolved in 1 teaspoon water)
¾ cup (3 oz/90 g) dry breadcrumbs
For serving:
6 tablespoons sugar
6 tablespoons water
½ teaspoon fresh lemon juice
walnuts

❖Preheat oven to 400°F (200°C). Butter a 9-in (24-cm) round cake pan. Melt the butter over low heat in a small saucepan and let cool. Finely chop the walnuts in a food processor.
❖Combine the egg yolks with ⅔ cup (5 oz/150 g) sugar and whisk until the mixture doubles in volume and is pale in color, about 10 minutes. Fold in the butter, rum and coffee extract, then the breadcrumbs and walnuts.
❖Beat the egg whites to soft peaks, then gradually add the remaining sugar and beat until smooth and shiny. Gently fold the egg whites into the walnut mixture. Pour the batter into the prepared pan and bake until browned, about 35 minutes.
❖Meanwhile, combine the 6 tablespoons sugar, water and lemon juice in a small saucepan and bring to boil. Cook until a dark caramel forms.
❖Turn the cake out onto a serving plate. Pour the caramel over and decorate with walnuts. Let cool completely before serving.

SERVES 8

SAVOY SPONGE (top) AND GRENOBLE
CARAMEL WALNUT CAKE (bottom)
PETER JOHNSON

GLOSSARY

ANCHOVIES, SALTED OR IN OIL: salted anchovies are fresh anchovies preserved in brine. They are sold by weight. Anchovies in oil are salted anchovies separated into fillets, rinsed, drained and marinated in oil. They are sold in tins or jars.

ANISE LIQUEUR: a liqueur flavored with star anise, much appreciated in the South of France, where it flavors many desserts.

ARAIGNÉE: this long-legged crab — hence its name, spider crab or *maia squinado* — is caught in the Mediterranean and Atlantic, especially in Aquitaine and the Basque region. Its firm, fine-textured and delicate flesh is much appreciated.

ARMAGNAC: a spirit, distilled from wine, which is produced in a defined area of Gascogne — essentially within the *département* of Gers. The region is divided into three areas of production: Bas-Armagnac, which produces a first-class brandy; Ténéraze, with its fragrant brandies; and Haut-Armagnac, where the brandies are less well defined. Armagnac is labeled *"monopole," "selection"* or *"trois etoiles"* (three stars) if it has been aged for at least a year; "VO" (very old), "VSOP" (very superior old pale) or *"réserve"* after at least four years of aging; and "extra," *"napoléon," "vieille réserve"* (old reserve) or *"hors d'âge"* when aged for more than five years. Armagnac is excellent for drinking at the end of a meal, and is also used in many main dishes and desserts to add strength and aroma.

ARTICHOKE: the large Breton artichoke is always eaten cooked, while the small purple artichoke of Provence is superb whether cooked or not — like the little *poivrade* artichokes that are munched raw.

BAGUETTE: this is the most familiar form of French bread. It is a long, crusty stick weighing 8 oz (250 g), most commonly prepared with bleached white flour.

BASIL: this herb has symbolized Mediterranean cuisine since the invention of *pistou*. There are several varieties, with smaller or larger leaves and with a more or less pronounced flavor. A decorative purple basil is also available.

BEANS: Broad bean: known for thousands of years, broad beans are most particularly appreciated in all the southern parts of France. Fresh in summer and autumn, they are sold in shells enclosing between five and ten beans of a green color, covered with a skin which must be removed before eating them, raw or cooked. Dried broad beans are also available; they must be soaked before cooking, like other dried beans.

Haricots verts: French green beans are cultivated mostly in the Val de Loire and in Provence, and are eaten from late spring until late fall. Several sizes are available, from thick to extra thin; the thinnest beans are considered the tastiest.

Flageolets: these beans are found ready to be shelled in all markets during late summer and in the fall. Out of season, they can be purchased dried, and should then be soaked for around 12 hours before cooking. These pretty beans, of a delicate green color, can be replaced by any other shelled white beans — navy beans, for example.

BOUQUET GARNI: a combination of herbs and flavorings tied together and used to flavor stocks and simmered dishes. The basic composition includes thyme, bay leaf and parsley, but according to the region and the type of dish, it might also include celery stalks, branches of fennel, leek leaves, orange rind.

BROUSSE DE BREBIS: as the name implies, this is a ewe's milk cheese. It comes fresh in a hemispherical shape, drained in wicker baskets or, today, in plastic cartons. The cheese is white, soft, very mild and flavorful. It is just as delicious in savory preparations (stuffings, tarts) as in desserts (cakes, mousses, charlottes).

BUTTER: a very important ingredient in French cuisine, particularly delicious when farm-made from unpasteurized milk. Most often it is sold in pasteurized form. It is important to differentiate unsalted butter from *demi-sel* or lightly salted butter, a Breton specialty. The best unsalted butters come from Normandie, Charentes and Deux-Sèvres.

CALVADOS: a spirit distilled in Normandie from cider. It is very good used in cooking, and excellent for adding an apple flavor to cakes and pastries. In Bretagne and Normandie a *"café-calva"* is served: the calvados comes with the coffee, and is either drunk after it or poured into the hot coffee before drinking.

CANTAL: a cheese with 45% fat, produced in Auvergne from cow's milk. It is semisoft and comes in the form of a cylinder about 16 in (40 cm) in diameter and 16 in (40 cm) high, weighing about 40 kg. The greyish crust hides a pale-colored cheese, firm and somewhat crumbly, its flavor slightly biting.

CAYENNE PEPPER: a fine red powder often known simply as "cayenne", made from the dried and powdered fruits of the cayenne pepper. These slender, long, pointed and very hot fruits are known as "bird peppers" in the Antilles.

CHEESES: the varieties of French cheese are by now too numerous to mention. Some of them are used mainly as the final addition to a dish; Gruyère or Parmesan, for example, is simply grated over pasta or rice or used in various stuffings. Others, however, are an integral part of a recipe — for example, in Savoie *comté* cheese is used in the celebrated local soufflé and in chicken dishes (see recipes). We should also note the many regional recipes using *beaufort*, goat cheese, *tomme* (made with cow's, goat's or ewe's milk depending on the region) or roquefort (a ewe's milk cheese with veins of blue mold that develop during the aging process).

COCKLE: a pale-shelled mollusk found in the Mediterranean, Baltic and American Atlantic. They can be eaten raw or cooked.

COGNAC: a spirit, distilled from wine, which is made in the area around Cognac, a town in Charentes. Cognac is labeled *"trois étoiles"* (three stars) if it has aged for at least two years; "VO" (very old), "VSOP" (very superior old pale) or *"réserve"* after at least five years of aging; and "extra," *"napoléon"* or *"vieille réserve"* (old reserve) when aged for more than seven years. Cognac is an excellent drink for the end of a meal; it is also used to add aroma to numerous main dishes and desserts. *"Fine champagne"* or liqueur cognac is a blending of the first two cognac vintages (*Grande Champagne* and *Petite Champagne*), containing at least 50% *Grande Champagne*.

CRAYFISH: there are numerous varieties of this little freshwater crustacean, which looks like a miniature lobster. The most famous, and the tastiest (with flavor like a lobster), is the crayfish *à pattes rouges*, with red claws. Unfortunately it is becoming more and more rare in our rivers and is most often imported or farmed.

CRÈME FRAICHE: a mature cream with a nutty, slightly sour tang. It can be made mixing two tablespoons of cultured buttermilk with two cups heavy cream; cover and let stand at room temperature until thick or leave overnight. Stir cream, then cover and refrigerate to thicken it further.

CRÉPINE: caul fat, a very thin membrane with veins of white fat which covers the internal organs of the pig. Used to wrap terrines and pâtés, it must always be soaked in warm water before use, to soften.

CROUTONS: small slices of bread fried in butter or oil, or simply toasted.

EMMENTHALER: a firm cheese, with 45% fat, prepared from cow's milk in the Franche-Comté or Savoie. It comes as enormous wheels 32 in (80 cm) in diameter and 10 in (25 cm) high, weighing as much as 180 lb (90 kg). The crust is smooth and yellow, the cheese mild and fruity, with large holes.

FAISSELLE: a fresh cow's milk cheese, solid in a *faisselle* (hence its name), a sort of colander in which the cheese drains.

GARLIC: it is important to differentiate the new season type from garlic that has been stored. The former appears in the markets around the end of spring and is available until the end of summer; it has a white or purplish bulb and a long stalk. The peeled garlic clove is white, mild and fruity, easy to digest (because the germ has not developed) and aromatic. As it dries, its flavor becomes stronger and more noticeable. Garlic braids can be kept for a whole year in a cool, dry place. After fall, the soft green germ, or shoot, starts to develop in the heart of the cloves. It is indigestible and should be removed, either after the clove of garlic is cut in half or just before it is eaten cooked whole.

GOOSE FAT: this is the fat from inside the goose, melted and then strained. Sold in jars and tins, it is very popular in the cuisine of the southwestern regions. Once used, it may be strained and stored in the refrigerator in a tightly sealed container for about one month. Take care; goose fat quickly becomes rancid.

GUINEA FOWL: this bird has tender flesh with a flavor resembling pheasant.

HAM, COOKED (*jambon cuit*): also known as *jambon de Paris*. Boned and cooked in water, it is traditionally prepared in most *charcuteries*. When the leg of pork is left whole with the bone in, it is called ham on the bone (*jambon à l'os*) or York ham. In both cases the meat must be pale pink and lean, and there must be no sign of moisture. This type of ham is generally served as is, in slices, for first course. It is also one of the most popular sandwich fillings.

HAM, UNCOOKED (*jambon cru*): The best known is certainly Bayonne ham, but every region has its local version, known as *jambon de pays*. Some uncooked hams are smoked. Uncooked ham is eaten as is for a first course, but it also contributes its incomparable flavor to many cooked dishes.

HERBES DE PROVENCE: a blend of dried herbs including thyme, rosemary, bay leaf, savory and lavender.

LANGOUSTINES: these little marine crustaceans – called *scampi* by the Italians and *gambas* by the Spaniards – are fished almost all year round along the Atlantic coast. The tail, from 10 to 15 in (15 to 30 cm) in length, has delicate flesh; the long pincers are almost without flesh. The langoustine's hue of pink, brick or salmon, marked with the finest of lines – showing its years – changes little in cooking.

MALAGA RAISINS: large black grapes dried as a bunch. They are very moist, sweet and flavorsome.

MARC: after the grapes have been pressed for making wine, a solid mass of skins, seeds and stems remains; this is distilled into alcohol known as *marc*. Different wine-growing areas produce *marcs* of different flavors — for example, *marc de Bourgogne* and *marc de Champagne*.

MUSHROOMS, CULTIVATED: white or pink *champignons de Paris* are availabe all year round. They must always be selected very fresh, with the caps firmly attached around the stalks. The white ones are a uniform ivory color, the pink ones a pinkish-brown. Both tiny and very large mushrooms are excellent; the small ones are used in sautés and gently simmered dishes, while the large ones are often stuffed.

MUSHROOMS, WILD: gathered in the fields and in woods, these mushrooms appear in French markets in spring and fall. Among the best known and most widely used are *cèpes* (boletus mushrooms or *porcini*, of which many varieties exist), the apricot-colored *girolles* (perhaps better known as *chanterelles*), morels, blewits, *pleurotes* (which these days are cultivated), *craterelles* (sometimes called in France "trumpets of death"), and of course truffles (q.v.) They are often expensive and sometimes scarce, and are most often served as a vegetable, sautéed briefly with garlic or shallots and sometimes with cream added. But they also add a wonderful flavor to all sorts of stews and simmered dishes. Abroad, and in France too, when out of season, they are often replaced by dried mushrooms.

MUSTARD: Dijon mustard, or strong mustard is a pungent, aromatic mustard, smooth-textured and highly-colored, prepared with white wine. This is mostly used in cooking. There are numerous other varieties of mustard, for the most part served as condiments to accompany cold meats or vegetables and in the making of all sorts of vinaigrettes. *Meaux* mustard is made with coarsely crushed seeds, which accounts for its characteristic texture. It is mainly used as a condiment.

NEW SEASON ONIONS: fresh onions, round or elongated, with green stalks, sold in spring and summer. They may be eaten raw or cooked, and are distinguished by their sometimes pungent flavor.

OIGNONS GRELOTS: small pickling onions, round or oval in shape and about ½ to ¾ in (1 to 1.5 cm) in diameter, principally used as a vegetable accompaniment.

OLIVE OIL: extra virgin or first cold-pressing olive oil is derived from the first crushing of the olives, by mechanical means and not steam. This oil is natural, pure, fruity and unrefined and it is the ideal oil for salads as well as for cooking.

OLIVES: green or black, olives are always treated in brine before being sold. They are sold in brine, or marinated in oil with flavorings, loose or in jars. Niçoise olives are very small olives, macerated in oil and flavorings and prepared in the Nice region.

OYSTERS: true oysters are flat, but the deep ones called *gryphaea* or "Portuguese oysters" are mollusks belonging to the same family. Flat oysters have yellow flesh and a nutty flavor that is sweet rather than savory. The only variety still in existence is the *belon*, which takes its name from the Belon River in which these oysters were once fattened. They are also cultivated in the north of the *départment* of Finistère. Flat oysters, with deep green shells and flesh that is almost colorless, are also found at Cancale, Bouzigue and Arcachon.

As for the deep variety, they came to France by accident: in 1868 a Portuguese boat carrying oysters to England lost its cargo off Arcachon. The oysters, which were still alive, reproduced and multiplied. Thus the Portuguese oyster, with its deep, long and narrow shell, was established in France.

The flesh of the oyster is more or less green according to the amount of time it has spent in the breeding park, where it feeds on the plankton that give it its unusual color. The *claires* ("pales") as their name indicates, are very light green in color, having spent only one month in the river basin; the *fines de claires* remain in the basin for three months, so they are greener and have a fuller flavor. As for the *spéciales*, which can stay in the basin for up to two years, they are best of all — a consistent green color, plump and delicate.

Belon and Portuguese oysters are classified by numbers: the 000 and 00 varieties are rare, very large and with a fatty flesh. Those numbered 0 and 1 are large, while no. 2s are medium-sized and no. 3s small. Finally there are the "butterflies," very small Portuguese oysters.

PÂTE À PAIN OR *PÂTE LEVÉE*: bread dough. This may be made at home, and it freezes very easily. In France it can be bought ready-prepared from the bakery, for making bread, all kinds of savory or sweet tarts, and cakes such as brioches, babas, kugelhopf, etc.

PÂTE BRISÉE: short pastry made from flour, butter, salt and water or milk. This is the simplest of French pastries, elastic and firm rather than delicate. Being fairly impermeable, it can be used for sweet or savory tart bases without precooking. It may be enriched with eggs, which make it still firmer.

PÂTE SABLÉE: flour, butter, eggs, sugar, salt and water. This is a delicate, very crumbly pastry which must be worked as little as possible. It is very rich, and is excellent for sweet tarts and cookies. For an even richer flavor, ground almonds may be added.

POIVRE MIGNONETTE: also known as "steak pepper". It is more or less finely crushed peppercorns, and may be white, black or a mixture of the two.

PORK BELLY: also known as *lard maigre*, lean lard. It is sold fresh, *demi-sel* (that is, salted; this must be parboiled before cooking), or smoked (salted, then smoked, and eaten raw or, more frequently, cooked).

PORK CAUL: can be replaced by thin slices of fatty bacon.

PORC DEMI-SEL OR *PORC SALÉ*: nearly all cuts of pork, such as shoulder, sparerib, rump, belly, flank, tail, feet, ears, etc, are salted. In the south, salted pork belly is referred to as *petit salé*. The salting is done with a pickling brine of salt, sugar, water and saltpeter, either by immersion or by injection with multiple needles. Salting times vary from one to six days; the longer the time, the saltier the meat will taste. Meat that has been salted for one day requires simply a rinse under running water; if it has been salted for several days, however, it should be soaked for 12 hours in several changes of water. If you do not have time to do this, you can blanch it for about 15 minutes in boiling salted water, then rinse it before cooking.

Meat can be salted at home, by rubbing it with coarse sea salt (flavored with thyme, rosemary, bay leaf or crushed peppercorns if you wish) and then keeping it buried in additional coarse sea salt in the refrigerator, where it will keep for six days. You must take care that it is always covered with salt; if the salt dissolves, add more. Rinse off the salt under running water and leave the meat to soak, or else blanch it before using.

PORK RIND: this must be trimmed of all fat and blanched before using, particularly in slow-simmered dishes. It gives a marvelous syrupy, slightly gelatinous consistency to the sauce base.

PRALINE: almonds cooked in caramel. Once cooked, the mixture is spread on a marble slab and cooled, then crushed to powder.

QUATRE-ÉPICES: a blend of spices used in France for many years to flavor meat terrines, pâtés and all kinds of charcuterie products. It is made of equal quantities of powdered white pepper, nutmeg, cloves and ginger. According to the end use, chili, cinnamon or mace may also be added.

RICE: Camargue, a small, long-grained rice grown in the Camargue. It is delicate and perfumed. Long-grain, the type of rice used when preparing boiled rice or pilaf. The grain is long and off-white in color. Short-grain, a type of rice with short, white grains, used in desserts because of its sticky properties.

SAUSAGES: there are two different types of sausage. Dry ones are eaten as is, thinly sliced — with drinks before dinner, as a first course in sandwiches, with baguette or coarse country bread accompanied by butter and gerkins, and so on. Cooking sausages are made from ground meat and fat, either alone or with truffles or pistachios added; they may be smoked or unsmoked. They must always be pricked several times with a fork before being slowly poached in barely simmering water for about 20 minutes.

SHALLOTS: there are two varieties: pink shallots, simply called shallots, and the grey type. The former are more common and more frequently used; they are a pinkish-brown color and much less aromatic and milder in flavor than the grey variety. The latter are greyish-brown in color and are covered by several thick layers of skin.

STOCK: used to poach fish fillets, prepare a *blanquette de veau* or poach pieces of beef suspended by a string, but just as important for cooking rice or making a soup. Stocks prepared from bouillon cubes or flavorings extracts are not perfect substitutes. If you have a little time to spare, make your own stocks. They can be frozen in 6 tablespoon (100 ml) portions in plastic bags.

TOMATO PUREE: tomatoes, cooked and reduced to a lightly concentrated puree. It is sold in cardboard packs. A flavorful natural product, it has many very practical uses.

TRUFFLE: There are two kinds of truffle, white and black. The white or Piedmontese truffle is rare in France; it grows under oaks and linden trees in winter, at a depth of 2 to 20 in (5 to 50 cm) beneath the ground, and looks rather like a large potato ranging from grey to ocher in color. It is superb and very delicate. The black truffle, called the "black diamond" of cooking, is certainly better known. This black tuber, which can measure up to 6 in (15 cm) in diameter, is covered with little pyramidal warts; it grows spontaneously and ripens throughout the winter and up to early spring underneath oak, ash and hazel trees. Today black truffles are cultivated in the Vaucluse and Périgord areas in plantations of truffle-producing oak trees. Fragrant and delicious, they form the basis of many special-occasion dishes. Out of season and abroad they are to be found bottled or tinned.

VANILLA SUGAR: superfine (caster) sugar flavored with natural vanilla (in which case it is called vanilla sugar) or artificial vanilla (in which case it is called vanillin sugar, vanillin being a synthetic vanilla flavoring). It can be bought in 15 lb (7.5-kg) envelopes in packs of five or ten. If you are unable to find it, you can make it yourself: ½ cup (4 oz/125 g) sugar, add 1 tablespoon powdered vanilla or a vanilla bean split in two. Keep this in an airtight jar for several months; more vanilla may be added as desired.

VENTRÈCHE: pork belly, salted, seasoned and formed into a roll. It should be cut into thin slices, like *poitrine fumée*. Most commonly used in the southwest.

VERMOUTH: a fortified wine, 18% alcohol, flavored with aromatic herbs. It may be red or white, dry or sweet. The dry white vermouth is the one most commonly used in cooking.

VINAIGRETTE: this sauce is a mixture of oil and vinegar or lemon juice, with the possible addition of salt and pepper. It is traditionally used to dress green salads but also for all kinds of *crudités*, vegetables, fish and cold meats. Various other ingredients may be added, such as chopped shallots, onions or fresh herbs, crushed garlic, crumbled anchovy fillets, chopped hard-cooked egg, *tapenade*, or various kinds of mustard. Different types of oil and of vinegar may be used — walnut, hazelnut, olive or peanut (groundnut) oil, wine vinegar, cider vinegar or flavored vinegar.

VINEGAR: obtained by a fermentation process that changes the alcohol of a wine into acetic acid. It is most often made with red or white wine, but can also be based on champagne or cider. Wine vinegar can be flavored with tarragon, basil, garlic, shallots, berries, etc.

WHELKS: they generally have a brownish or greyish shell and are found on both sides of the Atlantic Ocean although the North American variety is much larger.

INDEX

agneau rôti de Pauillac (roast lamb of Pauillac) 172, *172*
aillade gasconne (veal with garlic) 175, *175*
alouettes sans têtes (beef rolls) 161, *161*
anchoïade (anchovy spread) *28-29*, 33
anchois au txakoli (anchovies in txakoli wine) 96, *96-97*
anchois grillés à la moutarde et à l'estragon (grilled anchovies with mustard and tarragon) 105, *105*
anguilles au vert (eels in green sauce) 113, *113*
araignée farcie (stuffed spider crab) 63, 78, *79*
artichauts à la barigoule (braised artichokes) 204, *205*

baba (rum baba) 225, 230, *230*
baeckeoffe (baked meat and potatoes) *6-7*, 87, 180
bagna cauda (anchovy dip) 33, *33*
bar farci (stuffed sea bass) 106, *107*
barbouiado de fèves et d'artichauts (braised broad beans and artichokes) 210, *211*
barbue à l'oseille (brill with sorrel) 103, *103*
barbue au cidre (brill in cider) 103, *103*
barquettes d'oranges (orange tartlets) 235, *235*
beans
  braised broad beans and artichokes 210, *211*
  cousinat 212, *213*
  green beans with garlic 200, *201*
  haricot beans in cream sauce *202*, 203
  haricot beans, Périgord-style *202*, 203
  stewed broad beans 198, *198*
beef
  aromatic braised beef with vegetables 160, *161*
  baked meat and potatoes *6-7*, 87, 180
  beef braised in beer 162, *163*
  beef braised with calvados *152-3*, 176
  beef rolls 161, *161*
  boatman's grill 165, *165*
  boiled beef and miroton 158, *158*
  braised beef with anchovies 162, *163*
  buckwheat pudding with meat and vegetables 166, *167*
  Burgundy beef 119, 154, 164, *164*
  Corsican stew with pasta 162, *163*
  oxtail stew *6-7*, 168
  pepper steak 166, *166*
  poached beef on a string 154, 158, *159*
  Provençal braised beef 160, *160*
  rib steaks, Bercy-style, with French fries 154, 168, *169*
beignets de legumes (vegetable fritters) *8-9*, 200
beuchelle (creamed kidneys and sweetbreads) 174, *174*
biscuit de Savoie (Savoy sponge) 121, 250, *251*
blanquette de veau (veal in white sauce) 155, *159*, 174
boeuf à la ficelle (poached beef on a string) 154, 158, *159*
boeuf à la gordienne (Provençal braised beef) 160, *160*
boeuf bourguignon (Burgundy beef) 119, 154, 164, *164*
boeuf mode (aromatic braised beef with vegetables) 160, *161*
bohémienne (tomato and eggplant casserole) 208, *208*
bouillabaisse *10*, 110, 148
bouillon de volaille (chicken stock) 34
bourride *10*, 109, 150
bourride de lotte à la sétoise (bourride of monkfish, Sète-style) *99*, 100, 150
brandade de morue (puree of salt cod) 108, *108*, 150
bread dough 41
brochet de l'Ill à la crème (pike in cream sauce) 103, *103*
brochets grillés aux noix (grilled pike with walnuts) 94, *95*
broufado (braised beef with anchovies) 162, *163*

cabbage
  buttered cabbage 200, *201*
  stuffed cabbage 206, *207*
calmars au riz (squid with rice) 70, *71*
calmars farcis (stuffed squid) 69, *69*
canard à l'orange (duck with orange) 136, *137*
canard à toutes les herbes (duck with herbs) 138, *139*
canard aux navets du Pardailhan (duck with glazed turnips) 135, *135*
canard aux olives (duck with olives) *12-13*, 138
canard Montmorency (duck with cherries) 136, *136*
carbonnades (beef braised in beer) 162, *163*
carpe farcie (stuffed carp) 112, *112-113*
cassoulet (Toulouse casserole) 150, 178, *179*
castanhet (chestnut cake) 244, *245*
cèpes à la bordelaise (cèpes, Bordelaise-style) 204, *205*
cèpes farcis (stuffed mushrooms) 203, *207*
cervelle de canut (herbed cheese spread) *36*, 37
chaudrée *97*, 98, 188
cheese
  cheese and walnut omelette 46, *46*
  cheese beignets 195, *195*
  cheese pastry "hats" 48, *49*
  cheese tart 241, *241*
  Comté cheese soufflé 44, *45*, 118
  herbed cheese spread *36*, 37
chestnut-flour polenta 196, *197*
chestnut patties 208, *209*
chicken
  Basque chicken 131, *131*
  boiled chicken, Toulouse-style 130, *130*
  chicken casserole 124, 127, *127*
  chicken with Comté cheese 118, *131*, 132
  chicken with crayfish *122-3*, 131
  chicken with cream and tarragon *133*, 134
  chicken with forty cloves of garlic 128, *129*
  chicken with mushroom sauce 132, *133*
  chicken with rice *131*, 132
  chicken with vinegar 120, *122-3*, 127
chicken stock 34
chipirons en su tinta (squid cooked in their own ink) *69*, 70
chou farci (stuffed cabbage) 206, *207*
choucroute (sauerkraut with pork and sausages) *6-7*, 87, 157, 180
civet de langouste au banyuls (rock lobster in Banyuls wine) 74, *75*, 151
civet de lièvre aux spätzele (hare in red wine with egg noodles) 141, *141*
clafoutis (baked cherry custard) 230, *230*
confit de canard (preserved duck) 126, 138, *138*
coq au vin (chicken casserole) 124, 127, *127*
coques à la façon de Roz-sur-Couesnon (cockles with garlic and parsley) *73*, 74
coquilles saint-jacques à la landaise (scallops, Landes-style) 68, *68*
coquilles saint-jacques au beurre blanc (scallops with beurre blanc) 68, *68*
coquilles saint-jacques d'Étretat (scallops, Étretat-style) *60-61*, 68
cornets de Murat (cream horns) 242, *242*
corniottes (cheese pastry "hats") 48, *49*
côtes de veau à la normande (veal chops, Normandy-style) 173, *173*
cotriade 27, 91, 106, *107*
courgettes au broccio (Corsican-style stuffed zucchini) 196, *197*
cousinat 212, *213*
crabe farci (stuffed crab) *60-61*, 80
crème caramel (vanilla custard with caramel sauce) 236, *236*
cremets (cream molds with fruit) 239, *239*
crêpes suzettes (orange liqueur crêpes) *222-3*, 225-6, 250
crevettes au cidre (shrimp (prawns) in cider) 72, *72-73*
croquants (crisp honey cookies) 240, *240*
cul de veau à l'angevine (veal pot roast, Anjou-style) *152-3*, 173

daube d'Avignon (Avignon lamb stew) *170*, 171
daurade à la provençale (baked bream, Provençal-style) *101*, 102
daurade au muscadet (baked bream in Muscadet) 98, *99*
desserts
  Albi rings 234, *234*
  almond and raisin cake 87, 224, *243*, 244
  Alsatian apple tart 236, *237*
  Angevine pears *231*, 232
  apricot pastry 227, *227*
  baked cherry custard 230, *230*
  Basque cake 248, *249*
  bee's nest cake 224, *243*, 244
  buttered pastry 225, 228, *229*
  caramel rice pudding 247, *247*
  cheese tart 241, *241*
  chestnut cake 244, *245*
  chestnut meringue 234, *234*
  cream horns 242, *242*
  cream molds with fruit 239, *239*
  crisp honey cookies 240, *240*
  flourless chocolate cake 227, *227*
  gingerbread 118, 248, *248*
  Grenoble caramel walnut cake 250, *251*
  ice cream plombières 245, *245*
  kirsch soufflé 232, *232*
  lemon tart *4*, 238
  madeleines 86, 242, *242*
  meringues chantilly *222-3*, 224, 231
  Metz cake 241, *241*
  Nancy cake 235, *235*
  Nancy macaroons 86, 242, *243*
  Normandy cookies 240, *240*
  orange liqueur crêpes *222-3*, 225-6, 250
  orange tartlets 235, *235*
  pastry puffs *4*, 247
  pear cake 233, *233*
  praline butter cream cake *222-3*, 246
  Provençal fruit loaf 149, 238, *239*
  prunes cooked in wine 231, *231*
  puff pastry with almond filling 228, *228*
  pumpkin cake 245, *245*
  rum and butter cake 225, 239, *239*
  rum baba 225, 230, *230*
  Savoy sponge 121, 250, *251*
  snow eggs *222-3*, 232
  strawberry tart 236, *237*
  strawberry water ice 233, *233*
  sugar tart 86, 224, 240, *241*
  sweet bread *234*, 235
  Swiss chard pie *4*, 238
  upside down apple tart 59, 246, *246*
  vanilla custard with caramel sauce 236, *236*
  warm prune tart 225, 228, *229*

échine à la bière (pork cooked in beer) *6-7*, 178
écrevisses au champagne (crayfish in champagne) 76, *77*
eggplant
  eggplant charlotte 212, *213*
  tomato and eggplant casserole 208, *208*
embeurrée de chou (buttered cabbage) 200, *201*
endives à la flamande (endives, Flemish-style) 200, *201*
entrecôtes Bercy, pommes frites (rib steaks, Bercy-style, with French fries) 154, 168, *169*
épaule d'agneau à la boulangère (shoulder of lamb with potatoes) 170, *170*
épinards aux pignons (spinach with pine nuts) 208, *209*

faisan en chartreuse (pheasant Carthusian) 134, *134*
falette (stuffed breast of veal) 175, *175*, 220
far (warm prune tart) 225, 228, *229*
fèves en ragoût (stewed broad beans) 198, *198*
first course
  Allymes tart *47*, 48, 120
  Alsatian tart 41, *41*
  anchovy dip 33, *33*
  anchovy spread *28-9*, 33
  bread and garlic soup 38, *38*
  carrot soup 38, *38*
  cheese and walnut omelette 46, *46*
  cheese pastry "hats" 48, *49*
  Comté cheese soufflé 44, *45*, 118
  cooked whole duck liver terrine 52, *52-3*
  duck pâté, Amiens-style 42, *42-3*
  egg and bacon quiche 51, *51*, 86
  eggs with tomatoes and peppers 30, *41*, 42
  fish soup *37*, *37*
  French onion soup 34, *34*
  herb pie *47*, 48
  herbed cheese spread 36, *37*
  leek tart *43*, 44
  little pies from Béziers 50, *51*, 150
  milk soup *38*, 40
  mushroom soup *40*, 41
  Niçoise salad *28-9*, 32, 50, 148
  olive spread *34*, 36
  parsleyed ham 34, *35*, 119
  pissaladière 46, *47*, 148
  poached eggs with red wine sauce 33, *35*, 119
  pork spread 36, *36*
  potato omelette, Auvergne-style 46, *46*
  pumpkin soup 38, *39*
  ravioli 45, *45*, 148
  stuffed vegetables of Provence *28-9*, 50, 148
  vegetable soup with basil *28-9*, 40
fish
  aïoli feast *88-9*, 93, 149
  anchovies in txakoli wine 96, *96-7*
  baked bream in Muscadet 98, *99*
  baked bream, Provençal-style *101*, 102
  baked sardines with spinach 104, *104*
  bouillabaisse *10*, 110, 148
  bourride *10*, 109, 150
  bourride of monkfish, Sète-style *99*, 100, 150
  brill in cider 103, *103*
  brill with sorrel 103, *103*
  chaudrée *97*, 98, 188
  cotriade 27, 91, 106, *107*
  eels in green sauce 113, *113*
  escabèche of red mullet 105, *105*
  fish and onion stew 111, *111*
  grilled anchovies with mustard and tarragon 105, *105*
  grilled pike with walnuts 94, *95*
  grilled sea bass with fennel 90, 100, *101*, 148
  marinated mackerel 96, *96-7*
  matelote of freshwater fish in Riesling 87, 110, *110*
  mullet in raïto *99*, 100
  pike in cream sauce 103, *103*
  puree of salt cod 108, *108*, 150
  quenelles 109, *109*
  red mullet, Nice-style *101*, 102
  salt cod, Brest-style 108, *108*
  salt cod with beet greens and currants 108, *108*
  sole meunière 90, 93, *93*
  sole with shrimp and mushrooms 94, *94*
  stuffed carp 112, *112-13*
  stuffed sardines 104, *104*
  stuffed sea bass 106, *107*
  trout in Riesling 112, *112*
  trout with almonds 112, *112*
  ttoro 91, *97*, 98
  tuna, Languedoc-style 102, *102*
  whiting in mustard cream sauce 106, *107*
flamiche aux poireaux (leek tart) *43*, 44
fleurs de courgette farcies (stuffed zucchini flowers) *8-9*, 199
foie de veau à la lyonnaise (calf's liver, Lyons-style) 119, 155, 173, *173*
foie gras en terrine (cooked whole duck liver terrine) 52, *52-3*
foie gras frais aux raisins (fresh foie gras with grapes) *12-13*, 140
fougasse (Provençal fruit loaf) 149, 238, *239*

galette bretonne (rum and butter cake) 225, 239, *239*
game
  breast of duck with garlic sauce *12-13*, 135, 185
  duck with cherries 136, *136*
  duck with glazed turnips 135, *135*
  duck with herbs 138, *139*
  duck with olives *12-13*, 138
  duck with orange 136, *137*
  fresh fois gras with grapes *12-13*, 140
  guinea fowl stuffed with girolles *122-3*, 130
  hare in red wine with egg noodles 141, *141*
  pheasant Carthusian 134, *134*
  preserved duck 126, 138, *138*
  rabbit, Corsican-style 142, *143*
  rabbit in cider 126, *133*, 140
  rabbit parcels 128, *129*
  rabbit with mustard sauce 126, 142, *143*
  rabbit with prunes 140, *140*
  saddle of hare in cream sauce *122-3*, 128
  stuffed hare 142, *142*
gâteau au potiron (pumpkin cake) 245, *245*
gâteau basque (Basque cake) 248, *249*
gâteau de Metz (Metz cake) 241, *241*
gâteau de Nancy (Nancy cake) 235, *235*
gigot d'agneau à la bretonne (leg of lamb, Brittany-style) 156, *167*, 170
gigot farci (stuffed leg of lamb) 171, *171*
gimblettes d'Albi(Alibi rings) 234, *234*
glace plombières (ice cream plombières) 245, *245*
gnocchi 196, *196*
grand aïoli (aïoli feast) *88-9* , 93, 149
gratin dauphinois(Dauphiné-style potato gratin) 120, 198, *199*
gratin de queues d'écrevisses (gratin of crayfish) *75*, 76
gratin de sardines aux épinards (baked sardines with spinach) 104, *104*
gratin savoyard (potato gratin, Savoy-style) 210, *210-11*
gratinée à l'oignon (French onion soup) 34, *34*
grenoblois (Grenoble caramel walnut cake) 250, *251*
grillade des mariniers (boatman's grill) 165, *165*

haricots à la périgourdine (haricot beans, Périgord-style) 202, 203
haricots blancs à la crème (haricot beans in cream sauce) 202, 203
haricots verts à l'ail (green beans with garlic) 200, *201*
hochepot (oxtail stew) *6-7*, 168
homard à l'americaine (lobster, American-style) 80, *81*

homard au curry (lobster in curry sauce) 73, 74

huîtres en brochettes (grilled oysters on skewers) 66, 67

jalousies (apricot pastry) 227, 227
jambon persillé (parsleyed ham) 34, 35, 119

kig-ha-farz (buckwheat pudding with meat and vegetables) 166, 167
kouign amann (buttered pastry) 225, 228, 229
kugelhopf (almond and raisin cake) 87, 224, 243, 244

lamb
  Avignon lamb stew 170, 171
  baked meat and potatoes 6-7, 87, 180
  lamb with spring vegetables 159, 172
  leg of lamb, Brittany-style 156, 167, 170
  roast lamb of Pauillac 172, 172
  shoulder of lamb with potatoes 170, 170
  stuffed leg of lamb 171, 171
langoustines de Guilvinec (langoustines, Guilvinec-style) 63, 72, 72-3
lapin à la moutarde (rabbit with mustard sauce) 126, 142, 143
lapin à l'istrettu (rabbit, Corsican-style) 142, 143
lapin au cidre (rabbit in cider) 126, 133, 140
lapin aux pruneaux (rabbit with prunes) 140, 140
lapin en paquets (rabbit parcels) 128, 129
le nègre (flourless chocolate cake) 227, 227
lentilles à l'auvergnate (Auvergne-style lentils) 207, 214
les baisers (kisses) 70, 71
lièvre en cabessal (stuffed hare) 142, 142
limousine d'écrevisses (crayfish, Limousin-style) 75, 76
loup au fenouil (grilled sea bass with fennel) 90, 100, 101, 148

macarons de Nancy (Nancy macaroons) 86, 242, 243
madeleines de Commercy (madeleines) 86, 242, 242
magrets grillés sauce aillade (breast of duck with garlic sauce) 12-13, 135, 185
maquereaux marinés (marinated mackerel) 96, 96-7
matelote au riesling (matelote of freshwater fish in Riesling) 87, 110, 110
meringues à la chantilly (meringues Chantilly) 222-3, 224, 231
merlans de Lorient (whiting in mustard cream sauce) 106, 107
millas (cornmeal mush) 202, 203
Mont Blanc (chestnut meringue) 234, 234
morilles à la crème (morels in cream sauce) 211, 211
morue aux blettes et aux raisins secs (salt cod with beet greens and currants) 108, 108
morue brestoise (salt cod, Brest-style) 108, 108
mouclade (mussels in wine and cream sauce) 65, 65, 188
moules à la crème (mussels in cream) 60-1, 66
moules aux épinards (mussels with spinach) 65, 67
moules marinière (mussels in white wine) 66, 67
muge en raïto (mullet in raïto) 99, 100
mushrooms
  cèpes, Bordelaise-style 204, 205
  morels in cream sauce 211, 211
  stuffed mushrooms 203, 207

navarin printanier (lamb with spring vegetables) 159, 172
nid d'abeilles (bee's nest cake) 224, 243, 244

oeufs à la neige (snow eggs) 222-3, 232
oeufs en meurette (poached eggs with red wine sauce) 33, 35, 119
omelette brayaude (potato omelette, Auvergne-style) 46, 46
omelette quercynoise (cheese and walnut omelette) 46, 46
oreillettes (pastry puffs) 4, 247

pain d'épices (gingerbread) 118, 248, 248
palets de marrons (chestnut patties) 208, 209
palourdes farcies à la lorientaise (stuffed clams, Lorient-style) 78, 105
papeton d'aubergines (eggplant charlotte) 212, 213
Paris-Brest (praline butter cream cake) 222-3, 246
pastis landais (sweet bread) 234, 235
pastry

choux pastry 247
puff pastry 44
short (shortcrust pastry) 50
sweet short (shortcrust) pastry 246
pâte à choux (choux pastry) 247
pâte à pain (bread dough) 41
pâte brisée (short (shortcrust) pastry) 50
pâte feuilletée (puff pastry) 44
pâte surcrée (sweet short (shortcrust) pastry) 246
pâté de canard d'Amiens (duck pâté, Amiens-style) 42, 42-3
paupiettes (veal rolls) 175, 176
petits farcis provençaux (stuffed vegetables of Provence) 28-9, 50, 148
petits pâtes de Béziers (little pies from Béziers) 50, 51, 150
petits pois à la vendéenne (green peas, Vendée-style) 214, 214
pets de nonne (cheese beignets) 195, 195
pintade farcie aux girolles (guinea fowl stuffed with girolles) 122-3, 130
pipérade (eggs with tomatoes and peppers) 30, 41, 42
pissaladière 46, 47, 148
pithiviers (puff pastry with almond filling) 228, 228
pochouse (fish and onion stew) 111, 111
poires belles-angevine (Angevine pears) 231, 232
poirier d'Anjou (pear cake) 233, 233
polenta de châtaignes (chestnut-flour polenta) 196, 197
pommes Anna (potatoes Anna) 198, 199
pommes de terre à la bretonne (potato casserole) 198, 199
pommes sarladaises (potatoes, Sarlat-style) 210, 210-11
pommes soufflées (puffed potatoes) 214, 215
porc au lait (pork cooked in milk) 177, 177
porc aux châtaignes (pork with chestnuts) 180, 181
porc aux deux pommes (pork with potatoes and apples) 177, 177
porc aux pruneaux (pork with prunes) 59, 157, 181, 181
pork
  baked meat and potatoes 6-7, 87, 180
  pork cooked in beer 6-7, 178
  pork cooked in milk 177, 177
  pork spread 36, 36
  pork with chestnuts 180, 181
  pork with potatoes and apples 177, 177
  pork with prunes 59, 157, 181, 181
  sauerkraut with pork and sausages 6-7, 87, 157, 180
  Toulouse casserole 150, 178, 179
pot-au-feu et miroton (boiled beef and miroton) 158, 158
potage aux cèpes (mushroom soup) 40, 41
potage Crécy (carrot soup) 38, 38
potatoes
  Dauphiné-style potato gratin 120, 198, 199
  gnocchi 196, 196
  potato casserole 198 199
  potato cream pie 207, 212
  potato gratin, Savoy-style 210, 210-11
  potatoes Anna 198, 199
  potatoes, Sarlat-style 210, 210-11
  puffed potatoes 214, 215
pothine de boeuf (beef braised with calvados) 152-3, 165
poule au pot à la toulousaine (boiled chicken, Toulouse-style) 130, 130
poule au riz (chicken with rice) 131, 132
poulet à la crème à l'estragon (chicken with cream and tarragon) 133, 134
poulet au comté (chicken with Comté cheese) 118, 131, 132
poulet au vinaigre (chicken with vinegar) 120, 122-3, 127
poulet aux écrevisses (chicken with crayfish) 122-3, 131
poulet aux quarante gousses d'ail (chicken with forty cloves of garlic) 128, 129
poulet basquaise (Basque chicken) 131, 131
poulet vallée d'Auge (chicken with mushroom sauce) 132, 133
pruneaux au vin (prunes cooked in wine) 231, 231

quenelles 109, 109
quiche lorraine (egg and bacon quiche) 51, 51, 86

râble de lièvre à la crème (saddle of hare in cream sauce) 122-3, 128
ratatouille 190-1, 195
raviolis (ravioli) 45, 45, 148
rillettes (pork spread) 36, 36
risotto des Baux (herb risotto from Les Baux) 204, 204

rognons à la moutarde (veal kidneys in mustard sauce) 176, 177
rougets à la niçoise (red mullet, Nice-style) 101, 102
rougets en escabèche (escabèche of red mullet) 105, 105

sablés normands (Normandy cookies) 240, 240
salade d'araignée (salad of spider crab) 63, 78, 79
salade niçoise (Niçoise salad) 28-9, 32, 50, 148
sardines farcies (stuffed sardines) 104, 104
shellfish
  cockles with garlic and parsley 73, 74
  crayfish in champagne 76, 77
  crayfish, Limousin-style 75, 76
  gratin of crayfish 75, 76
  grilled oysters on skewers 66, 67
  kisses 70, 71
  langoustines, Guilvinec-style 63, 72, 72-3
  lobster, American-style 80, 81
  lobster in curry sauce 73, 74
  mussels in cream 60-1, 66
  mussels in white wine 66, 67
  mussels in wine and cream sauce 65, 65, 188
  mussels with spinach 65, 67
  rock lobster in Banyuls wine 74, 75, 151
  salad of spider crab 63, 78, 79
  scallops, Étretat-style 60-1, 68
  scallops, Landes-style 68, 68
  scallops with beurre blanc 68, 68
  shrimp (prawns) in cider 72, 72-3
  squid cooked in their own ink 69, 70
  squid with rice 70, 71
  stuffed clams, Lorient-style 78, 105
  stuffed crab 60-1, 80
  stuffed spider crab 63, 78, 79
  stuffed squid 69, 69
sole à la normande (sole with shrimp and mushrooms) 94, 94
sole meunière 90, 93, 93
sorbet aux fraises (strawberry water ice) 233, 233
soufflé au comté (Comté cheese soufflé) 44, 45, 118
soufflé au kirsch (kirsch soufflé) 232, 232
soup
  bread and garlic soup 38, 38
  carrot soup 38, 38
  cotriade 27, 91, 106, 107
  fish soup 37, 37
  French onion soup 34, 34
  milk soup 38, 40
  mushroom soup 40, 41
  pumpkin soup 38, 39
  vegetable soup with basil 28-9, 40
soupe au lait (milk soup) 38, 40
soupe au pistou (vegetable soup with basil) 28-9, 40
soupe de poissons (fish soup) 37, 37
soupe de potiron (pumpkin soup) 38, 39
steak au poivre (pepper steak) 166, 166
stufatu (Corsican stew with pasta) 162, 163

tapenade (olive spread) 34, 36
tarte au citron (lemon tart) 4, 238
tarte au fromage blanc (cheese tart) 241, 241
tarte au sucre (sugar tart) 86, 224, 240, 241
tarte aux fraises (strawberry tart) 236, 237
tarte aux pommes à l'alsacienne (Alsatian apple tart) 236, 237
tarte flambée (Alsatian tart) 41, 41
tarte tatin (upside down apple tart) 59, 246, 246
tâtre des Allymes (Allymes tart) 47, 48, 120
terrinée (caramel rice pudding) 247, 247

thon à la languedocienne (tuna, Languedoc-style) 102, 102
tian de courgettes (baked zucchini with tomatoes and onions) 8-9, 211
tomates à la provençal (tomatoes, Provençal-style) 190-1, 195
tomatoes
  eggs with tomatoes and peppers 30, 41, 42
  tomato and eggplant casserole 208, 208
  tomatoes, Provençal-style 190-1, 195
tourain (bread and garlic soup) 38, 38
tourte aux blettes (Swiss chard pie) 4, 238
tourte aux herbes (herb pie) 47, 48
truffat (potato cream pie) 207, 212
truites au riesling (trout in Riesling) 112, 112
truites aux amandes (trout with almonds) 112, 112
ttoro 91, 97, 98

veal
  calf's liver, Lyons-style 119, 155, 173, 173
  creamed kidneys and sweetbreads 174, 174
  stuffed breast of veal 175, 175, 220
  veal chops, Normandy-style 173, 173
  veal in white sauce 155, 159, 174
  veal kidneys in mustard sauce 176, 177
  veal Marengo 152-3, 176
  veal pot roast, Anjou-style 152-3, 173
  veal rolls 175, 176
  veal with garlic 175, 175
veau Marengo (veal Marengo) 152-3, 176
vegetables
  Auvergne-style lentils 207, 214
  baked zucchini with tomatoes and onions 8-9, 211
  braised artichokes 204, 205
  braised broad beans and artichokes 210, 211
  buttered cabbage 200, 201
  cèpes, Bordelaise-style 204, 205
  Corsican-style stuffed zucchini 196, 197
  cousinat 212, 213
  Dauphiné-style potato gratin 120, 198, 199
  eggplant charlotte 212, 213
  endives, Flemish-style 200, 201
  gnocchi 196, 196
  green beans with garlic 200, 201
  green peas, Vendée-style 214, 214
  haricot beans in cream sauce 202, 203
  haricot beans, Périgord-style 202, 203
  herb risotto from Les Baux 204, 204
  morels in cream sauce 211, 211
  potato casserole 198, 199
  potato cream pie 207, 212
  potato gratin, Savoy-style 210, 210-11
  potato omelette, Auvergne-style 46, 46
  potatoes Anna 198, 199
  potatoes, Sarlat-style 210, 210-11
  puffed potatoes 214, 215
  ratatouille 190-1, 195
  spinach with pine nuts 208, 209
  stewed broad beans 198, 198
  stuffed cabbage 206, 207
  stuffed mushrooms 203, 207
  stuffed vegetables of Provence 28-9, 50, 148
  stuffed zucchini flowers 8-9, 199
  tomato and eggplant casserole 208, 208
  tomatoes, Provinçal-style 190-1, 195
  vegetable fritters 8-9, 200

zucchini
  baked zucchini with tomatoes and onions 8-9, 211
  Corsican-style stuffed zucchini 196, 197
  stuffed zucchini flowers 8-9, 199

ACKNOWLEDGMENTS

The publishers would like to thank the following people and organizations for their assistance in the preparation of this book: Appley Hoare Antiques of Mosman, Corso de' Fiori, Chatswood, Villeroy and Boch, Hale Imports, The Chef's Warehouse, John Normyle of Paddington, Sentimental Journey, Mosman Portobello, for photographic props; Inger Marchant, Maureen Simpson, David Furley and Linda Byak for the use of privately-owned items kindly lent for photographic propping; Jackie Wisbey, Elizabeth McLeod and Michelle Gorry for photographic and styling assistance; Penny Pilmer, Doreen Grézoux, Laurine Croasdale, Rosemary Wilkinson, Shelley Bright, Helen Cooney, Annette Crueger and Tristan Phillips for valuable editorial and administrative assistance.